10"
IRISH

Joyce's Catholic Comedy
of Language

Joyce's Catholic Comedy of Language

Beryl Schlossman

The University of Wisconsin Press

Published 1985

The University of Wisconsin Press
114 North Murray Street
Madison, Wisconsin 53715

The Univerity of Wisconsin Press, Ltd.
1 Gower Street
London WC1E 6HA, England

First printing

Printed in the United States of America

For LC CIP information see the colophon

ISBN 0–299–10160–6

Contents

Acknowledgments

This book was written as a *doctorat de troisième cycle* at the *Université de Paris VII* under the direction of Julia Kristeva; Jacques Aubert and Jean-Louis Houdebine were the other committee members. I would like to thank them for their critical guidance and encouragement.

I am grateful to Richard Macksey, Josué Harari, and Gregory Lucente for their extremely generous attention and support during the period of translation and revision; to David Hayman, J. Hillis Miller, and Gregory Lucente for their critical readings; to Fritz Senn, Eugene Vance, Susan Willey, and Jean-Michel Rabaté, who read parts of the manuscript; to Philippe Sollers and *Tel Quel*, who published an early version of part of the French text; to the staff of the University of Wisconsin Press; to Irwin, Lin, and Mark Schlossman.

It is a great pleasure to note my special thanks to David Hayman for his enthusiastic support of the publication of this book.

Preface

The sacred is at the heart of Joyce's writing experience. A brief overview of the biographical context shows the formulation of the sacred in Joyce's background and education. In my reading of the Joycean trajectory, I hope to analyze the influence of the liturgical scene on writing, the intersection of Catholic flesh and art in the Passion of the Word: for Joyce, oddly enough, this Passion is fully Catholic only when it is outside the boundaries of the Church. The exceptional quality of Joycean Catholicism implies an ambivalent attitude toward religious belief in general and the Church in particular; and yet certain forms of literary criticism have undercut the dimensions of Joyce's position by reducing it to the biographical identification of Joyce as apostate or obedient Catholic. In order to interpret the role of the sacred in *Ulysses* and *Finnegans Wake*, however, the reader must examine Joyce's Catholicism as an aesthetic focus and a symbolic source, inscribed in the writer's biography and imagination. Indeed, Joyce's investment in Catholicism is such that he considered it essential to the Irish experience.[1]

Joyce's parents seem to incarnate the ambivalence or ideological dissonance noted by certain critics: Joyce's mother was pious, an exemplary Catholic, whereas his father ridiculed the Church and spent much of his time in pubs. Noted for his wit, John Joyce transmitted his taste for humor and blasphemy to his son James; indeed, Joyce owed much of his comic repertoire to his father.

The influence of Catholicism seems to have dominated

Joyce's childhood. According to the earliest memories of his brother Stanislaus, Joyce dramatized the story of Adam and Eve—and he himself played the role of the devil.[2] In the Jesuit school of Clongowes, Joyce became an altar boy and received his initiation as a protagonist in Catholic ritual. He wrote a hymn to the Virgin Mary and learned the order of priestly functions.[3] As an adolescent, Joyce continued his Jesuit education at Belvedere; he attended a religious retreat echoed in fictional form in *A Portrait of the Artist as a Young Man*.

After "a severe crisis of repentance"[4] and its sequel of prayer and self-mortification, Joyce began to question his faith. Exile takes shape on the terrain of sexuality: crisis and repentance are the outgrowth of the first sexual experiences. In turn, desire overflows the boundaries of piety and invalidates the attempt at self-castration implicit in the religious crisis. Desire is divided into the "pure" attachment to the Virgin and the sexuality associated with the evils of prostitution. This ambivalence is at the core of the Joycean knot of religion, sexuality, and aesthetics. The young Joyce, encouraged to join the order by his Jesuit teachers, leaves for Paris. On Good Friday, 1903, he attends mass at Notre Dame, "standing in the rear of the Church to compare, with the aid of a missal from Ireland, the French style of *Tenebrae*."[5] Joyce returns to Dublin where his dying mother tries to convince him to make confession and take communion, but he refuses.[6]

The refusal to engage in the "false homage" of ritual is counterpointed by Joyce's preoccupation with Catholicism, documented by Francini Bruni[7] and others, particularly Stanislaus Joyce and Mary and Padraic Colum.[8] His Catholic identity is specifically Jesuit.[9] Joyce himself described the effect of his Jesuit upbringing as related to logical hierarchies of meaning and texts; the Jesuits taught him "how to gather, how to order, and how to present a given material."[10] After hearing Bach's *Matthäus Passion*, Joyce told Budgen: "I simply cannot understand how any man can mix the synoptic gospels with the gospel according to Saint John."[11] Logic slides toward theology: Joyce's aesthetic is mediated by a Jesuit's hierarchy of signification. His vision of Catholicism simultaneously integrates meaning or signification within its hierarchy and disperses or distances meanings rooted in Catholicism, placing them in other contexts. This double strategy indicates a peculiarly Catholic ambivalence within the Joycean trajectory. For the filtering through Catholicism excludes nothing, interpreting everything—monotheism, paganism, politics. Joyce himself integrates elements as diverse as the maneuver of Odysseus with the Cyclops and the Irish tragedy of Parnell within the configuration of the sacrifice of Christ.[12] This filtering productive of variations and interpretations ranging from transcendence to parabasis and parody is only possible given an initial stability of hierarchies.

Thus Joyce's Catholicism, often dismissed as an artefact,[13] is at the source of his symbolic vision and its imaginative constructs; it led him to read the writings of the great mystics[14] and perhaps to conceive of his own experience of language in their terms. This experience implies the undermining of the limits of identity, as the subject posits an identity in order to go beyond it. Joyce in Ireland assumes the identity of the apostate or iconoclast associated with a European image; he is Irish only in exile, as he is Catholic only outside the Church. His ambiguity as Catholic locates him between derision and jubilation: "Sometimes he recited the litany of the Blessed Virgin—a cherished prayer of Stephen Dedalus in *A Portrait*—'Rosa mystica, ora pro nobis; Turris Davidica, ora pro nobis; Turris eburnea, ora pro nobis . . .' with a half-mocking expression."[15]

These motifs of the disaffected Catholic, the Irishman exiled on home ground, and the mystical experience through writing are knotted together in Joyce's Catholic experience and are reflected in the *figura* of Saint Patrick. Joyce's identification and fascination with Saint Patrick seal his own configuration as Catholic, played out until the end of *Finnegans Wake*. In 1931, Joyce marked his birthday celebration with some Clos de Saint Patrice. He told James Stephens: "Saint Patrick is the only saint a man can get drunk in honor of. But he waited too long to write his Portrait of the Artist."[16] According to Jacques Mercanton, Joyce was still talking about Saint Patrick toward the end of his life. Joyce told him "that Saint Patrick's intervention was indispensable for the conclusion of his book. . . . Then with a sigh: 'Without the help of my Irish saint, I think that I would not have been able to go *jusqu'au bout*.'"[17]

Joyce's debt to the domain of the sacred is the point of departure for a reading, through Catholic resonances, of his poetic language—its pluralized, anagrammatic character and its version of theological infinity. Elements of a psychoanalytical reading permit the interpretation of the engendering of writing through Joycean subjectivity, through desire and the exigencies of the symbolic. The desire of the reader implies an interpretive passage toward the continent posited by others as Joyce's "unreadability"—the object of ignorance or repression. The possibilities of revealing the signification of "unreadability"—its beauty and singularity—are here figured through the passage and the voice of one reading. In the following pages, this reading will be elaborated through *Ulysses* and *Finnegans Wake*.

Reading Joyce

How is it possible to talk about Joyce? What positions, taken by the reader, allow the author's style and signature to be deciphered? The reading in question must be simultaneously unified and pluralized, attentive to the single focus of all of Joyce's fiction, and open to the dazzling complexity of *Ulysses* and *Finnegans Wake*. The point of departure of this oxymoron-like configuration is an interpretation of Joyce's Catholicism—as it affects him biographically and scripturally. Joyce's interest in the aesthetic aspect of Catholicism (its rituals, the drama of paschal ceremony, its written liturgy) is rooted in his focus on theology; both the aesthetic and theological concerns find their way into the early fiction of *Dubliners*, *Stephen Hero*, and *A Portrait of the Artist as a Young Man*. Although the Joycean exposition of the sacred takes on new depth and richness in *Ulysses* and *Finnegans Wake*, its presence in the early writings posits a series of questions, readings, and articulations that influence both the writing and reading of the two later texts.

For Joyce, the symbolic venture of writing itself is inseparable from his *own* version of Catholicism. Joyce's Catholicism takes an unprecedented set of turns: it implies both an oblique passage into the Catholic position (as noted by a character in *Ulysses*) and a subversion of this position; it enters into the configuration of the spiral, the interlace recalling the Celtic illumination that makes Catholicism into an art; its torsion leads to a Borromean structure, the knot figuring the dimensions of subjectivity—its impossibility and its truth. Joyce gives voice to a religious discourse that itself impels him to speak—as writer. Joyce's religious position is ambiguous and even ambivalent. Catholicism defines his Irish exile; his solitude as sinner; his *interior experience*, to echo Bataille; his *mysticism*—the mystery of the letter and its limits. From this stance (within Catholicism and yet at its margins), Joyce accosts the borders of languages and, in the *Wake*, the limits of literature. Joyce's Catholicism creates the necessity of a double reading of the sacred and the comic, working its passage through the scripture of *Ulysses* and *Finnegans Wake*.

An interpretation of the Joycean text necessitates a reading of Catholic tradition and its engagement in Joyce's writing—through a series of responses to religious transcendence. On the other hand, a reading of the language(s) deployed in Joycean subjectivity—the seemingly endless writing of the subject's theological positions and the sin that exceeds them[1]—arouses a psychoanalytical reading. Not an exclusively analytical reading, but rather an interpretation *open* to the Freudian and Lacanian dimensions of the word. In order to decipher the marks of truth and, especially, the process of its revelation; and the blackness out of which this revelation comes forth. Analytic discourse allows for the explication not only of Joycean Catholicism but also of what encroaches upon it as intruder. The *jouissance* (that is, the double register of sexual and symbolic *jouissance*) of the Catholic sinner will become the sublimation of the artist.

Beginning with *Dubliners*, Joyce presents Catholicism as halfway between truth and parody. The dramatization central to the Joycean word is here introduced: theology and sexuality, or Catholicism as the infinite access to grace and the Fall, to scriptural truth and its parodic undoing. To this arrangement *Stephen Hero* adds the artist-to-be Stephen Dedalus, counterpointed by the aesthetic approach to theology through the Passion of Christ. The pervasive Catholicism of *Dubliners* becomes the backdrop for the subject turning religion inside out—uttering a refusal of the Church as a religious "institution" or normative agency, while anticipating an entry into paternity and the drama of Trinitarian liturgy.

This anticipation is confirmed in the rewriting of *Stephen Hero* as *A Portrait of the Artist as a Young Man*. The rejection of the Church is further integrated in the vision of sexuality and theology; the sinister, deviant Catholic, exiled within his own version of Catholicism, confronts sin and the Word. In the *Portrait* Joyce reveals the enormous conflict between Catholicism and that which overflows its boundaries, translated into the creation and the dissolution of meaning. The survival of the symbolic structure depends on a *transmission*. Joyce's portrait focuses this transmission on Stephen, and the word effects its passage: Stephen rejects the Church in order to become, theologically, Catholic. He will be a writer rather than a priest. As a figure of the artist, he will be a "deviant" or "twisted" priest, inscribing his illicit *jouissance* at the heart of the radiant, eucharistic sublimation of writing.

Joyce sets down on paper the limits of Catholicism and their overflow, starting with the *jouissance* canalized by the Church. He stages the two sides of this enjoyment: the symbolic, Trinitarian aspect as contrasted with the carnal or Marian one. Joyce's writing is simultaneously dramatic, theological, and comic, or "spiritual"—bewildering, through a forbidden illumination. Joyce's heterogeneous sublimation invites a reading from this stance, as he indicates himself, with some irony, in the scene of the *Portrait* centered on the writing of the villanelle. Joycean Catholicism is symbolic, sexual, scriptural: it circles toward the transmission of the Pentecost, the gift of tongues.

In the *Portrait*, Joyce posits the enunciation of *Non serviam* that allows him to navigate through the diverse identifications of language and sexuality. The ambivalent position of Lucifer opens out toward the infinite operation of languages and *jouissance* constitutive of Joyce's unique Catholicism. The latter reveals the Trinitarian status of writing: the call of the voice (the song of Dedalus the father, the sounding of a single, repeated note emanating from an infinite sky); the call of the image (giving flesh to filiation through the Virgin, the birdlike girl); the transfiguration of the name (Stephen's name, transformed, becomes the proper name of the artist).

The theological framework outlined in the *Portrait*—and in our preliminary discussion or point of departure—anticipates the enterprise of Joyce's later works. Our reading, then, moves out of the *Portrait* and into *Ulysses*, where Stephen Dedalus' conflict with the Church shifts toward the locus of language: desire and theology intertwine as filial flesh and *Verbum*. In *Ulysses* the center of Joycean subjectivity takes a new turn toward symbolic and artistic sources, fictionalized through the representation of Bloom. The theological structure of biblical light in darkness marks the relationship of the Son to the Father: through Bloom, Joyce engages the paternity of Judaism and Scripture, counterpointed by an aesthetic exploration of voice, song, and poetic language formulating *love's bitter mystery*. The question of the Passion emerges, linking autobiography to the Trinity. On a fictional plane, Joyce elaborates the encounter between Father and son as a vision, face to face, of language and exile. *Modus peregrinus* implies a way of writing, leading toward a new enunciation as Joyce operates the mysterious disappearance of fictional characters into a voice—feminized, for Joyce's most exquisite enjoyment— that opens a passage toward the "Irish stew" of *Work in Progress*.

Joyce confronts Judaism with the enunciation of the Virgin. The somewhat paradoxical result is the hyper-Catholic passage into *Finnegans Wake*—simultaneously Judaic and Catholic, constructed as a knot of sin, felicity, and the word. At this juncture, a specific focus on the Easter cycle in *Finnegans Wake* allows for the textual deployment and theoretical exploration of this knot as it affects the sacred discourse absorbed or engaged in the Joycean enterprise.[2]

Joyce's account of the Crucifixion filters autobiography through the fictional and stylistic elements of the *Wake* via echoes of sacred Scripture and Catholic dogma. The stage of suffering and enjoyment is set for the focus of the paschal experience, the nocturne of Holy Saturday. Here Joyce's integration of liturgy into the textual design becomes explicit within the formulation of the sacred and comic; Holy Saturday reveals the experience of negativity leading toward the *felix culpa*. The inscription of the speaking subject marks the convergence of autobiography and theology: the enigmatic experience of negative passage opens into the repressed sources of Catholicism, i.e., Judaism, articulating the Name and its signatures. The heterogeneity resulting from this return to Judaism is further implicated in the temporal dimensions of the paschal experience; here the Irish Church maps out its links to Judaism, sustaining Joyce's specifically Celtic-Catholic position. The Resurrection marks this turn with its Catholic focus, the counterpoint of the *felix culpa* rendered as revelation, vision of the invisible, the *call* that stylistically records jubilation in the series of exclamations underpinning Book IV of the *Wake*. It then becomes possible to read the text as a *paschal enunciation*, implicating the negativity of passage in the weave of names creating *Work in Progress* and transmuting it into *Finnegans Wake*—via the naming of James Joyce. The climax of the paschal experience and its revelation occurs at the Pentecost, countersigning the symbolic return in the moment of transmission. Ultimately, the margins of Catholicism unfold to reveal the mystical theology of Judaism; at its core is the mystery of the Name, the eucharistic heart of poetic language. The Joycean *punctum* is located with respect to one of the last formulations of *Wake* heterogeneity—the Catholic comedy of meaning and vocalization, "sense" and "sound." In support of this view, the Appendix provides a stylistic illustration of Joyce's Catholic comedy which locates the effects of Celtic illuminated manuscript in the art of Joycean interlace—the gift of tongues passing through *Finnegans Wake*.

"Dubliners," "Stephen Hero," "A Portrait of the Artist as a Young Man"

Thematic references to Catholicism play a considerable role in Joyce's work. At the same time this Catholic presence (the thematic content) slips into the interstices of the text as its symbolic power affects other themes (politics, friendship, mythology, and so on). Thus Joyce's Catholicism exceeds the limits of thematic content;[3] a proliferation of Catholic resonance is the result, particularly in *Ulysses* and *Finnegans Wake*.

In *Dubliners*[4] religion makes an ambiguous appearance. Joyce himself seems to vacillate between the true and the parodic, between that which engenders meaning and that which dissolves it. In the story "Grace," Joyce rejects the Church as a totalitarian institution consigning the failure of Catholicism:

here the Church is guilty of a kind of simony, acquiring power over the community in exchange for the meaning of its history and Scripture—its symbolic weight. On the other hand, in "The Sisters" and "The Dead" (the frame of the book), Joyce's bias is thoroughly Catholic. The fictional characters fall into the abyss of corruption, according to the Catholic location of sin in the desiring body. The broken chalice of Father Flynn emblematizes the permanence of sin. But this broken chalice, so significant on the sexual level, resonates above all on the level of theology. Confession and the mass are travestied or falsified in "The Sisters" and "Grace," and overturned in "The Dead"—where substance is ineluctably corrupted and the word (particularly that of Gabriel) does not receive transmission. Joyce marks his interest in theology in the narrator's speech ("The Sisters"), in the characters' lack of comprehension ("Grace"), and especially in the sketch of a Christly itinerary ("The Dead"): annunciation, birth, passion, and death, experienced or perceived by Gabriel, the bearer of the Word. . . . Gabriel's desire is displaced by the *passion* of another who had loved his wife and whose death rendered that love infinite. But within Joyce's negative framework, neither the drama of the Eucharist that impresses the boy in "The Sisters" nor the Passion glimpsed by Gabriel in "The Dead" gives rise to an enduring Word; all seem to be swallowed up by death.

In the fragments of the first long version of the *Portrait*,[5] an autobiographical character is portrayed in opposition to the Church; Stephen attempts to free himself from all authority and to establish his identity outside Catholicism. The limited scope of *Stephen Hero* focuses on the doubt undermining Stephen's Catholicism; rewritten as the *Portrait*, Stephen's refusal is posited in a theological context that imbricates sin, femininity, and the Word. In *Stephen Hero* sexuality forms an obstacle limiting Stephen's confrontation with theology since desire, sin, and femininity appear as the maternal body of the Church, the virgin mother of God. Stephen flees the eroticism of the Church by invoking the example of Christ. He moves beyond the doubt attributed to him, and he rejects Protestantism on theological grounds. This rejection is linked to Stephen's attraction to Catholicism as a focus on the tragic dimensions of Christ—on the liturgy as a vehicle for artistic beauty: "Jesus had a very pure tragic manner. . . . Do you imagine the Church could have erected such elaborately artistic sacraments about his legend unless the original figure had been one of a certain tragic majesty?" (166). Stephen's emphasis on the paschal drama of darkness and light foreshadows the symbolic arrangement of Joyce's later work. He evokes the dramatic horror of Tenebrae ("Isn't it strange to see the Mass of the Presanctified—no lights or vestments, the altar naked, the door of the tabernacle gaping open, the priests lying prostrate on the altar steps?" [106]) and the transformation of Christ ("The corpse has become a paschal candle with five grains of incense stuck in it instead of its five wounds" [107]). Stephen here refers to the benediction of the new fire, the Christly illumination of darkness, in the dramatic and musical representation preparing the Resurrection. It is this tragedy turned into jubilation that fascinates Stephen. The drama of Christ gives rise to the theological dimensions of *Stephen Hero*; outside the Church, Stephen is more Catholic than ever.

Rewritten as *A Portrait of the Artist as a Young Man*, the trajectory of the central character is staged through his interpretation of Catholicism; his rejection of the Church becomes a pivotal moment of the narrative within a new perspective centered on the articulation of sin and theology. At the moment of Stephen's refusal of priestly seductions, the Church is posited as an institution of social order opposed to the symbolic singularity of the individual: "When the soul of a man is born in this country there are nets flung at it to hold it back from flight. You talk to me of nationality, language, religion. I shall try to fly by those nets" (203). The anticipated flight of exile is founded in the encounter with sexuality (sin) and the symbolic—with the flesh and the Word. As in *Stephen Hero*, the Church is seen as an extension of maternal authority: after an argument with his mother, Stephen declares, "I will not serve." The supposed mother tongue of Gaelic and the fatherland join religious discourse as obstacles to Stephen's freedom: "I will not serve that in which I no longer believe whether it call itself my home, my fatherland or my church" (247).

The declaration of flight leads Stephen into the infinite realm of sin, in Stephen's negative exploration of the sacred. He abandons himself to the forbidden alterity of femininity and abjection, the dark night that overflows the boundaries of his imagination: "He had sinned mortally not once but many times and he knew that while he stood in danger of eternal damnation for the first sin alone, by every succeeding sin he multiplied his guilt and his punishment" (103). The imaginary unity of the body is fractioned by desire: it is flesh. Joyce records the Catholic strategy of the integration of flesh as the locus of sin, destined to rot in the abyss of Hell. The sinner is maintained in negativity in order that his sinfulness may be transformed into holiness. He must abandon the world and its enjoyment: Stephen attempts to deny the flesh and return to the putative innocence of childhood. This strategy entails a brush with castration in order to save Stephen from the hell implicit in *jouissance*: "The serpent, the most subtle beast of the field" (118).

Since the writing of Genesis, the separation between sin and purity has been interpreted as a fall. The Catholic version of sin, however, carries the traces of beatitude or purity within it: sin is condemned from within the structure without being completely expelled. Sin functions like the negative sign of beatitude, its symmetrical subversion: "These devils, who were once beautiful angels, have become as hideous and ugly as they once were beautiful" (123). Catholicism is thus the impossible synthesis of a non-synthetic contradiction—a split between spirit and body. The doubled, or heterogeneous, status of Christianity persists even in Hell; sin contains its own intimate refusal of the sacred as an interiorized double: "Sin, remember, is a twofold enormity. It is a base consent to the promptings of our corrupt nature to the lower instincts . . . and it is also a turning away from the counsel of our higher nature, from all that is pure and holy, from the Holy God Himself" (127).

Stephen attempts to counteract his abandon in sin by dedicating himself to the Virgin. Displaced from the instance of the Symbolic, the Virgin gives her fleshly being to God in the form of the Son. The Virgin provides a screen masking the demoniacal quality of flesh: "There was still time. O Mary, refuge of sinners, intercede for him! O Virgin undefiled, save him from the gulf of death!" (125). The Virgin plays a central role in the Catholic doubling of sin. Her cult marks the convergence of imagery, music, symbols: *like the morning star which is thy emblem, bright and musical, breathing purity, telling of heaven and infusing peace* (139). The signs of the Virgin proliferate—spices, vestments, plants, flowering trees. The femininity that attracts Stephen leads him alternately to prostitutes and to the Virgin. After the retreat, he seems to identify his own abandonment with that of the Virgin herself—"virginal self-surrender." His soul is woman/spouse/virgin, giving itself over to the amorous inaudible voice of the Song of Songs, considered by the mystics to be a holy voice speaking to the soul: "A faded world of fervent love and virginal responses seemed to be evoked for his soul by the reading of its pages in which the imagery of the canticles was interwoven with the communicant's prayers. An inaudible voice seemed to caress the soul telling her names and glories . . . bidding her look forth, a spouse . . . and the soul seemed to answer with the same inaudible voice, surrendering herself: *inter ubera mea commorabitur*" (152).

The call of sin is now filtered through a Catholic disguise of eroticism. Although Stephen seems to be taken in by his own Catholic ruse, he echoes the terms of his fall into sin, imagining the femininity of his soul: eroticized with respect to the voice, seduced and seductive, he answers the call interiorizing the abyss and the unnameable. This call of the flesh[6] works its way through the sexual and linguistic gamut of positions; it is perverted in the abjection of institutional hierarchy. Stephen utters *Non serviam* in response to the Church—and begins his trajectory toward the Word.

The confrontation with sin and religious exile leads Stephen toward the symbolic domain of a noncarnal birth: the flight of the soul, beyond the nets of repression. This repression establishes two types of barriers. The first is the repression (in the specifically psychoanalytic sense) of representations linked to the drives (to pleasure); Catholicism makes pleasure into *jouissance*, and the repression of substance becomes a repression of the flesh. Second, the symbolic sense of repression focuses on the Christly *Verbum*, whose Incarnation is the effect of sin (the carnal mystery). In the lifting of repression, the access to the Word comes forth as an erotic venture—through flesh and through a representation of the Word itself.

Stephen responds to the paternal voice: "He smiled to think that it was this disorder, the misrule and confusion of his father's house and the stagnation of vegetable life, which was to win the day in his soul" (162). His brothers and sisters sing, recalling the song of his father in the Victoria Hotel, "the tender tremors with which his father's voice festooned the strange sad happy air" (88). The father's style of singing transmits the undecidable emotion through the tremolo effects—trembling, beating, vibration, sign—mingled with the lyrics, putting them into relief. When Joyce's own son began a singing career, Joyce wrote to him: "Pensa alle parole, ti supplico. Il canto non è che un linguaggio alato."[7] The voice brings about a transfiguration, like the erotic moment envisioned by the child Stephen, troubled by "the unsubstantial image" of Mercedes: "They would be alone, surrounded by darkness and silence: and in that moment of supreme tenderness he would be transfigured" (65). The representation passes through a voice (of the father, of God on Mount Thabor), through a magical mysterious figuration, an unsubstantial image: the body of Christ become like the sun (Matt. 17:2), the flesh of the Virgin bearing the *Verbum*, the bread and wine transformed into God. Symbolicity is approached through figuration—the image of the body, the fluid "substance" of language: "the liquid letters of speech" (223). But the symbolic is not absorbed by this multiple figuration. In the Bible, God manifests himself through natural phenomena that do not contain him; and then he speaks. As if to show that the prophetic vocation or Incarnation operates through a *passage* (*transitus*): a Passover.[8]

Stephen awaits the call of the Word. Having refused ordination, his interest in religious discourse is displaced toward language itself, "the rhythmic rise and fall of words . . . the contemplation of an inner world of individual emotions mirrored perfectly in a lucid supple periodic prose" (166–167). Stephen makes a distinction between words and things, concentrating on the musical qualities of language, *linguaggio alato*, recalling the voice of the father's song. He receives the call of language through music: "A voice beyond the world was calling" (167). It calls him by name: "Hello, Stephanos! . . . Stephanos Dedalos! Bous Stephanoumenos! Bous Stephaneforos!" (167–168). "His strange name seemed to him a prophecy" (168): his name signs him as artist, creator of "a new soaring impalpable imperishable being" (169). The flight of the mythical artist Daedalus slips toward the flight Stephen defines through eucharistic symbolism: "His soul was soaring in an air beyond the world and the body he knew was purified in a breath and delivered of incertitude and made radiant and commingled with the element of spirit" (169). Symbolic *jouissance* is made possible by the Word; as "uncreated conscience" or spirit, it will take form in Stephen's art. The mythical Daedalus and the father who sings converge in the name of the father calling the artist toward his Trinitarian configuration, the linking of Father and Son through the Holy Spirit.

The call is crystallized in the feminine *image* posited as the subversion of sin. In Catholic logic, God takes on human form through the intermediary of the Virgin. At the end of the fourth chapter of the *Portrait*, the Incarnation is condensed in the instant of the call, the signifier coming forth, establishing the temporal break of before/after. With a symbolic gesture, the feminine receptacle becomes the vessel of the Word; her glance rendered as a sign, she marks the spiritual flight of Stephen with her heterogeneity. As a womanly figure at the edge of the sea (the significant element of reproduction, the biological site) and as a Daedalian bird (the paternal sign of artistic flight), the bird-like girl calls Stephen to creation: "Her image had passed into his soul forever and no word had broken the holy silence of his ecstasy. Her eyes had called him and his soul had leaped at the call" (172). In his erotic relation to the Virgin, Stephen surrenders once again to the flesh that will give him life: "His soul was swooning into some new world, fantastic, dim, uncertain as under sea, traversed by cloudy shapes and beings. . . . Glimmering and trembling, trembling and unfolding, a breaking light" (172). This birth is metaphorized through images of light, color, and the cyclic rhythms of poetic language projecting Stephen toward the *jouissance* of art.

Stephen's awakening to the Word echoes the context of the call: "O what sweet music! . . . Over his limbs in sleep pale cool waves of light had passed" (217). This passage is embellished with liturgical images of light, incense, bells, etc. Stephen's elaboration of the villanelle becomes part of the paschal celebration focused on the Holy Saturday benediction of fire and water. Joyce relates the Christly images of light to Stephen's access to poetic language: "waves of light," "point of light," "white flame," "rose and ardent light," "rays of rhyme," "smoke, incense ascending from the altar," "roselight" (217–218). In the liturgy, the Holy Spirit is asked to fecundate the baptismal water of grace: "His soul was all dewy wet. . . . A spirit filled him, pure as the purest water, sweet as dew, moving as music" (217). The celebrant breathes on the water while invoking the holy breath: *Descendant in hanc plenitudinem fontis, virtus Spiritus Sancti.* Stephen is filled with the Holy Spirit as he was filled with the image of the bird-like girl, whose form echoes that taken by the Spirit as dove: "A spirit filled him" (217).

In contrast to *Stephen Hero*, the *Portrait* explicitly assimilates the symbolic elaboration of the Trinity within artistic creation: According to Saint Thomas, "God's relation to created things is that of the architect to his works."[9] The Trinitarian venture includes the paternal voice (the call naming Stephen Dedalus—the proper name of the son and the name of the father, the paternal song, Stephen's scriptural enunciation, and the call of God the Father); the incarnated Word (Stephen's filiation and creation, through imagination and the forms of the Passion); and the Holy Spirit (the transmission of *ruah*, breath: gift, love, fire, effusion, etc.), linking the instance of the vocal enunciation with the Word it brings forth. The tongues of fire derive from a voice at their source and the incarnated Word; according to Stephen, the Holy Spirit offers itself—in scriptural creation, in love (encoded as the "enchantment of the heart"), in the "morning knowledge" of words. The Holy Spirit, the unity of Father and Son, is thus described in the liturgy of the Pentecost. Joyce marks its inscription with the liturgical color red, symbolizing fire, alternating with the whiteness of light.

In this moment of "inspiration," of "spirit . . . inbreathed,"

Stephen's writing seems to be catalyzed by its apostrophic object, Emma Clery. In the villanelle, liturgical figures of praise, enchantment, and eucharistic sacrifice are arranged around the central image of the sinner's Fall. The ambiguity of the poem stems from this *Fall*, involving the Passion of Christ, the God whose encounter with flesh begins in a woman's body. The fall locates sin—the transformation of pleasure into *jouissance*—in the line of vision of the Holy Spirit—identified by Saint Hilary as *jouissance* itself.[10] The Passion of the *Verbum* comes into view as the repetition of the Fall. In Joycean terms as in Catholic theology, the Word passes through a feminine vessel, where it takes on flesh, thus marking the split between the body of the Virgin and the desired flesh implicated in sin. Despite her purity, Emma lures the angels to their downfall. The Catholic consequence of this split, the *felix culpa*, will resonate in *Finnegans Wake*.

Joyce emphasizes the Catholicism he attributes to Stephen: "O! In the virgin womb of the imagination the word was made flesh. Gabriel the seraph had come to the virgin's chamber" (217). In a letter to Nora, Joyce elaborates the same figures concerning the text of *Dubliners*: "thinking of the book I have written, the child which I have carried for years and years in the womb of the imagination as you carried in your womb the children you love."[11] Gabriel announces to the Virgin her conception through the Holy Spirit: *Et concepit de Spiritu Sancto*. According to the femininity of Stephen's soul or imagination, the angels come to inspire him: *Et Verbum caro factum est*.

In this text the liturgical context of the Pentecost—the descent of the Holy Spirit on the Apostles—clarifies the relation between the Holy Spirit and the Word. The Holy Spirit is the illuminated breath of the Word, the gift of the voice in the whirlwind of tongues; language is infinitely divided into voices and the plurality of languages in order to "magnify God." In Peter's speech to the crowd, the tongues of fire are formulated through dream, vision, prophecy—the terms of Stephen's awakening: "a dream or vision," "augury," "symbol." Filled with the Spirit, Stephen writes the villanelle and then seeks a sign—or countersign—of prophecy: "A soft liquid joy flowed through the words where the soft long vowels hurtled noiselessly and fell away, lapping and flowing back and ever shaking the white bells of their waves in mute chime and mute peal and soft low swooning cry; and he felt that the augury . . . had come forth from his heart" (226). Joyce repeats the configuration of liturgical imagery heralding the Holy Spirit; the letter itself ("the liquid letters of speech") seems to share the fluidity of the forms taken by the Holy Spirit. The augury emerges from this fluidity in a symbolic and eucharistic form: "symbols of . . . mystery."

The Catholic focus of Joyce's text confronts the Church with the sin that overflows its boundaries, thus underlining the complicity between the Fall and the Passion—scandalously revealing the erotic subversion of order. The *Non serviam* of Lucifer introduces the theological dimensions of the Passion that ultimately lead Joyce toward the writing of the *felix culpa*. Stephen is the fictional focus revealing the passage through flesh of the *Verbum* as a passage through art—the feminine voice of theology: *"Et tu cum Jesu Galilaeo eras"* (244).

—————

Ulysses

1

―――

And the Light Shineth
in Darkness

Stephen: the refusal

In *Ulysses* the character of Stephen Dedalus is free of the institutional attachments confronted in the *Portrait:* the religious training, the retreat, and the call of the Jesuit Father are definitively relegated to the past. The articulation of *Non serviam* in the *Portrait* effectively prevents the Jesuit-influenced adolescence from seeping into the present tense of June 16, 1904; *Non serviam* became the verbal emblem (the *symbolum*) of the break anticipated at the end of the *Portrait*. This rupture took place between the *Portrait* and *Ulysses* but was instantly canceled by the mother's death. Stephen's detachment at the *Portrait's* conclusion, his flight past the institutional nets of society, religion[1] and family, is altered by the death of the mother who had attempted to reconcile him with the Church. But the effect of her death is to plummet the Daedalian Stephen back to Irish earth when he receives the telegram: "Mother dying come home father."[2] The call of father Daedalus at the end of the "Portrait" is reversed and brings the son back to the starting point: "Fabulous artificer, the hawk-like man. You flew. Whereto? Newhaven-Dieppe, steerage passenger. Paris and back. Lapwing. Icarus. *Pater, ait.* . . . Lapwing you are" (*U* 210). The failed flight is signaled by the paternal Daedalus, the terror of death and the "sins of hell"

3

(underlined by the maternal figure), and the filial character whose fall is qualified as exile form a constellation recalling Dante's descent into Malebolge. Joyce's Dantean identification is substantiated through Daedalus, particularly in light of the mournful exclamation Dante invents for Daedalus as he witnesses the fatal flight of Icarus: "Mala via tieni!" (*Inferno*, XVII, 111). The flight of Daedalus brings about the fall of Icarus; the fallen Stephen returns, lapwing, to his mother.[3] From this point on, his act of rupture or flight must be repeated—except that his mother has died, and his rejection of institutions resonates in the narrative account of her death. The problematic status of the breaking away has changed: Stephen's exile in Paris, thwarted but made *real* (in the Lacanian sense) by the mother's death, does not suffice to free him from the institution. The conflict, now internalized, sets the stage of signification in *Ulysses*. Stephen's sense of guilt and his mourning/melancholia lead him to confront the repressive agency—the nets he had attempted to elude, and primarily that of the Catholic institution.

The first scene of *Ulysses* concerns the rejection of the institution, specifically as regards the deceased mother. Mulligan accuses Stephen of diabolically killing his mother: "You could have knelt down, damn it, Kinch, when your dying mother asked you, Buck Mulligan said. . . . But to think of your mother begging you with her last breath to kneel down and pray for her. And you refused. There is something sinister in you" (5). For Mulligan, Catholic ritual is without meaning; Stephen's refusal seems to him absurd, skewed, perverse. Not only does Mulligan reject Stephen's identification, he finds it incomprehensible that Stephen can articulate a refusal of Catholicism while, at the same time, taking Catholicism seriously: "Etiquette is etiquette. He kills his mother but he can't wear grey trousers" (6). Stephen's Catholicism is perverse because it is divided, ambivalent. His rejection of the institution leads him to take a distanced, parodic position, in which the dissolving of meaning into nonsense puts in relief his exile from the Church; but his opposition to Mulligan (who calls him "fearful jesuit" [3], "priestified kinchite" [199], "inquisitional drunken jew jesuit" [216], "Jesified orchidized polycimical jesuit" [425]) indicates that neither the parodic dimension nor the rejection of the institution completely destroys the seriousness of Stephen's Catholicism. Stephen's refusal situates him in a Luciferian space: sinister (demoniacal), his Jesuit strain "injected the wrong way" (8), (twisted) Catholic.

But insofar as Stephen enjoys Mulligan's parody—his subversive, potentially atheistic distance from Catholic truth—even his refusal is double: the *Portrait's* binary articulation of Lucifer/Christ is echoed by another double relation to Catholicism, that of parody and slavery. Stephen is stymied by his own doubled positions. His denunciation of Mulligan's parody is therefore, problematic. He condemns Mulligan's subtraction of meaning from Catholicism, his untying of the Trinitarian knot: "*et unam sanctam catholicam et apostolicam ecclesiam:* the slow growth and change of rite and dogma like his own rare thoughts, a chemistry of stars. Symbol of the apostles in the mass for pope Marcellus, the voices blended, singing alone loud in affirmation; and behind their chant the vigilant angel of the church militant disarmed and menaced her heresiarchs. A horde of heresies fleeing with mitres awry: Photius and the brood of mockers of whom Mulligan was one" (20–21). Stephen's ambivalence is such that his defense of the Trinity crumbles into self-parody even as he condemns Mulligan's parody: "Hear, hear. Prolonged applause. *Zut! Nom de Dieu!*" (21).

Stephen's refusal makes him into a Catholic in exile because, in spite of his denegation, his Catholic stance is manifest. His self-excommunication looks suspiciously like an excommunication of the entire Church, thereby putting Stephen in the position of sole Catholic: "FLORRY: Are you out of Maynooth? You're like someone I knew once. STEPHEN: Out of it now. Clever" (519). The prostitute corrects Stephen's denegation: "FLORRY (*To Stephen*): I'm sure you are a spoiled priest. Or a monk" (523). Stephen has trouble making his refusal understood since his Ulyssean entourage (Mulligan, Haines, Bloom, etc., and Lynch in the *Portrait*) takes him for a Catholic. Thus he must act out his refusal, in symbolic terms—encoded, already in the *Portrait,* in the *Non serviam* uttered by Lucifer, "th'Apostate Angel."[5] In the general hallucination of "Circe," Stephen can no longer use denegation to fend off the

Catholic institution; it threatens and haunts him, leading him toward the maternal vacuum and death. In confronting this mother, Stephen repeats his denegation, directly addressed to her: "STEPHEN: *Ah non, par exemple!* The intellectual imagination! With me all or not at all. *Non Serviam!*" (582). Stephen's acting out, prelude to his fall, brings him beyond the repeated denegation he sustains with symbolic means in a theatrical catharsis:[6] "STEPHEN: Nothung! (*He lifts his ashplant high with both hands and smashes the chandelier. Time's livid final flame leaps and, in the following darkness, ruin of all space, shattered glass and toppling masonry*" (582). Stephen's cane functions like Siegfried's sword Nothung, the signifier of the father's name and death, and thus reinforces the nickname of Kinch: Stephen-Kinch, the onomatopoeia of a knife blade, cuts with his words.[7] Stephen's destructive gesture acts as a cut, a sacrifice, a rupture, actualizing denegation in the form of a catastrophe. Stephen gives himself over to this apocalyptic night, and thus the trial by fire to which he alludes at the end of "Oxen of the Sun"[8] resonates in the last flame of time: "She [Babylon] shall be utterly burned with fire," "There should be time no longer" (Apoc. 18:8; 10:6). In Joyce's rewriting of the Revelation of St. John the Divine, Stephen comes face to face with his mother as he awaits *her* revelation. But the dead mother engages in an institutional battle to save Stephen, who overturns the Revelation of the new Jerusalem (Apoc. 21) by locating Lucifer's refusal within it.

The catastrophe set in motion by Stephen, echoing Lucifer's catastrophe, indicates that the Catholic itinerary turns back to the time of the Creation and of Lucifer's dramatic leap into the dark void. Stephen too puts out the light; and the darkness associated with sin throughout *Ulysses* and particularly in "Circe" (the night of fantasy and abjection) seems to speak out both for him and for his refusal. The dimension of the real, as located in the mother's dead body, becomes the abject space of the institution, which shows itself incapable of eluding sin. After this scene, Stephen recognizes the interiorization of his refusal. Although it is still problematic and paradoxical, Stephen signals his breaking away from all exterior nets: "(*He taps his brow*) But in here it is I must kill the priest and the king" (589).

Nevertheless, Stephen's attempt to detach himself from the

Catholic institution is offset by other elements of his experience, other problems rooted in Catholicism. These elements are more or less personified: Mulligan represents parody, heresy; the phantom of Mrs. Dedalus is the focus of sin and love as well as the rejection of the institution; and several characters, notably Bloom, play a paternal role with Stephen. Indeed, Stephen seems to solicit a paternity which, through Bloom's intervention, takes a theological form: it brings together the problems and their solutions in a space of potential *jouissance*—in the sacred, violent, sexual space of art.

Catholic and pagan

Stephen opposes Mulligan, who plays the role of friend—the equivalent of the fraternal enemy, in Joycean terms.[9] Starting with the *Portrait,* Joyce brings into focus the position of the friend, in the battle between Stephen and the character who is his betrayer: the opposition is based on religion. In *Ulysses* the refusal of the institution is less central than in the *Portrait;* the Catholic venture is located elsewhere, on theological territory. It is Stephen who defends Catholicism.

Stephen vacillates between two positions—on the one hand, complicity with Mulligan's humor (mocking everything, thereby jeopardizing any seriousness; Mulligan ridicules others by playing the clown) and, on the other, the tragic implications of his own experience of Catholicism. Of filiation: in Stephen's family romance, the adopted son is created not so much by his parents as by the triune God via the Virgin vessel of the Word. But Stephen resists Mulligan's temptation: "God, Kinch, if you and I could only work together we might do something for the island. Hellenise it" (7).[10] Stephen's internal conflict is specifically rooted in the question of Hellenization; Stephen shares Mulligan's parody but without succumbing to paganism. And, too, the parodically powerful Mulligan seems to incarnate all of Stephen's fraternal enemies. Like Hce (and his sons) in *Finnegans Wake,* Stephen is brought to trial and judged.

Stephen opposes Mulligan with respect to the question of filiation. Mulligan seems to scorn the quasi-Oresteian drama of the mother's death; according to those passing judgment

(Mulligan and his aunt), Stephen is responsible for Mrs. Dedalus' death since he refused *to go through the motions* of prayer. The reproach addressed to Stephen the Jesuit is tantamount to a condemnation of Catholic truth.[11] Mulligan is remote from the filiation so crucial to Stephen, and he is thus left untouched by the Oedipal drama of desire. Mulligan consequently lacks any trinitarian theological dimensions, just as, regarding the castration complex, he is remote from the dimensions of the Word (*Verbum*) with its carnal, demoniacal passage. It is clear, then, that the conflict between Stephen and Mulligan is central to the venture of *Ulysses;* the depiction of Bloom and Stephen, and particularly of the obstacles they face, confirms this reading, as does the event which fleetingly ties them together at the threshold of a descent into night, of an entrance into sleep and dream—on the threshold of the death vigil/awakening of *Finnegans Wake.*

Mulligan advises Stephen to create semblances or appearances: "Why don't you play them as I do?"(16). Mulligan eludes or rejects truth in favor of the real; life and death are natural, bestial, without signification or symbolic weight. Any symbolic investment is a semblance, a parody. Mulligan returns to the pagan real-ness of nature from which Judeo-Christianity had disengaged itself.[12] He extols an agricultural, institutional sexuality ("Mr Malachi Mulligan, Fertiliser and Incubator, Lambay Island" [402]) destructive of eroticism—that is, of the signifying, linguistic dimension of human sexuality. According to the Freudian formulation, sexuality is not natural: it is *perverse,* obscene, and hence Catholic.[13]

Mulligan's version of the real is, moreover, "greeker than the greeks" (201). It is predicated on a repression of women as objects of desire: "An allocution from Mr Candidate Mulligan . . . postulating as the supremest object of desire a nice clean old man" (411).[14] "Greek" pleasure assimilates women as "natural"—as mothers—while eliminating feminine desire—flesh, obscenity, the horror of the Other. For Stephen, femininity links desire to death and horror.[15] When Mulligan mentions the mother's death, Stephen's thoughts focus on sacred ritual (the prayer of the dying, the bowl of bitter waters [Num. 5:15ff.]) in which the ground and theater of guilt is fleshly substance. The symbolic weight of words and things evoked by Stephen seems to counter Mulligan's accusations, thereby revealing the conflict between Stephen and his mother: "What is a ghost? Stephen said with tingling energy. One who has faded into impalpability through death, through absence" (188). Stephen confronts the crossing of death—absence, or invisibility representative of spiritual being—as nonsubstantial, trans-substantial.

Oedipus and the complex of meaning

Without father and mother, Mulligan lacks a sense of tragedy: through his intimacy with real substance, he makes of desire something natural, the body/detritus of paganism. The tragedy of his mother's death pins Stephen between *amor matris* and *Non serviam:* he oscillates between desire and revolt against her authority. But her death consigns him to the horror of a *culpa* which can never be rendered *felix:* "I could not save her. Waters: bitter death: lost" (46). Stephen is caught between the prayer and his own silence, between symbolic purification and the death that overruns it and bears it away. The repeated prayer filtering into the text is the emblem of desire's intersection with death. It is the emblem of the erotic wound Stephen suffers at his mother's death and his attempt to distance himself from death itself as well as from the Catholic authority integrating it. Stephen refuses to say the prayer; he rejects the fleshly death of his mother. Yet he cleaves to her, incestuously: she is the point of origin, of sin and flesh. He is thus suspended between the meaning of prayer (purification of death and the dead, separation of sinful flesh from the soul, the location of symbolicity)[16] and the erotic bias of his interpretation of Catholicism. Horrified by the flesh, he nevertheless cannot give it up; he would then risk total castration at the hands of a "Libidinous God" (assisted by his mother). Standing silently during the prayer uttered while his mother dies, Stephen refuses to engage in a ritual that will later haunt him. The prayer marks the symbolic renunciation of the flesh, the gift of the maternal body to *Dio boia*, the executioner—Joyce's libidinous God.[17] Stephen thus places himself in the abyss of sin, refusing to acknowledge the Catholic absorption of the female flesh, of his mother's sin. The abyss is represented by the sea, which has become a gigantic bowl of bile, "bowl of bitter waters." According to Numbers 5, the "jealousy offering" consists in a trial by internal abomination—she who dies after swallowing the bitter waters is a sinner, for her death proves that she has committed adultery.

Stephen finds himself in the double bind of sin and incest. His lack gives rise to a phobic horror that he cunningly projects as the abject sin of the mother (the vampire or "corpse-chewer") who has betrayed him by dying. On the other hand, his lack gives rise to desire, dramatically articulated in the *cut*, where Stephen's *jouissance* nails him to the flesh and incarnates him.[18] This double bind presents the subject with the following aporia: how is it possible to say No to the Church and Yes to sin, when the locus of sin is in a woman's body? Abjection is situated in a feminine space, as it is in the institution, an avatar of femininity, for the Church is the bride of Christ. The prayer crystallizes remorse bearing guilt, the "agenbite of inwit." Through a displacement, the prayer recited next to the bed is a sign of the impossible and pervasive death of Mrs. Dedalus—it constitutes a sublimation of abjection. The purity of virgins, of confessors carrying shining lilies *disguises* the demoniacal quality of death through an effect of reversal of meaning characteristic of dreams.[19]

When Mulligan accuses Stephen of having killed his mother, he accuses him rather of having loved her, of having incestuously sought paternity via the woman who made him her son. Moreover, Christly filiation is Oedipal since the father is absent, suspended, and his position is filled by the son. Mulligan's mockery of Stephen singles out his incestuous leanings: "*Ma mère m'a mariée*" (424). The gap separating Mulligan from the domain of the flesh distances him from language as well, for he can only function according to the parodic mode, marking the detours of meaning and the undoing of meaning. Parody is the pretender of language, the creator of semblances or illusions; thus Stephen, despite the doubts that tempt him toward parody, condemns the heretical character of Mulligan's parody of Catholicism. Joyce the writer, orchestrating these different voices, fully exploits the possibility of taking seriously the object of parody.[20]

Through parody, Joyce presents Stephen on the brink of non-sense, thereby countering the positivism of the institution of Catholicism. Parody reflects the Joycean ambivalence regarding Catholicism—and Mulligan personifies the risk entailed by that ambivalence. It is through parody (the Eucharist, "the ballad of Joking Jesus," "Everyman his own Wife," Yeats's "Baile and Ailinne," etc.) that Mulligan inflicts erotic wounds on Stephen. Mulligan's intimacy with substance seems to call forth parody: his repetitions and nonsense are ultimately demoniacal. His universe is circumscribed by the violence of the real, which he describes as "beastly." In this kingdom of abjection, he plays the "stage irishman" with his caricatures and multiple roles. But he emphasizes the automatism of nonsense, which tends to devour meaning: like Prospero's book drowned in the sea, language is swallowed by corporality. Thus even if Stephen asks his mother for the Word, it is in order to follow the opposite trajectory—incarnation. Mulligan attempts to deprive Stephen of symbolic discourse in order to sink him in the maternal sea and reduce him to silence. He consigns Stephen to psychosis ("That fellow I was with in the Ship last night, said Buck Mulligan, says you have g.p.i. . . . General paralysis of the insane" [6]) in order to prevent him from creating poetic language ("He can never be a poet"[249]). Because of this, Mulligan condemns the creative process, Yeats, Stephen's Shakespearean theory, and writing itself; he is hostile to Stephen's potential filiation, and he mocks Simon Dedalus, Bloom, Shakespeare, and Christ. In this context, his reply (in "Scylla and Charybdis") to Stephen's evocation of Thomas Aquinas is particularly significant: "Saint Thomas, Stephen began . . . *Ora pro nobis*, Monk Mulligan groaned, sinking to a chair. There he keened a wailing rune. *Pogue mahone! Acushla machree!* It's destroyed we are from this day! It's destroyed we are surely!" (205). Instinctively, Mulligan recognizes his enemy in the symbolic system of theology.

Stephen: the theological dimension

The Trinitarian knot is nearly undone by the refusal of the institution and by the comedy undermining Catholicism—

comedy being the point of no return for the totalizing system of theology. The break with the institution gives access to the sovereign laughter that defies enslavement: "Dieu-esclave demande mon esclavage au second degré dans l'établissement de chaînes sans fin. Rire de l'univers libérait ma vie. J'échappe à la pesanteur en riant. . . . Aucune limite à partir d'un rire assez violent."[21] Having interiorized his enslavement, Stephen laughs only halfheartedly: he is ambivalent, or double. Thus he functions, according to Freud's *Witz,* in a compromise between slavery (the unity of meaning, serious discourse) and Mulligan's parody (the mocking destruction of meaning, which seems to be swallowed up by corporality). Stephen incarnates the two dimensions—his parody can be read as "incurring debtorship for a thing done," i.e., bearing the burden of its serious statement (*énoncé*) before turning into a pulverized enunciation. In this territory of the double, the subject mocks itself and, indeed, the subject *becomes* subject in the battle with the unified agency of authority, whereas Mulligan uses parody only as a mask, covering up his lack of a subjective stance in language.

The opposition between serious discourse and parody reinforces the interiorized split of religion in the *Portrait.* In the conflict between Stephen and Mulligan, the split between Catholic and profane, purity and sin, is articulated even in the style of the characters' spoken language. Religious doubles are even more important in *Ulysses* than they were previously, and they reach their peak in *Finnegans Wake.* The split between sin and purity first takes place within Catholicism: in rejecting the Jesuits and turning toward the father, Stephen maintains his Catholic context, articulated as an identification with Lucifer/Christ. But sin is equivocal: although established within Catholicism through the interiorization of the desiring flesh, sin marks a vanishing point, leading the sinner into the world and outside the Catholic domain. Sin is thus midway between Catholicism and the "world," between soul and flesh, between truth and the real: it constitutes the knot of religious doubling.

As Joyce remarks in his essay on the Renaissance, medieval Catholicism is shunted aside by the modern world. Modern realism emphasizes sensation, materiality, and the body, thereby relegating Catholicism to the past.[22] Thus, for Joyce the modern writer, religion is doubled (or split) on several levels. Catholicism is necessary for Joyce's symbolic framework, but in order to put it into writing, he filters it through a setting of the modern world and its realism. The latter seems to open out in the light of subjectivity—deployed in the dream, in the interior monologue, in hallucination—thereby creating a heterogeneous dimension of tragicomedy. The doubling that Joyce (writing tongue in cheek) uncovers in the Renaissance reveals his slant on religious questions. Between medieval and modern, between purity and sin, religion in *Ulysses* becomes the object of a scriptural expansion of Catholic meaning. Its double articulation is reflected in the Joycean treatment of the split subject, which is at the foundation of Joyce's stylistic invention.

What allows us to distinguish Stephen's Catholicism from the destruction of meaning implied by Mulligan's parody? We must again invoke the religious doubles inherent in the function of Catholicism, but, in this instance, as they operate within dogma itself. It is through the intervention of heresy that dogma remains vigorous; heresy introduces doubt to the realm of truth, thereby undermining truth from within. Throughout the history of Catholicism, what is at stake in the venture of theology is formulated as the problematic of the Trinity:[23] "quod Trinitas sit unus et solus et verus Deus, et quam recte Pater et Filius et Spiritus sanctus unius ejusdemque substantiae vel essentiae dicatur, credatur, intelligatur" (the Trinity is a single, sole and true God, and it is correct to say, to believe, to think that Father, Son, and Holy Ghost are of a same and unique substance or essence). Saint Augustine evokes knowledge received "per speculum in aenigmate" in his discussion of knowledge or vision of a God impossible to represent, inconceivable without grace. The Trinitarian heresies are evidence of this representational difficulty—they maintain either the One or the Three: "In the sovereign Trinity there are three Persons, however this Trinity of Three Persons is more inseparable than the Trinity of one alone." "One essence (or substance) and three Persons"—this is what Augustine calls "marvellously ineffable or ineffably marvellous."[24] For Stephen, despite his tendency to dissolve discourse in laughter, the Trinity holds its own.

Mulligan's irony calls forth Stephen's meditation on the creed followed by a condemnation of heresy: "Symbol of the apostles in the mass for pope Marcellus, the voices blended, singing alone loud in affirmation: and behind their chant the vigilant angel of the church militant disarmed and menaced her heresiarchs" (21).

The symbol (or creed) at the heart of Catholicism casts Trinitarian meaning in the form of musical *jouissance,* and this Catholic art dismisses the claims of the heretics. Thus, Stephen conceives of himself as a defender of theology; and the Trinity, at the core of Catholic theology, is concentrated in the form of the *symbol* of Catholic law and Catholic language: "Est-ce à ces dons ou bien aux mots de passe qui y accordent leur non-sens salutaire, que commence le langage avec la loi? Car ces dons sont déjà symboles, en ceci que symbole veut dire pacte, et qu'ils sont d'abord signifiants du pacte qu'ils constituent comme signifié."[25] At the crossroads of Catholicism and psychonalysis, "la symbolisation dans l'être" stands out. It presents itself, literally, in speech—at the meeting point of music and voiced language: "La musicalisation de la langue, à rebours, remonte à ces bases de la fonction sémiotique: articulation de marques vides (phonèmes liées aux charges pulsionnelles + représentation, passage au signe. Le langage poétique retire dans l'ordre *symbolique* la musicalité et la gestualité fondamentales de la *semiosis.*"[26] The theological question is henceforth inseparable from the artistic venture or, more specifically, from that of poetic language. The *jouissance* or artistic fruition of the symbolic structure of the Trinity first implies a process of sublimation (the displacement of drives toward artistic production).[27] Then, an anchoring or a position in symbolicity allows for a passage through the territory of the drives. This economy is outlined in some of Stephen's remarks. Taking the Trinity as its point of departure, Catholic art confronts the erotic phenomena marginalized by the Trinitarian configuration; Joyce takes up this perspective and attempts to re-create it, through the beauty of a "realistic" art focused on the intertwining of desire and violence.

The condemnation of heresy is repeated in the Shakespeare discussion. Mulligan's arrival is marked by the reference to heresy followed by a mocking version of the medieval *symbolum.* The musical score of the Gloria is played as punctuation: veils, flowers, and bells are ciphers or figures of the sung music. This Catholic interval acts as an intermission within the discussion. The heretic knows the limits or boundaries of dogma, for when Stephen evokes Hamlet "the son consubstantial with the father" Shakespeare, King Hamlet, Mulligan answers: "Amen!" "You were speaking of the gaseous vertebrate, if I mistake not? he asked of Stephen" (197). It is Mulligan who renders explicit the reference to the Trinitarian model with respect to Shakespeare.

Stephen links theology to art through an interpretation of the Shakespearean experience and its transformation into poetic language. This transformation is spun out after what might be termed the semiotic awakening to *sin,* described thus by Stephen: "It is in infinite variety everywhere in the world he has created" (212). Shakespeare's creation begins with an incarnation, a passage through the flesh modulating language, or that which must be said by the artist. Ann Hathaway's seduction and betrayal erotically wound the writer; these wounds (the sacrifice of what had taken on flesh) become the path toward a kind of dis-incarnation, a decantation, of the Word carrying the traces of its passage through flesh—the Word surviving this flesh: "What is a ghost? Stephen said with tingling energy. One who has faded into impalpability through death, through absence" (188). Stephen relates Shakespeare's experience to his own desire and horror of death, the erotic wound of his mother's dying: "Mother's deathbed. Candle. The sheeted mirror. Who brought me into the world lies there, bronzelidded, under few cheap flowers. *Liliata rutilantium.* I wept alone" (190). Stephen's horrified reaction to love is designated by Hamlet (who reacts to incestuous love, displaced by his uncle) as integral to the scandal of desire: Hamlet's horror as well is focused on a murder. One is always in the proximity of an *incestuous murder,* rooted in original sin and revealing itself through the "horror of incest" analyzed by Freud. It is the scandal of abjection, revelation as betrayal, and Passion that allows for the possibility of writing, the *jouissance* of flesh rising into signs.

The flowering of signs takes as its starting point an X, a crucifixion signed Shakespeare ("He has hidden his own name, a fair name, William, in the plays, a super here, a clown there, as a painter of old Italy set his face in a dark corner of his canvas. He has revealed it in the sonnets where there is Will in overplus" [209]), or Joyce ("O Jamesy let me up out of this pooh sweets of sin whoever suggested that business for women" [769]). The holocaust brings about the delineation or wake of creation, punctuated by the proper name[28]—the most subjective, anaphorical, signifying *symbolum* of all.

Through the experience of the Passion, then, he who awaits his hour will incarnate the Word. Since the Father gives his Word to be incarnated and equal to him, filiation establishes itself in the hearing, in the ear. Stephen's definition of paternity fixes it in the symbolic domain: "It is a mystical estate, an apostolic succession, from only begetter to only begotten. On that mystery and not on the Madonna . . . the church is founded and founded irremovably because founded, like the world, macro- and microcosm, upon the void. Upon incertitude, upon unlikelihood" (207).

Stephen's "mystical estate" of paternity, its foundation upon the uncertainty of interpretation and the void (a biblically infinite hole), is operative for him as an elision of the troubling sexual reality materially constituted by his mother and theologically represented by the Madonna. This opposition, rather than being binary, takes the form of a knot. In Lacan's theory (throughout his career, but most specifically in the 1974–1975 *R.S.I.* Seminar published in *Ornicar?*), the Symbolic and the Real combined with the agency of the Imaginary to form the Borromean knot—a singularly tenuous and minimal kind of knot. At the risk of oversimplifying an immensely complex and subtle formulation of psychic reality as encountered in the analytic experience, we may perhaps paraphrase Lacan's description of that assemblage of holes that is the Borromean knot. The Real is that which is expelled from meaning (*sens*); it is the unthinkable. The Imaginary takes as its point of departure the reference to the body, which, as image, forms the basis of representation: of *sens* or meaning. Lacan contrasts *sens* to equivocation or ambiguity (*équivoque*) characteristic of the Symbolic, defined as that which sustains the unconscious (the latter being, according to Lacan's famous formulation, "structured like a language"). The triadic configuration of the Borromean knot is approximated, by Lacan, as follows: the

Imaginary operates as consistency or *consistance;* the Real operates outside of *consistance* and outside of the signifying domain of the Symbolic, and therefore the Real functions as *ex-sistence;* and the Symbolic operates as an irreducible, inviolable hole (*trou*).

Joycean paternity is at the frontiers of the real. Its displacement from a biological status to a configuration of desire gives it access to the symbolic domain, or, in Judeo-Catholic terms, "spirituality." Whence Stephen's meditation on the relation between father and son: "What links them in nature? An instant of blind rut. Am I father? If I were?" (208). Desire is transformed into divinity, taken outside the reality of biological temporality. This ambiguity, the event of Creation situated in the real and, beyond it, in the symbolic, is theological—even Christological—in its double, enigmatic aspect: "The corpse of John Shakespeare does not walk the night. From hour to hour it rots and rots. He rests, disarmed of fatherhood, having devised that mystical estate upon his son. . . . Fatherhood, in the sense of conscious begetting, is unknown to man. . . . Paternity may be a legal fiction. Who is the father of any son that any son should love him or he any son?" (207).

It is in the Trinitarian model that Stephen, attempting to elude the clutches of the Real, situates the foundations of the Church—thereby marking the displacement of the Virgin (or rather of the Madonna/Mother). Stephen affirms the Trinity as the central mystery of Catholicism by insisting on the *void* or vacuum constitutive of the paternity taken on at the moment of the mysterious transmission from John Shakespeare to William; from William Shakespeare to Hamlet; and thus from William Shakespeare to Stephen Dedalus. And it is at this juncture that Stephen's search for a father comes into play, thereby parrying the problematic identification occasioned by maternity. But the Real slips into the void, becoming an obstacle not only within maternity but within paternity as well—despite Stephen's protestations that fathers and sons are "sundered by a bodily shame so steadfast that the criminal annals of the world, stained within all other incests and bestialities, hardly record its breach" (207). Stephen is haunted by sin; nevertheless, he attempts to affirm the doubled articulation of divine/artistic paternity and divine/artistic filiation leading toward a *true* paternity: "Well: if the father who has not a son be not a father can the son who has not a father be a son? When Rutlandbaconsouthamptonshakespeare or another poet of the same name in the comedy of errors wrote *Hamlet* he was not the father of his own son merely but, being no more a son, he was and felt himself the father of all his race, the father of his own grandfather" (208).[29]

The Trinitarian model, thus rendered explicit, unfolds in Bloom's paternal presence. While Stephen's conflict with his past (and with those who threaten to condemn him to its horror) leads him toward the wreckage of the apocalypse—the dead end of mimetic desire and, more important, the partial objects of drive—the strategic move toward Bloom manifests itself as the solution to Stephen's problems. Bloom enables Stephen to go beyond or to pass over all that waylays his encounter with theology.

2

Love's Bitter Mystery
Blumenlied

Paternity in the desert

Stephen's encounter with theology seems problematic, given the set of contexts that situate him, menacing his subjective stance. Authority (the institution of the Church, political powers, the nightmare of history) establishes itself at the expense of its subjects: murdered, ruined, or castrated, they are deprived of their singularity. Mulligan's fantasy of pagan authority (eugenic medicine, bestiality, etc.) is no exception. Authority leads to an overflow of substance and detritus. On the other hand, the Irish Renaissance (confronted by Stephen in "Scylla and Charybdis") advocates the non-corporeality so evident in the uncomprehending reaction to Stephen's theory. The sexual repression characterizing the Irish Renaissance attitude in *Ulysses* creates a displacement or distancing from both biography and interpretation. And Joyce, in opposition to Irish repression, often represents sterility of the flesh as contrary to symbolic creativity. Within this context, marked by the rejection of eroticism (and, at the same time, of sin and theology: Stephen alone, comparable to Hamlet, hears the words of the invisible spirit), Bloom comes forth, as the solution to Stephen's tragic situation—in order that his *culpa* may become *felix*. It is through Bloom that Joyce extends the religious panorama of the *Portrait* to Judaism, via the specifically theological bias on paternity. Bloom's paternity involves fleshly, religious, and scriptural points of origin. The attribution of the complementary roles of Father and Son to Bloom and Stephen is the object of an immense figuration throughout the text of *Ulysses:* the differentiation of the two characters takes effect only after they have been knotted together or linked by resemblance.[1]

The narrative representation of Bloom's paternity begins, in "Calypso," with the distancing of his daughter and the evocation of his dead son: "Her first birthday away from home. Separation. Remember the summer morning she was born, running to knock up Mrs Thornton in Denzille street. . . . She knew from the first poor little Rudy wouldn't live" (66). This biographical indication of Bloom's failure motivates his desire with respect to Stephen in the narrative; his sense of having fallen or of having failed (underlined by a deathly continuity linking his father's suicide to the loss of his son) as an *expiration* of his own paternal and filial roles—as a condemnation to death—inspires his sense of horror. In this particular abyss, Bloom's paternity is reinforced by his desire for a son, precisely at the moment when the *name* of Bloom is dying out since Milly's childhood is definitively over. Her detachment from Bloom thus dissipates the Oedipal romance: "*O Milly Bloom, you are my darling. . . .* Milly too. Young kisses: the first" (63, 67).[2] In the drama of desire, Milly joins Molly: introduced into the world of the feminine Other, she becomes a source of erotic wounds. Object of desire, obstacle, she is expelled from the realm of filiation and transmission of meaning and, similarly, of the name: "Boys. . . . Mine. Slieve Bloom" (58).[3] Bloom's thoughts glide from his dead son to the topologizing of the name—for its space, like that of a burial ground, conceals a death. Bloom's wounded masculinity requires a son since all women are merely pale substitutes for Molly and, thus, reminders of his fall in the loss of his son. It follows, then, that his idea of adopting Stephen is produced by his desire to utilize him as a means of re-seducing Molly.[4]

Given these historical and sexual circumstances of Bloom's paternity, his reaction to the advertisement of Agendath Netaim seems inevitable, since it situates the religious and specifically Judaic bases for his suspended paternity. The advertisement, found at the counter of the pork butcher, Moses Dlugacz, concerns plantations in Palestine: "You pay eight marks and they plant a dunam of land for you with olives, oranges, almonds or citron. . . . Nice to hold, cool waxenfruit, hold in the hand lift it to the nostrils and smell the perfume" (60).[5] The advertisement transmits a message of renewal— the desert will be made to *flower*, or *bloom*. This message of Zionist resurrection impresses Bloom with its sensuality, and the names attached to it reappear several times in his thoughts. The signifiers of oranges, citrons, almonds, and perfume return when Bloom buys soap and Molly's lotion; the motif of flowering becomes explicitly attached to Bloom's desires in a passage of "Lestrygonians": "All for a woman, home and houses, silk webs, silver, rich fruits, spicy from Jaffa. Agendath Netaim. . . . Perfume of embraces all him assailed. With hungered flesh obscurely, he mutely craved to adore" (168). In Bloom's search for a renewal of love, objects serve as relays, monuments, and symbols. Bloom's *jouissance* can be deciphered as the flowering of the desert; the root of his *jouissance* lies in Judaism and it will manifest itself, in the course of *Ulysses*, through his relation to paternity.

The signifying network of Bloom's desire, thus evoked, confronts the emptiness constituting the truth of his paternity. His fall interrupts the flight of renewal, denying it: "No wind would lift those waves, grey metal, poisonous foggy waters. Brimstone they called it raining down: the cities of the plain: Sodom, Gomorrah, Edom. All dead names. A dead sea in a dead land, grey and old. Old now. It bore the oldest, the first race. . . . Now it could bear no more. Dead: an old woman's: the grey sunken cunt of the world. Desolation. Grey horror seared his flesh" (61). The source of Bloom's reflection, i.e., the destruction of the Old Testament cities, becomes confused with the Dead Sea, metaphorized as the genitals of an old woman. And, in a typically Bloomian misinterpretation, Edom is included with the cities of the plain. In fact, Edom is evoked principally in Numbers 20, when the Lord announces the punishment of Moses and Aaron—A Pisgah Sight of Palestine. When Edom refuses passage to Israel, Aaron dies, prefiguring the death of Moses in that he too is refused entry into the Promised Land.[6] A counterpoint of horror slips into Bloom's paternity: this fall into irrevocable death is here interiorized in Judaism. Rooted in an Old Testament perspective, Bloom's horror echoes Stephen's horror. It does so in a repeated version of abjection localized in the pervasive and obsessive sin of the mother (both woman and ocean). Judaic paternity and Catholic filiation abruptly come together on the Irish terrain of death, thus marking the place where *jouissance* becomes erotic wound.

Desire and writing

Bloom's wound, as well as that of Stephen, occupies a specifically signifying space. It can be interpreted, according to Lacan's analysis of the entry into speech, as related to the rupture or cut that every instance or act of discourse, constitutive of the subject, brings into relief.[7] The erotic wound can be articulated within the framework of the experience of castration, but in reversed form: in the Joycean experience of lack, the symbolic order "repairs the damage," stemming the "internal hemorrhage"[8] of melancholia. At the site of lack, where the subject glimpses its own abject displacement in death, the desire for the lost object is painfully insistent in the signifying chain. The artist exploits the insistence of flouted desire—or fallen desire—by investing its intensity with artistic form. Whence the cry of Don Giovanni Joyce: without conquests to add to the list, he locates the call toward writing, the scriptural vocation, on the virginal page of fiery desire: "Youth has an end: the end is here. It will never be. You know that well. What then? Write it, damn you, write it! What else are you good for?"[9] With Bloom and Stephen, Joyce plays out the possibilities in the relation between desire and the word—of which the message, reversed in the hearing, goes beyond the limits of the subject who utters it: this is manifest in the strategy of multiple parallels between the thoughts of the two characters, moving toward their encounter.

The erotic investment of speech gravitates toward music and, specifically, toward song. Since music supports or sustains speech in singing (*linguaggio alato*), the poetic quality of language would derive from musicality overflowing the boundaries of the sign.[10] Joyce's poetic language can be formulated as a plenitude sustained by the void, the abyss, the emptiness of breath. In Joyce's version of Catholicism (and in that of Stephen Dedalus as well), the true and the beautiful stand face to face. Desire has become desire of the infinite, the *jouissance* of sublimation: in the rhythmic passage through meaning, presence is sustained by absence, or an illusion of presence is created by the absence constitutive of *ec-stasis*—an ecstasy of art. *Jouissance* comes closest to the letter in the Passion of Christ: torn by an erotic wound, the sufferer turns it around and recovers it in an enduring Word. Submitted to passion, the word is multiplied in *Finnegans Wake* into a Trinity, a "trifid tongue" confronting the multiplicity of languages, locations, and identities.

The passion and the ear

Bloom's wound eroticizes language and puts eroticism into words: Bloom has a good ear. He compares the voices of Molly and Mrs. M'Coy, and describes the latter: "Reedy freckled soprano. Cheeseparing nose. Nice enough in its way: for a little ballad. No guts in it. . . . Can't he hear the difference?" (76). And again, in "Sirens": "M'Coy valise. My wife and your wife. Squealing cat. Like tearing silk. . . . Gap in their voices too. Fill me. I'm warm, dark, open. Molly in *Quis est homo:* Mercandante. My ear against the wall to hear. Want a woman who can deliver the goods" (282). Joyce here elaborates the site of Bloom's lack. Feminine voice and sex are conflated in the Sirens' seduction precisely at the moment of Boylan's rendezvous with Molly—the seduction of Molly by someone else, hollowing out Bloom's erotic grave. Causing his fall. The aria "Là ci darem" from *Don Giovanni,* as sung by Molly, often slips into Bloom's thoughts: the seduction of Zerlina by Masetto (of Molly by Bloom himself) gives way to that of Zerlina by Don Giovanni (of Molly by Boylan), under the auspices of sung passion, marked by the drives: "*Mi trema un poco il.* Beautiful on that *tre* her voice is: weeping tone. A thrust. A throstle" (93). Bloom's thoughts bring together the beauty of the voice, the eroticism that passes through it, and the words that transmit them. This ensemble or knot of Bloomian thought is articulated in religious signifiers.

Surrounded by women, Bloom observes Holy Communion. He thinks of the Mass as a bodily relation ending in oral satisfaction: "Nice discreet place to be next some girl. Women knelt in the benches. . . . The priest bent down to put it into her mouth, murmuring all the time. Latin. . . . What? *Corpus*. . . . Now I bet it makes them feel happy" (80). Bloom admires the usage of wine, Latin, music, and sacred art. It is this signifying quality that he pinpoints as the source of religious *jouissance*. He refers to the paschal suffering encoded in the Christly monograms, I.H.S. and I.N.R.I.: "I have sinned: or no: I have suffered, it is. And the other one? Iron nails ran in" (81), according to Molly's interpretation. Bloom's position is clear: "Good idea the Latin. Stupefies them first. . . . Letters on his back. . . . Wine. Makes it more aristocratic. . . . Some of that old sacred music is splendid. . . . Those old popes were keen on music, on art and statues and pictures of all kinds" (80–82). Bloom considers Latin superior to the English used in the liturgy of the Irish Church: "The service of the Irish church, used in Mount Jerome, is simpler, more impressive, I must say. Mr. Bloom gave prudent assent. The language of course was another thing" (105). The Latin is fascinating, seductive, as *letter:* monogram and multiple anagram (or paragram). Latin, become a code of unreadability and sonorous arabesque, enters into the domain reserved to poetic language.

As he evokes religious passion and its means of expression, Bloom anchors them in his own passion and in the echoes (received by his own fine ear during the day of June 16, 1904) of his desires, wounds, and pleasures, all mediated through Molly's singing: "Molly was in fine voice that day, the *Stabat Mater* of Rossini. . . . Music they wanted. . . . I told her to pitch her voice against that corner. I could feel the thrill in the air, the full, the people looking up: *Quis est homo!*" (82). The relation between Bloom's fall (into death—Molly's infidelity is its consequence and extension) and the signifying display of eroticism, the seductions of religion, is noted prior to the end of the Mass. Bloom imagines a scenario including a betrayed husband and a sinful wife; the latter makes of her seduction the origin of a *jouissance* disguised as repentance. Bloom sees adulterous satisfaction as inseparable from mariolatry and its accessories: "Repentance skindeep. Lovely shame. Pray at an altar. Hail Mary and Holy Mary. Flowers, incense, candles melting. Hide her blushes" (83). The scandal of the Church consists in a mixture of betrayal, seduction, confession, and salvation. This mixture is also evident in the tragic celebration of the Passion, in which suffering is the condition of *jouissance.* Jealousy and betrayal catalyze Bloom's passion: it is the pleasure of the *other* that creates a suffering rendered into *jouissance,* per-versely so.

The "Sirens" chapter displays the seduction (operated by signifiers) of speech dramatized in song. At the hour of Boylan's rendezvous with Molly (at the hour of *Don Giovanni*), Bloom listens to Simon Dedalus sing "M'appari" (from Flotow's *Martha*). In this scene, the decline and marginal grandeur of Stephen's father are evident; this portrait cuts close to the bone of the paternal function as experienced by Joyce himself.[11] However, unlike descriptions of biographical anecdotes, Stephen in *Ulysses* does not hear his father's song. He is absent from the scene, and the transmission of the paternal function ("a mystical estate, an apostolic succession") is left in silence. What does take place, however, is a "lateral" transmission, from the biological father to the "spiritual" father, from Simon to Bloom, through song. (In the narrative, this transmission is anticipated at the beginning of "Hades" when, in a carriage with Dedalus, Power, and Cunningham, Bloom the father glimpses Stephen, while Dedalus himself does not see him [88]).

Simon Dedalus, like Bloom ("Yes. All is lost") and Stephen ("I could not save her. Waters: Bitter death: lost"), is in mourning (273, 46). This shared mourning is deployed in song. The call to the lost woman brings together, through a coincidence of signifiers, the losses of Lionel (Martha, in the opera), Simon (Mary-May, his wife), and Bloom (Marion-Molly); the circuit closes on Bloom's literary affair with Martha: "Martha it is. Coincidence. Just going to write. Lionel's song. Lovely name you have" (275).[12] The last words of the song are punctuated by the union of Simon and Bloom *in the signifier itself:* "*To me!* Siopold! Consumed" (276).[13] The *consummation,* as both sacrifice and resurrection, introduces Simon Dedalus' voice within Bloom: this event precedes the act of assuming paternity toward Stephen. Bloom's entry into the Judeo-Christian domain is supported by this *translation,* in the etymological sense of the word, of paternity.

"What's his name? Ikey Moses? Bloom"

Through the character of Bloom, Joyce fully reveals the Judaic foundation of Catholicism[14]—or of those elements of Catholicism which impress him, as well as the symbolic and fictive residue of his youth personified by Stephen Dedalus in *Ulysses.* Bloom's ear, refined by his wounds and *jouissances,* projects him in the direction of filiation (bearing and speaking for paternity). Bloom will find himself in a prophetic role, or, rather, at the site of the Old Testament prophetic resonances that lead to the assembly of prophets around Christ in the synoptic narrations of the Transfiguration in the New Testament.

Bloom's Judaic identification (for Bloom does identify with Judaism, even though he does so through a denegation) focuses on Moses, the essential nominative signifier of what constitutes Judaism in *Ulysses.*[15] The name of Moses resonates in anti-Semitic discourse, in the journalists' conversations, and in Bloom's thoughts. In "Aeolus" Joyce specifically approaches the subject of Moses, through the characters of Bloom, J. J. (James Joyce?) O'Molloy, MacHugh, and Stephen. Despite the disjunction of Bloom and Stephen in this chapter (the references to Moses are uttered in Bloom's absence and, moreover, Bloom glimpses Stephen from far away, without hearing him), the series of references will take conclusive form at the end of the book, when Stephen[16] describes his Pisgah Sight of Palestine to Bloom (685).

The deaths of Bloom's father and of Dignam invade Bloom's thoughts as he makes the connection between the inverted printing type and the Hebrew writing of the hagaddah, the Passover liturgy. The title in large type, "AND IT WAS THE FEAST OF THE PASSOVER" (122), with its connotations of *both* paschal celebrations,[17] alludes to the encounter between the Old and New Testaments. Bloom's references to the Judaic ritual of Passover reveal his condition of exile as the disappearance of meaning at the heart of the Mosaic enunciation, and the comic aspect of his mistakes of memory and interpretation further pinpoint the permanent Fall that constitutes exile. When Moses orders the annual celebration of Passover, he says: "Remember this day, in which ye came out from Egypt, out of the house of bondage" (Exod. 13:3). According to Bloom: "All that long business about that brought us out of the land of Egypt and into the house of bondage" (122). Bloom's slip is at the core of the predicament of the exile identified as Moses/Bloom/Joyce: the expulsion from Egypt does not put an end to exile, which is ongoing. The expulsion from exile becomes another version of exile itself—from relay to relay, one deferral to the next, the arrival in the Promised Land will never occur.[18] Bloom thinks: "Next year in Jerusalem"; this fragment of Passover ritual marks the desire of every Jew to celebrate the following Passover in Jerusalem. Repeated year after year, this desire ultimately underlines the ever-present condition of exile itself. But Bloom casually and effortlessly affirms his Mosaic position by saying: "*Shema Israel Adonai Elohenu.* No, that's the other." Moses, the prophet par excellence (see Deut. 18:15; John 1:21), utters (outside the paschal context, but at the moment of the presentation of the Law) a key statement of Judaic monotheism; "Hear O Israel: the Lord our God is one LORD" (Deut. 6:4).

Following Bloom's departure, Irish orators are quoted on the subject of Moses: their discourse resonates according to the identification of Bloom with Moses via Stephen's presence as listener. First, Michelangelo's *Moses* is described in Christly terms as "the human form divine" and the eternal Word, "that eternal symbol of wisdom and prophecy" (140); finally, this *Moses* located by O'Molloy in the Vatican is, with its creator, subject to the Transfiguration: "soultransfigured" and "soultransfiguring." Moses and the Christ appear as doubles. The articulation that makes of Moses both the subject and the agent of the transfiguration adumbrates the context of mediation between God and his chosen people. The knot constituted by this mediation can perhaps be read in terms of the Lacanian interpretation of the Symbolic.[19] The place of the prophet and that of the artist are identical in the sense that the manifestations of the signifier (the divine site of the Other) become, in the event of the word (or of art), a transfiguration of the subject itself: the word imposes itself on the subject by and through language. The word bears the traces of its passage through the whirlwind of figuration: the "transfigurer" re-creates language, ritual, forms, colors. The signifier sustaining transfiguration is the transfiguration itself: "I AM THAT I AM" (Exod. 3:14): in the circularity of the proper name and its performative nomination, being is inseparable from the anaphoric event of its designation as such. Transfiguration is at the pivotal position between that which receives the spirit (the transfigured subject) and that which is transmitted or delivered by it—as a gift. The subject transfigures its own tongue: figuration being that which, because of a disparity or deviation, modulates language *as such*, i.e., less its signification:[20] the signifier, or the letter, is abandoned to the arabesque that constitutes it.

It is in this context that the "stony effigy, horned and terrible" of Moses establishes the first Transfiguration. According to Exodus 34:29–35, "the skin of his face shone" when Moses came down from Mount Sinai. This illumination is "expressed by the verb *qaran*, derived from *qeren*, "horn", thus the literal translation of the Vulgate: "cornuta esset facies sua", "his face had horns."[21] Exodus, Passover, the Law, and the illumination of Moses are assembled in "FROM THE FATHERS," a discourse comparing the Irish to the Hebrews. The attentive ear of Stephen (the Irishman in exile on home ground) and the evocation of the absent Bloom (the Jew in exile) through the intermediary of Moses come together in a prefiguration of their meeting "face to face."

"Elijah is coming": the whirlwind of the prophetic word

The chapter of "Aeolus" ends in "*A Pisgah Sight of Palestine*," or "Moses and the promised land" (149). Three paragraphs later, in "Lestrygonians," Bloom receives an advertisement. He misreads his name (a visual slip) in the reference to Christ:

"Bloo . . . Me? No. Blood of the Lamb. . . . Elijah is coming" (151). Through a satirical presentation of "the church in Zion," a sect named after the Promised Land, Bloom identifies himself (literally: through his name) with the *agnus dei* as well as with the prophet Elijah. The identification with Elijah is sparked by a parapraxis of reading, and this slip marks Bloom's prophetic autonomy in the *instant* of his reading—which is also an instant of comedy. The Freudian domain of parapraxes, or slips, is on the threshold of the dimension of truth in the enunciation of the word as it operates within two domains essential to the text of *Finnegans Wake:* the domain of the dream, related to prophetic vision (in religion, particularly in Judeo-Christianity), and that of *Witz* (the comedy of the letter).

A major biblical event of *Ulysses* occurs in "Cyclops": in the bar ruled by the Citizen, or Irish patriot, Bloom slips from his Mosaic role of expelled scapegoat to the role of Christ. The explicit identification with Elijah, the fundamental Bloomian identity in this chapter, can be interpreted as a pivotal point between the Old and New Testaments. Elijah's position uncovers the *series* of prophetic enunciations, the nexus of which is constituted by Moses, Elijah, and Christ, embodied by the polysemic character (HCE: Here Comes Everybody) of Bloom.

"Cyclops" includes a discussion of the nightmare of history and its laws. Bloom engages in the discussion, emitting some extraordinary remarks that lead to his expulsion: "And J. J. and the citizen arguing about law and history with Bloom sticking in an odd word. Some people, says Bloom, can see the mote in others' eyes but they can't see the beam in their own" (326). Bloom paraphrases the Gospel of Christ (Matt. 7:3).[22] Through his own nonviolence, his sympathy for victims, and through his state of exile as wandering Jew, crowned by the exile to which Molly condemns him this June 16, 1904, Bloom gains access to his prophetic and Christly role. He denounces violence as the fabric of history: "Persecution, says Bloom, all the history of the world is full of it. Perpetuating national hatred among nations" (331). The knowledge of the expelled victim is expelled, in turn, by the representative of patriotism and racism: "The citizen said nothing only cleared the spit out of his gullet and, gob, he spat a Red bank oyster out of him right in the corner" (331). Attacked, Bloom defends himself as Jew: "And I belong to a race too, says Bloom, that is hated and persecuted. . . . Right, says John Wyse. Stand up to it then with force like men" (332). Bloom, like Christ, rejects mimetic violence: Bloom's rejection of "manly" strength motivates what Joyce calls the "feminization"[23] of his personality—a trait shared with Stephen Dedalus and, apparently, with Joyce himself, especially concerning his Judaic identification.

Bloom opposes life and love to mimetic violence, thus uttering the evangelical message of the Kingdom of Heaven. Like Christ, he announces his absence and anticipated return: "But it's no use, says he. Force, hatred, history, all that. . . . And everybody knows that it's the very opposite of that that is really life. —What? says Alf. —Love, says Bloom. . . . I must go now, says he to John Wyse. . . . If he comes just say I'll be back in a second. . . . A new apostle to the gentiles, says the citizen. Universal love" (333). During his absence Bloom's messianic identity is ridiculed: "That's the new Messiah for Ireland! says the citizen" (337). Cunningham remarks the anticipation of the Messiah as common to Jews and Christians, but the others deride Bloom the Judaic Messianic Father, particularly his virility: "Well, they are still waiting for their redeemer, says Martin. For that matter so are we. —Yes, says J. J., and every male that's born they think it may be their Messiah. . . . Do you call that a man? says the citizen. — I wonder did he ever put it out of sight, says Joe . . . One of those mixed middlings he is" (337–338). When Bloom returns, the Citizen throws him out: Joyce operates a lifting of the Catholic repression concerning its Judaic origins. This truth is intolerable to the patriotic and anti-Semitic audience, as becomes clear following Bloom's declaration. The Citizen attacks Bloom: "By Jesus, says he, I'll brain that bloody jewman for using the holy name. By Jesus, I'll crucify him so I will. Give us that biscuitbox here"(342).

The sacred identifications are knotted in the final paragraph of the chapter, written in a biblical style. In this transformation scene, Joyce filters the return to the Bible evident in the narrative both into and through his style. The laughter directed at Bloom is subverted into transcendental joy: "When lo, there came about them all a great brightness and they beheld the chariot wherein He stood ascend to heaven. And they beheld Him . . . clothed upon in the glory of the brightness, having raiment as of the sun . . . that for awe they durst not look upon Him. And there came a voice out of heaven, calling: *Elijah! Elijah!* And he answered with a main cry: *Abba! Adonai!*" (345).[24] Joyce rewrites the taking-up of Elijah (2 Kings 2:11), integrating within it the prophetic vocation and the call to God as well as the luminosity of the transfigured Christ. Elijah and Christ thus converge, and Joyce notes the essential points of the Transfiguration and the prophetic vocation (the act of naming in God's call, the dialogue, the location of being in the name itself). But Joyce indicates yet another aspect of the prophetic vocation, the effusion of the prophetic spirit that cannot be transmitted except by God: "And they beheld Him even Him, ben Bloom Elijah, amid clouds of angels ascend to the glory of the brightness" (345). When Elijah leaves Elisha, the latter asks of him: "I pray thee, let a double portion of thy spirit be upon me." Elijah answers: "Thou hast asked a hard thing: nevertheless, if thou see me when I am taken from thee, it shall be so unto thee; but if not, it shall not be *so*" (2 Kings 2:11). Elisha sees him and receives the prophetic "inheritance." Prophetic succession echoes the apostolic succession desired by Bloom and Stephen. Joycean laughter resonates throughout the discord of dissonances (sordid gossip, ecclesiastical miracles, Irish caricatures) of the scene, leading to the "disparition élocutoire" (the elocutionary disappearance of the author, reminiscent of Mallarmé) of Elijah, Bloom, and Joyce.

The biblical event of "Cyclops" sets the stage for the leap into language (echoed by a leap outside the maternal body) that brings Bloom into Stephen's radius[25] (or that brings Stephen into the world, beginning with Bloom's anticipated paternity). Joyce evokes the leap into the Word constituting the Incarnation (the formulation of paternity and filiation). Prior to their encounter, Bloom and Stephen find themselves together in "Oxen of the Sun," where Mina Purefoy gives birth to a male child. Once the prophetic series is established by Moses and Elijah, Bloom must demonstrate its Judaic continuity through Christ: in "Circe," the Crucifixion of Christ takes place through the sacrifice of Bloom. This is the culmination of the prophetic series, hence the identification of Stephen, the eternal Son,[26] in a Trinitarian configuration.

"Circe," the Transformation scene,[27] takes place in Night-town, the chaotic matrix of sexuality and language. The descent into Nighttown becomes operative through the parodic incarnation of Stephen, who stages a Last Supper (the paschal event to be repeated in transsubstantiation). Stephen states: "Now drink we, quod he, of this mazer and quaff ye this mead which is not indeed parcel of my body but my soul's bodiment" (391). At the point of entry into Nighttown, the city of Sin, Stephen-Christ designates in Bloom the operation of the lifting of repression as concerns the Judaic origin of Christ. Lynch whispers: "Who the sooty hell's the johnny in the black duds?" Stephen answers: "Hush! Sinned against the light and even now that day is at hand when he shall come to judge the world by fire. Pflaap! *Ut implerentur scripturae*" (428–9). Taking up Deasy's anti-Semitic explanation of the wandering of the Jews,[28] Stephen reshapes it with respect to the Last Judgment; he integrates Judaic sin[29] within the instance of divine Judgment in the Johannine Apocalypse ("johnny in the black duds"). The consequence of sin is the enigmatic apocalypse in which the end of the world and the world without end offset each other. Bloom's "mission" seems to be recognized as specifically Christlike: he appears in order that the Scriptures might be fulfilled, notes Stephen (John 19:24), alluding to the division of Christ's robes. In fact, it is just that Christlike position that is divided between Bloom and Stephen, linked by the discourse of the "gospeller." Elijah returns, announcing the coming of Christ: "Elijah is coming washed in the blood of the Lamb" (428).[30]

The gamut of religious positions represented throughout the book is recapitulated and reformulated through the hallucinations of "Circe." Fantasies and visions are played out in theatrical format, i.e., with the active participation not only of the character supposedly producing the hallucinations, but with that of the entire world composing *Ulysses* as well. This explains the apparent autonomy of statements, details, characters, and the like, all of which take on new life in this chapter. The reader witnesses a generalized incarnation of the Signifier: its miraculous dimension (the impossible mastery of the Real?) is located in the realm of prophecy. In "Circe," Joyce marks the convergence of sexuality and religion, particularly through the hallucinatory itinerary of Bloom, from Father to Son. As in *Finnegans Wake,* the entire Bible is re-created, from Egypt ("my client's native place, the land of the Pharaoh") to the new Jerusalem (Apoc. 21:2) ("the new Bloomusalem in the Nova Hibernia of the future" [463, 484]).

The Dantesque descent of Bloom into Hell triggers his confrontation with his own sexual guilt[31]—in the terms of biblical abomination, adultery, seduction. The painful accusations raised against this victim of the "Sweets of Sin" make Bloom into a scapegoat ("I am being made a scapegoat of" [457]) and an *abject*[32]: masculine-feminine, apostate Jew, betrayed and potentially adulterous husband, "Street angel and house devil" (460). Bloom's perversion gets him arrested by the sergeants, put on trial, and condemned to death. Through Bloom's abjection, Joyce takes up the questions of desire and the paradoxes of *jouissance:* fullness and lack, life and death, flesh and Word. The shared and visible mourning worn by both Bloom and Stephen brings them together.[33] As a consequence of their encounter and his new paternity, Bloom sees himself as Mayor of Dublin, Leopold the First, and Messiah. He announces himself, moreover, in a biblical style: "Yea, on the word of a Bloom, ye shall ere long enter into the golden city which is to be, the new Bloomusalem" (459). He delivers the Law of Moses (484); he is the Messiah, of whom the *liber generationis* is recited. He is a scapegoat, according to an adaptation of Leviticus 16:22. Having sinned and having suffered (544), he is put to death: "BLOOM: (*In a seamless garment marked I.H.S. stands upright amid phoenix flames*) Weep not for me O daughters of Erin" (498).[34]

The doubling of Judaism and Christianity, of Moses and Christ, sets the scene for Bloom's encounter with Stephen by revealing both the sacred/spiritual stake inherent in the relations of paternity and filiation and the signifying impetus behind these relations as they function in the prophetic enunciation. Bloom makes his way through paternity toward an encounter with filiation: Elijah subtly indicates the leap from

Bloom-Stephen to Blephen-Stoom (682) when, in the whore-house, he speaks of erotic power and of the *jouissance* of eternity dividing up the body of Christ in a communion of the Word: "If the second advent came to Coney Island are we ready? Florry Christ, Stephen Christ, Zoe Christ, Bloom Christ, Kitty Christ, Lynch Christ, it's up to you to sense that cosmic force. . . . Are you all in this vibration? I say you are. You once nobble that, congregation, and a buck joyride to heaven becomes a back number" (507–508). In the last lines of the Old Testament, it is through Elijah that the leap from Moses to Christ is traced: "Behold, I will send you Elijah the prophet before the coming of the great and dreadful day of the LORD: And he shall turn the heart of the fathers to the children and the heart of the children to their fathers. . . ."

3

Modus Peregrinus
The Trinity

The *Passion* (a jubilatory tragedy of love and death) is thus the Bloomian experience of eroticism, music, and language: its focus on *parole pleine*, the fullness of signification in the spoken word, is played out in the Judeo-Christian symbolic framework. In Joyce's characterization of Bloom, the Judaic element[1] precedes and founds the symbolic dimension located in Catholicism; Bloom's reflections circulate between the two, starting with his entry into the immeasurable depths of signification (the powers of word and voice) identified by him with paternity and the rupture of paternity caused by apostasy: "Poor papa! . . . The scene he was always talking about . . .—Nathan's voice! His son's voice! I hear the voice of Nathan who left his father to die of grief and misery in my arms, who left the house of his father and left the God of his father. Every word is so deep, Leopold" (76). At the point of recognition of a death that must be countered or overcome (the end of sacrifice, since in the kingdom of Love advocated by Christ/Bloom, there will be no more whitened sepulchers, no more deaths to conceal), the figure representing the defeat of apostasy comes forth: Christ. What leads Bloom toward the encounter with Stephen is precisely this state of continuity and rupture which shapes *his* coming-forth and makes of him the father of his race (Christ-Shakespeare). His paternity is then revealed as a "contransmagnificandjewbangtantiality." In this sense, he transmits his paternity to Stephen even as he maintains it, while Stephen the future writer will make of this paternity a creation in tongues. An impossible structure, in which the same and the other are inextricable: the Trinity.

Paternity and spiration

The Bible: a single itinerary of the sacred in language, a double configuration of the instance possessing symbolic power. Through Christ, the Trinity sets off a break with the Old Testament even as it establishes a continuity with it through paternity, through symbolicity. The Creation (Genesis) is relit, repeated, retransmitted.

The Trinitarian model takes up Judaic paternity as the cause of the Catholic filiation that overlaps it. With respect to the Old Testament God, the Word constitutes, simultaneously, a *rupture* and a *continuity*. This apparatus is implied by the engendering of meaning through signs.[2] The principal event of *Ulysses* is sustained by the Judeo-Christian form of the Trinity. In this framework, the Shakespearean event of literary creation is rendered explicit as an instance of paternity in filiation. Joyce takes up this problematic, revealing its specifically *dramatic* proportions: theological and artistic creation cannot bypass a confrontation with sexuality. Eliminating this confrontation entails the risk of falling into the theosophical trap— the caricature of Catholicism, eluding the scandalous relations through which the Word reaches its heights. Sexuality brings the subject beyond institutional limits (*Portrait of the Artist*): in *Ulysses* the risk of incest punished by castration is revealed as the negative version of the heterogeneity constituted by the Passion of the Word in flesh. Having indicated the domain of truth in Catholicism, exceeding the institution in the double articulation Lucifer/Christ, Stephen risks all in the confrontation with the demoniacal element, the only possible means of access to *jouissance*. Stephen, however, cannot accomplish this alone; the Incarnation of Christ necessitates a Father who functions as truth rather than as semblance. In Aquinas' terms: "The Father notifies himself to us through paternity and spiration; as 'Principle which has no principle,' he notifies himself in that *he does not come from another:* and there, precisely, is the property of innascibility, which is signified by the name of *Unengendered.*"[3]

The Son, engendered by the Father, "a pris son corps humain: dans le ventre d'une femme juive":[4] Bloom's encounter with Stephen takes place in the feminine body of the whorehouse (that of Mrs. *Cohen*, descendant of Judaic priests, of Aaron?) in the context of hallucinations of femininity. Between Molly's apparition (to Bloom) and that of Mrs. Dedalus (to Stephen), Bloom and Stephen see themselves united in the horned[5] image of Shakespeare, who speaks to them from the mirror reflecting their two transformed faces: "(*Stephen and Bloom gaze in the mirror. The face of William Shakespeare, beardless, appears there, rigid in facial paralysis, crowned by the reflection of the reindeer antlered hatrack in the hall*)" (567). After the erotic trial of betrayal and the deathly consequences of a woman cutting herself off from a man, the resulting lack acts as an open wound: "The shadow of the object fell upon the ego," Freud writes of the psychic constellation of the melancholic: "An object-loss was transformed into an ego-loss."[6] The divine instance[7] of the Other opens this space of lack ("hole" and "overflow") displayed in "Circe." For Joyce, this lack leads to an unfolding of signs, a deployment of signification—a *jouissance:* from a pre-text of fantasy and a mocking derision of fantasy. Sin and parody reign in Mrs. Cohen's brothel (through a drama of emasculation and murder, linking Bloom, Stephen, Shakespeare, Othello, and Hamlet) as the point of origin of writing and the truth that writing is there to tell. Hamlet the Father is not invisible: he is Shakespeare. He is reflected in Stephen, who, as he sees him in the mirror through (the Other/the Same) Bloom, enters the impossible, aporetic domain of the Trinity: the procession by generation of the Son.

"Darkinbad the Brightdayler"

It is through two series of images that Joyce symbolically brings together Christ and Shakespeare. The unity of the two series is underlined by the Prologue to the Gospel of Saint John, running through the text of *Ulysses:* "And the light shineth in darkness, and the darkness comprehendeth it not." Joyce's oeuvre marks the wavering, tension, and distancing between darkness and light, night and day, sin and grace: these oppositions are profoundly Catholic. And at the same time, they are as if surprised at being so, confronted by all the "profane" blackness and drive staged by Catholicism.

First, the shadow, Freudian indication of the object, indicative of the divinity invested in the cloud: the pillar of the cloud guides Moses out of Egypt (Exod. 13:32). The cloud spotted by Stephen[8] takes on its Mosaic context when Bloom returns home in the morning: "A cloud began to cover the sun wholly slowly wholly. Grey. Far" (61). Forbidden to enter the Promised Land, Bloom relives the diaspora and the horror of death. In "FROM THE FATHERS" (142) the role of the "pillar of the cloud" guiding Moses in exodus is evoked in Stephen's presence. When Stephen speaks of the nominative/scriptural/ erotic path taken by Shakespeare, he links Moses to Shakespeare and, implicitly, to himself: "A star by night, Stephen said, a pillar of the cloud by day" (210). Bloom is added to this series. In "Circe," he becomes Mayor of Dublin: "*The pillar of the cloud appears*" (480). Moreover, the ascension of Ben Bloom Elijah takes place amid "clouds of angels"; and Stephen attributes his "collapsus" to "the reapparition of a matutinal cloud (perceived by both from two different points of observation, Sandycove and Dublin) at first no bigger than a woman's hand" (667). These circumstances are evocative of the cloud "small as a man's hand" indicating the end of the drought to Elijah's servant (Elijah had announced: "As the LORD God of Israel liveth, before whom I stand, there shall not be dew nor rain these years, but according to my word" [1 Kings 17:1]). Elijah's cloud opens the prophetical series discussed earlier. It is the mark of temporal phenomena subsumed under divine power. This cloud is like a trace of the holy Word painted in the sky, whence its inclusion in the series of images associated with the pillar of the cloud.

Stephen recasts the narration of Exodus (13:22) by substituting a star for the pillar of fire lighting up the night in order to modulate his Mosaic narrative according to the biographical and astrographical variants of Shakespeare: "A star, a daystar, a firedrake rose at his birth . . . and by night it shone over delta in Cassiopeia, the recumbent constellation which is the signature of his initial among the stars" (210).[9] The star juxtaposes a divine and Christly sign with the Hebraic sign of the cloud. However, the Christly star maintains a certain ambivalence between the demoniacal and the sacred, between the morning star (Lucifer) whose fall, according to the Fathers, figures that of the Prince of demons[10] and the Star venerated in the form of *Lumen Christi,* the flame sparked by the cornerstone, according to the benediction of the new fire of Holy Saturday: the coming of Christ will be "like lightning" (Matt. 24:27). According to tradition, the mystery of the Incarnation is evoked even as far back as the oracles of Balaam (himself a spokesman of ambivalence, literally cornered between benediction and malediction), who predicts: "there shall come a Star out of Jacob, and a Sceptre shall rise out of Israel" (Num. 24:17). *Orietur stella ex Iacob:* the prediction refers to the coming of David, and of Christ. The star noticed by Stephen thus seems to be demoniacal and holy, Judaic and Christian, Bloomian and Shakespearean. When, at the end of "Proteus," Stephen sees the cloud, he implicates himself in the astral distribution: "Come. I thirst. Clouding over. . . . Allbright he falls, proud lightning of the intellect, *Lucifer, dico, qui nescit occasum.* No" (50). Stephen slips into the series of prophetical and liturgical enunciations. Jesus on the cross says: "I thirst" (John 19:28); Isaiah notes the fall of the morning star (Isa. 14:12) assimilated to that of Lucifer saying No: the Latin sentence refers to the Star that does not decline (Christ, the paschal candle) in the Exultet of Holy Saturday.[11] The vertiginous doubling of fraternal enemies in *Finnegans Wake* takes as its starting point the doubling of sacred and demoniacal. It begins with the opposition between Stephen and Mulligan, evident in the passage cited: Stephen's No marks a decision to wander, in "his my sandal schoon" through the night and through exile, rather than return to the tower. While marking a pulverization (a catastrophe or "collapsus") of individual identity, of which the polysemic aspect is at the heart of writing, the multiplication of images of the Judeo-Christian star indicates a path through symbolic discourse toward the Word; and the demoniacal trial is summed up in the Fall. The trial is imposed through the double—that which troubles identity—the sliding outside the self, the body or the sex, outside the realm of the superego or divine instance, even to fatal abjection. He who does not founder among the dead, like the light in darkness, subject to resurrection, may move toward a lightning-like *jouissance*.[12]

In "Circe," Stephen is submitted to the trial of the Passion. His fall impresses itself on the wounded Bloom, the agent of the resurrection. That this resurrection be that of a son links it to the redemption of Bloom himself;[13] Stephen and Bloom play out the Trinitarian drama of the same and the other. When Stephen sees his mother in a hallucination, he denies *amor matris,* the archaic, pre-verbal *institutional* union with her; which is not to say that the "mystery of love" and of incest is erased, since, before putting out the light and plunging into Luciferian darkness, Stephen asks his mother to make a gift of language to him. Stephen attempts his own incarnation beginning with this word (a paschal word: the passage or trajectory through death) which comes from the Other. This demand or request is made in proximity of Bloom, the holder of a transcendent paternity brought to life by a new possibility of filiation (the encounter with Stephen): "STEPHEN: (*Choking with fright, remorse and horror*) They said I killed you, mother. . . . THE MOTHER: (*A green rill of bile trickling from a side of her mouth*) You sang that song to me. *Love's bitter mystery.* STEPHEN: (*Eagerly*) Tell me the word, mother, if you know now. The word known to all men. THE MOTHER: Who saved you. . . . Repent, Stephen. . . . FLORRY: (*Points to Stephen*) Look! He's white. BLOOM: (*Goes to the window to open it more*) Giddy. THE MOTHER: Repent! O, the fire of hell! STEPHEN: (*Panting*) The corpse-chewer! Raw head and bloody bones!" (581). Stephen's mother eludes the demand of the word. The horror of her death is integrated in the institution. Maternal decay and the corruption of the Church overflow the Prayer of the Dying, its virgins singing joyous canticles, its purification. Faced with the maternal refusal and invaded by abjection, Stephen refuses the dead mother's offer of salvation and puts out the light.[14]

Liliata rutilantium

Religion takes charge of the mute, inassimilable horror of death by means of repression, the effect of prayer (*Liliata rutilantium . . .*). The abyss of death is hollowed out by original sin.[15] The refusal of the institution enunciated by Stephen is, in fact, a denunciation of the repression as maintained by the prayer, i.e., at the price of the mother's split into virgin and prostitute—victim sacrificed to *dio boia* and sinner. The split brings about Stephen's downfall until June 16, 1904.[16] According to the Joycean interpretation, distinguishing the corrupt institution from the Trinitarian trajectory, Christ operates a lifting of repression, a crossing that takes up the problem of original sin—whence the *felix culpa* announced in the Exultet.

At the beginning of the novel, Stephen remembers the Yeats song "Who Goes with Fergus?" that he had sung to his dying mother: "It lay behind him, a bowl of bitter waters. Fergus' song: I sang it alone in the house, holding down the long dark chords. Her door was open: she wanted to hear my music. . . . She was crying in her wretched bed. For those words, Stephen: love's bitter mystery" (9). In "Circe" the mother evokes "love's bitter mystery" again. It is through this poetic signifier,[17] marked for Joyce by the letter of Irish subjectivity, that the seductions of the semiotic domain (voice, song, rhythm) are traversed by symbolicity: death, love, and loss are to be transmitted by spiration, "the gift of tongues."[18]

Love's bitter mystery: something along the lines of the Christly Word, enduring through death, returning in a resurrection. Through Bloom's paternity, the bowl of bitter waters indicating sin in a feminine body turns its bitterness into the joy of the Christly mystery, transsubstantiation, at the moment of Bloom's communion with Stephen: "They drank in jocoserious silence Epps's massproduct" (677).[19] The tragedy cut short by jubilation is "jocoserious": founded by the Trinitarian event—the generation of the Son and the spiration (the procession of the Holy Spirit), gift of love linking the Father and the Son.

The mother does not answer the demand or request for a gift of the word; she merely stresses Stephen's guilt, leading him to share her deathbed of institutionalized abjection. It is

Bloom who "answers" in her place, after Stephen's fall. On the other hand, when Bloom *answers,* picking Stephen up off the ground, a resurrection occurs, thanks to his paternity. In the interval of Bloom's paternal lack, the apparition of his son Rudy comes forth: the empty space is taken by Stephen, who murmurs Yeats's poem. The fact that Bloom hears a girl's name, "Miss Ferguson," underscores the importance of desire in this "jocoserious" (sacred and comic) mystery: "STEPHEN: Who . . . drive . . . Fergus now. And pierce . . . wood's woven shade? . . . BLOOM: Poetry. Well educated. Pity. . . . Ferguson, I think I caught. A girl. Some girl. Best thing could happen him" (608). The poetic letter is definitively allied with the sacred letter of the Law; and in this process begins the production of the Joycean word. The fact that Rudy reads from right to left, kissing the page, indicates that he is reading the Torah. Thanks to the intervention of Bloom the father, Stephen gains access theologically, in the letter, to *jouissance.* The Passion according to Joyce: the cuckoo *sings,*[20] the erotic wound opens to jubilation, in song.

Jew and Greek

If the vision of Rudy puts Stephen in the line of Judaic filiation, Stephen himself marks Bloom's paternity with Christ's act of rupture: *"Ex quibus . . . Christus* or Bloom his name is" (643). The Trinitarian truth of their encounter is located in their doubled identity: "Jewgreek is Greekjew. Extremes meet" (504). The meeting point of Jew and Greek is Christ, according to Paul: "For there is no difference between the Jew and the Greek: for the same Lord over all is rich unto all that call upon him" (Rom. 10:12). In this context, we may note the Greek name of Dedalus, as well as the Homeric display spread through *Ulysses:* a Greek skeleton (of Semitic origin, according to Joyce) fleshed with Trinitarian language according to Shakespeare. The communion in tongues as well as in drink joins the two series (Bloom-Shakespeare-Ulysses and Stephen-Hamlet-Telemachus) in Christ: "Light to the gentiles" (677).

The multiplicity (or seriation) of roles, identities, and cross-circuiting symbols links the characterizations of Bloom and Stephen. In "Ithaca" their Irish exile comes into relief on a religious level. Like Christ, accomplishing the union between Jew and Greek, between the Hebrew and the Greek of the Bible, Ireland[21] is for Joyce the crossroad of paganism and monotheism—whence the equation Greece = Ireland = Zion. Stephen's evocation of the conversion of Ireland from the Druid cult to Christianity by Saint Patrick (666) marks this crossroad, this heterogeneous continuity, with its Christly specificity. This intermingling explains why, during the exchange in tongues (or the spiration—the linking of love, in language), Stephen sings in Gaelic: "What fragments of verse from the ancient Hebrew and ancient Irish languages were cited with modulations of voice and translation of texts by guest to host and by host to guest? By Stephen: *suil, suil, suil arun, suil go siocair agus, suil go cuin* (walk, walk, walk your way, walk in safety, walk with care). By Bloom: *Kifeloch, harimon rakatejch m'baad l'zamatejch* (thy temple amid thy hair is as a slice of pomegranate)" (687–688). Stephen's song links him, "wandering Aengus of the birds," "the most innocent son of Erin," to Bloom, "the wandering jew" (214,217). This passage bears witness to a double wandering, and to the desire that, in establishing lack and the cut that founds it, makes of it an exile. Bloom responds with a Hebrew citation from the Song of Songs (4:3 and 6:7), a verse sung by the lover to the beloved. This fragment of a biblical love song found in the five scrolls [22] stresses not only that which, at the heart of the Law, threatens its boundaries with an erotic overflow, but also the love, *jouissance,* and suffering that Bloom offers Stephen with his invitation to spend the night. He not only offers him an incestuous relationship with Molly but also eventually, fantasmatically, a legal, Mosaic, and erotic filiation through marriage to Milly: "Why might these several provisional contingencies between a guest and a hostess not necessarily preclude or be precluded by a permanent eventuality of reconciliatory union between a schoolfellow and a jew's daughter? Because the way to daughter led through mother, the way to mother through daughter"(695).

What seems to be at stake in the communion linking Bloom and Stephen is language itself. Their exchange in song and in writing underlines the symbolic equivalence between Jew and Irishman. Each of them writes four characters of the exiled tongue. The two languages and their respective traditions are knotted together by a series of analogies combining fantasy and history: "What points of contact existed between these languages and between the people who spoke them? The presence of guttural sounds, diacritic aspirations, epenthetic and servile letters in both languages: their antiquity, both having been taught on the plain of Shinar 242 years after the deluge in the seminary instituted by Fenius Farsaigh, descendant of Noah, progenitor of Israel, and ascendant of Heber and Heremon, progenitors of Ireland: their archeological, genealogical, hagiographical, exegetical, homilectic, toponomastic, historical and religious literatures comprising the works of rabbis and culdees, Torah, Talmud (Mischna and Ghemara) Massor, Pentateuch, Book of the Dun Cow, Book of Ballymote, Garland of Howth, Book of Kells: their dispersal, persecution, survival and revival" (688). The reference to Noah, as well as to the presumed antiquity of the two tongues, situates their origin according to Genesis 11 in the period of the tower of Babel. The "progenitors" of Israel and Ireland are linked by genealogy, which is itself implicated in the teaching of the two languages. With his predilection for encyclopedic knowledge, Joyce brings together all imaginable kinds of sacred writing.[23] He arrives at the parallel between specifically Judaic sacred texts and the specifically Irish sacred texts of the illuminated manuscripts (in which Irish decoration and graphics are used to represent an evangelical text, the Book of Kells being the most spectacular example).[24] The culmination of this list of analogies is the mention of the double destiny through exile, ritual, and politics: Bloom sings the national anthem in Hebrew. Thus the parallel trajectory of Bloom and Stephen dates from biblical antiquity (Genesis) and continues through political contexts contemporary to the two characters, and even beyond. Bloom and Stephen as characters seem surpassed and submerged in the vast unfolding of time. But they simultaneously endure through their Trinitarian figuration, as they gather all languages, or rather all forms of writing (689) from hieroglyphics to Morse code, in their "common study."

It is the Trinitarian axis of their figuration that is at the heart of their sharing of hidden identities.[25] Simultaneously, Stephen sees in Bloom "the traditional figure of hypostasis," the image of Christ "as leucodermic, sesquipedalian with winedark hair," and Bloom hears in Stephen, "the traditional accent of the ecstasy of catastrophe" (689), the *jouissance* of the Fall. This chapter in the form of a catechism marks the final disappearance of Bloom and Stephen as characters in a novel and their entry into figuration, their infinitization in language. Thus opens the path of access to the Word, its Incarnation, in Molly's monologue at the threshold of *Finnegans Wake*. Catechism precedes communion, which takes place, presumably, in Molly's chamber music,[26] terminating the series of feminine receptacles and overturning the bowl of bitter bile of the dying mother. The exchange of signs between Bloom and Stephen stands out against the Judeo-Christian trajectory: the exile in tongues of the Tower of Babel is undone in the "gift of tongues" of the Christly Word. Transmitted by the Holy Spirit at Pentecost, the word overturns the confusion of Babel as well as the abject nakedness, impossible to behold, of the drunken Noah. The reversal takes place in a flash of jubilation: "And they were all filled with the Holy Ghost, and began to speak in other tongues, as the Spirit gave them utterance" (Acts 2:4). The encounter between father and son leads to an *ebriography*, the writing of intoxication in tongues. These "cantraps of fermented words"[27] are related to the Pentecostal tongues of fire: "And they were all amazed, and were in doubt, saying one to another, What meaneth this? Others mocking said, These men are full of new wine" (Acts 2:12, 13).

Signatures and readings:
the name and the letter

At their meeting, Bloom and Stephen speak, sing, and write in a symmetrical, reciprocal act: they reflect themselves in each other, in a fleeting event of union. The foundations of Catholicism and literature in transcendental language, evident in Stephen's remarks, do not seem to preoccupy Bloom—thus potentially limiting not only his role of absorbing the word of prophecy but also the extent of his paternal relationship with Stephen. But such is not the case. Joyce directly operates Bloom's Transfiguration, *in actu* (in sacred and performative enunciation), while Stephen (like Hamlet, the speaker-addressee of his own inability to act—he can only talk) argues, meditates, discusses, without quite succeeding in *translating* himself onto paper. He cannot create art: "That answer and those leaves, Vincent said to him, will adorn you more fitly when something more, and greatly more, than a capful of light odes can call your genius father" (415).

If Bloom's paternal position is defined by his entry into the Trinitarian circuit, he arrives at this position through language. Between the position of prophetical enunciation and the vision of Shakespeare linking Bloom to Stephen in the mirror, a series of events or acts of writing takes place, anchoring Joyce's experience in the Bible and in Shakespeare. Bloom sketches the trajectory of reading-writing that locates the writer.[28] The prophetical position reaches its peak here, coming close to the point of emergence of being in language: the Christly position recapitulates the prophetic experience of the Old Testament, but this occurs in the impossible space where the triune divinity incarnates the spoken word. The heterogeneity of man and god, of flesh and spirit, gives rise to this *borderline* state (on the edge: the strand, border between land and sea, between father and mother, is a privileged space of the Joycean domain of the true and the Real—the *vréel*).[29]

For Bloom, the Other who is the Letter, whose presence on paper is constantly fleeing the gaze of others, hidden because of the scandal it consigns, circulates between love and death until its "revelation," its coming to light, its entry into an equally fleeting *jouissance*. Of his exchange with Stephen in "Ithaca," Joyce writes: "Bloom and Stephen thereby become heavenly bodies. . . . The last word . . . is left to Penelope. This is the indispensable countersign to Bloom's passport to eternity."[30] Thus the response to lack (as felt by Stephen) turns out to be a coming-forth of the word out of the strange femininity in which the Jew, successor to the dead mother, gains access to his paternity in the language . . . come from the Other. Joyce extends the femininity he attributes to Bloom to the Jewish people as a whole, in order to make of Judaism the feminine space where "Jesus Christ a pris son corps humain." It is thus that Stephen's Oedipal crisis is overturned, and the Oedipal path reversed: the father (Bloom) intervenes in order to heal (suture?) the cut. In re-creating the mother-child dyad (Molly-Stephen), Bloom retrieves his threatened masculinity. In this context, castration is the effect of *Dio boia,* the devouring God or the "libidinous God."[31] This strange form of divine paternity disguises death and the Real; and Bloom's strange paternity reconstitutes its Symbolic dimension through the archaic reality of mother and child.

Bloom is surrounded by signifiers. His day is punctuated by the letter, circulating the imprint of the Other. He receives a note from his daughter Milly, and, under the name of Henry Flower, a letter from Martha Clifford, his "mistress" (only on paper). He discovers Molly's betrayal when he sees Boylan's letter to her (66, 77–78, 61, 63). Several times he thinks of the letter his father left for him before committing suicide (97, 499, 723). He answers Martha's letter (279–80) and remembers an anonymous valentine he once sent to Josie Powell (Mrs. Breen) (444). A poem he wrote in childhood appears in "Ithaca," as well as a series of anagrams of his name and a love poem to Molly containing the acrostic "POLDY" (678).

The focus of Bloom's letters is seduction itself, sexual adventure on the terrain of the other—or of the other revised according to the exigency of its infinitization, or *magnification*—leading it toward the capital O of the Other. Bloomian *jouissance,* eliding "natural" sexuality, takes place primarily on writing paper, or stationery: in this space, his *jouissance* (as well as his wound, inflicted by Molly's infidelity) is woven out of linguistic effects.[32] For Bloom, the letter sustains the name (of paternity) that he seizes as his own (or that he rewrites metaphorically as "Flower"). In this sense, he nonchalantly gains access to symbolic discourse weighted with emotion, or drive. With a writer's delight, he arranges the meanings that come forth out of the realm of non-sense.

Such is the search for the letter in letters—the name is hidden, figured, anagrammatized in the text [33] of seduction and of the "night of being" that Joyce conceived of as feminine. Obscenity works its way into theology and holds its own, with all the drive it can muster.[34] Indeed, obscenity seems to be the underbelly of theology, the flesh of *parlêtre* that haunts it (talking its way through corporeal being, piercing the flesh with words like arrows). It is perhaps this region of the sacred which meshes being (*l'être*) and the letter (*la lettre*) according to an ultimately biblical conception that Joyce envisages as that which lies *beyond* seduction ("the seductions of music beyond which Ulysses travels").[35]

It is through writing that Bloom transcends seduction. He saves himself from a silent fall into the Real with the help of the letter's ink: his uses of *correspondence* are evocative of the figure of *metaphor,* essential to the (paternal) function of language.[36] In "Sirens," Bloom writes to Martha Clifford (as in "Nausikaa" he writes a few words, in the sand, to Gerty). The biographical model for Martha was Martha Fleischmann, a woman glimpsed in Zurich in 1918. Joyce saw her as a double of the bird-girl on the Dublin strand, herself an image of the Virgin (and of the call to sin and to life). Joyce's division of femininity into the roles of Virgin and whore is evident in the letters to Nora, particularly those of 1909;[37] in this context, it is pertinent to mention the name of Amalia Popper, the young Jewess admired by Giacomo in *Giacomo Joyce.* But the character of Gerty (Nausikaa), and Bloom's fantasmatic relation to her, is primarily reminiscent of Martha Fleischmann, to whom Joyce sent a postcard addressed to Nausikaa and signed Odysseus.[38] This Joycean missive is perhaps displaced toward the frontier of signatures, that of Jacob Boehme cum Stephen: the strand where the signatures of all things are inscribed, the borderline threshold of the inscription of Bloom/Ulysses to Gerty/Nausikaa. The topography of the Joycean borderline marks the passionate attainment (half engendering, half incarnation)[39] of flight in the letter. This flight at the edge of the sea produces *wavespeech:* the breaking of waves on the sand speaks for the *entre-corps,* the eroticism of margins.

Carried away by the music, Bloom includes some high-soaring lyricism in his letter: "Too poetical about that sad. Music did that. Music hath charms Shakespeare said" (280).[40] Bloom, Shakespeare, Joyce: these biographical, or biogrammatical, traces are confirmed in "Circe" when Bloom defends himself against the accusations of the plagiarized writer, Beaufoy, who calls him "a plagiarist. A soapy sneak masquerading as a literateur" (458).[41] Thus Joyce can only arrive at the comic and sacred trans-figuration of Stephen into Shem via Bloom the father. As Bloom himself remarks, after perceiving in the rhythm integrating the role of rhyme in blank verse that which leads to paternal repetition, the invisible has become visible only for the ear of the invisibly begotten: "That is how poets write, the similar sounds. But then Shakespeare has no rhymes: blank verse. The flow of the language it is. The thoughts. Solemn. *Hamlet, I am thy father's spirit Doomed for a certain time to walk the earth*" (152). Paternal repetition unfolds in the non-substantial body of language, in the flowing passage of signifiers. The enunciation, or rather its seriation begun in repetition, is projected or spread farther than the declaration it enunciates—thanks to rhythm itself, which sends it beyond.

At the moment when Bloom's gestures in writing are described, Joyce indicates their Judeo-Christian specificity. In "Circe," when Bloom and Stephen mathematically unite (in the gap between 16 and 22 years), Bloom writes: "*Bloom releases his hand and writes idly on the table in backhand, pencilling slow curves*" (563). These slow curves of an arabesque, from right to left, foreshadow Rudy's reading of Hebrew, also from right to left. The context (the hallucination of adultery, returning to the afternoon rendezvous of Boylan with Molly), as well as Bloom's enigmatic writing, seems to echo the Gospel account of Christ's equally enigmatic approach to writing during the confrontation with the adulterous woman: "But Jesus stooped down, and with *his* finger wrote on the ground, *as though he heard them not*" (John 8:6).[42]

The writing on the table recalls the message left for Gerty in the sand. Moreover, Bloom writes (and erases his writing) rather than confront Molly (381). Like Christ encouraged to threaten the adulterous woman, Bloom renounces mimetic violence toward Molly. He displaces his desire elsewhere, in the relation to writing.[43] Bloom thinks of Molly, Gerty, Martha's letter. When he sees the signature of his own face in the reflection of a pond, he interprets the strand as a response to his own subjectivity: "All these rocks with lines and scars and letters" (381).[44] The beach, its rocks, bear the traces of *wounds*. From the erotic wound to the letter: Bloom's narcissism is that of a god signing himself in the world he creates. His vision *in actu* (in language) is a kind of genetic begetting, a signature detached from him: "I. . . . AM. A." Bloom does not end his sentence, and it thus designates the anaphorical act of the sacred enunciation. Since it does not end, the signifying dimension of the sentence remains intact, untouched by the finite quality of the declarative statement, of which the meaning is manifest only at its end. The copula of being finds neither attribute nor predicate. "I" only designates itself or shows itself,[45] and its being-enunciation thus opens out toward theological infinity. This interpretation seems to be confirmed by the last words of *Finnegans Wake:* prior to the famous return to the beginning, "riverrun," the confrontation with the silence following the series "*A* x *a* x *a* x *a* x *a* x *the*" is unavoidable. Joyce wrote: "The book really has no beginning or end. (Trade secret, registered Stationers Hall.) It ends in the middle of a sentence and begins in the middle of the same sentence."[46] Yet Joyce also pronounced this description of the end of the *Wake:* "Cette fois, j'ai trouvé le mot le plus glissant, le moins accentué, le plus faible de la langue anglaise, un mot qui n'est même pas un mot, qui sonne à peine entre les dents, un souffle, un rien, l'article 'the.'"[47] The return to the beginning of the book is sketched out, the circuit is indicated, but the gap is there. One goes in and out of speech; yet as an act or event, it constitutes a *rupture.* Syntax (like capital letters, final periods, and other marks of punctuation), through its attempt to control the "fluidity" of language, seems to *deny* the *spiritual* (in the Freudian sense of *Witz*) event of the word, the coming-forth of meaning out of non-sense. Joycean epiphany provides ample testimony for this surge of the symbolic out of reality—a moment comparable to the mystery of the Incarnation.

At the end of *Finnegans Wake,* the proof that an ineluctable rupture has taken place is the "Paris, 1922–1939" marking the place of a signature, designating that particular infinity by its spatial and temporal axes. It is only after this moment that the reader can plunge back into the flux of enunciation, into that flow which conjures up all names, all places, and all times, re-begetting them and bringing them into the world again through HCE and ALP. The signature/monument does not allow the reader to forget that the squaring of the circle, throughout the text, does not occur by itself. Joyce goes out of the circle in order to find its borders; he stops time and re-creates it, plotting against the "temporal," the time of this world, the linear flow of syntax. He seduces this linearity and drives it toward a rhythmic, pluralized, serial *jouissance*. Such is the wake of linearity, of the narrative thread. Its burial is celebrated and it is brought back to life—otherwise, elsewhere: in the wake again/*Finnegans Wake*.

Bloom's writing elicits the text of Exodus 3:14: "And God said to Moses, I AM THAT I AM: and he said, Thus shalt thou say unto the children of Israel, I AM hath sent me unto you." According to Semitic tradition, divine being contracts itself to fit in the hollow of the name, but not exclusively; the name, then, does not confine being but comprehends its infinity. According to the prophets, moreover, the proper name indicates vocation and destiny. I AM is divine being that declares itself as "I"; it is the name unlimited by the "proper" of identification, but rather the name virtually in itself: and throughout the Bible, belief in God is expressed by naming His Name, He is blessed by His Name, acts are carried out in His Name. The Name of God is constructed from the instance of discourse designating itself as such, creating, from the emptiness of the speaking "I," the plenitude of being. The Creation, the *parole pleine* as the utterance filled with truth, surges forth (*ex nihilo*) from the abyss (emptiness without form, *tohu* and *bohu*).

The auto-nomination of the Mosaic God is also articulated in another context, that of God first and last. This is the world without end; Stephen sought its origins in "Proteus": "Aleph, alpha: nought, nought, one" (38). The letter "A," sign of the Creation *ex nihilo*, is written in Hebrew and then in Greek, linking the Bloomian "I. AM. A." to the enunciation of the revelation (Apoc. 1:8): "I am Alpha and Omega, the beginning and the ending, saith the Lord." According to the configuration of the Catholic letter, Stephen's symbolic position would be at the "O," insofar as the Son, accomplishing the knot of the Trinity, would be the Messiah prefigured by Elijah.[48] The sacred trajectory runs the gamut between the first letter and the last: the Alpha–Omega of Greek is expanded (according to the various alphabets) in *Finnegans Wake,* with the A–Z of English, et al. Bloom's scriptures give an indication of the extraordinary purification of that which supports symbolic discourse encoded in the Bible. The letter is breathed (*ruah*) and creates the world. So opens the dialogue between the object anchoring the letter and the virtuality of this letter: the airy, the invisible letter. The transmission of the sacred takes place in writing on the tablets of stone (the kingdom of the Father), then through the Incarnation in human flesh (the writing in the sand, the anaphorical dimension of the Son) and, finally, through a gesture—a breath airy as the flight of a dove, a word, an infinitesimal *rien* (the kingdom of the Spirit): the tongue of fire.

Bloom, Stephen, Scripture: a Trinitarian ensemble. As we have seen, Bloom is interested in the Church (the feminine body, the wife of Christ), in the Son, in children. Stephen is interested in origins; he seeks a Father, he seeks a solution to the separation from the Mother, the unavowable cut. He asks the question: Where do children come from? in order not to ask: How can I enter into the double realm of femininity, the night of being, the matrix of (auto-)enunciation? The encounter between Bloom and Stephen takes shape in terms of paternity. The rise of a fallen word becomes operative through a coincidence, a concatenation of events, by "chance" (but the letter knows all about chance, enough to suspend its operation).[49] At the conclusion of the dialogue that follows this encounter, the narrative (its realistic quality, or *vraisemblance,* that imitates reality[50] by revealing the gap constitutive of paternity) separates father from son. The irruption of paternity sets filiation to rights. Paternity operates in an instant,[51] coming forth out of a tohu-bohu, emptiness constituting symbolicity. The instant belongs to the category of the impossible, the unbelievable; and for this reason, it allows family romances[52] to multiply so easily under its aegis. Indeed, the impossible instant creates the need of "faith" so particularly Catholic because it is based on the mysterious leap into One Being that makes it Triune. This leap is sustained by the first leap, the divine throw of the dice that brought letters out of the voice in order to create the world. Stephen says this of paternity: "On that mystery . . . the church is founded and founded irremovably because founded, like the world, macro- and microcosm, upon the void" (207). Uncertainty, real and significant (the Mallarméan throw of the dice), surrounds the paternal event: the symbolic result of the encounter between Bloom and Stephen produces an elaboration of the Name-of-the-Father (Bloom and the letter) revealed as Judeo-Catholic (In the Name of the Father . . .). From that point, exile begins in the proper name, the gap between the subject and the being who, as his father, names him. After the instant, exile: "I'll leave you all where Jesus left the jews" (238).

The Trinitarian function of the artist undoes the separation or fills the gap through a strategy of all in all: "He [Shakespeare] is the ghost and the prince. He is all in all" (212).[53] The distance between Bloom and Stephen reunites them in a sharing of exile in order to, henceforth, incorporate exile in the gap that separates them. The hole is the pretext for an impossible, transsubstantiational *jouissance* of all in all. The impossible totality tests the possibilities of identity, and finally dissolves this identity in the night of being. The *vraisemblance* of the fictional characters shrinks, when the all in all of the Christ is established as the site of an enunciation in the present tense. Between the borders separating/uniting Bloom and Stephen in exile, Joyce allows negativity to speak the demoniacal underside of the impossible Trinity. Here the fiction of femininity, love and death, the womb and the tomb and the desire that holds them in an embrace with language, locates itself. Here Joyce creates himself as Word in the fictional flesh of Molly.

The fugitive instant and the retrospective ear

With the expedient of the instant, the Trinitarian event participates in eternity. Trinitarian temporality is elaborated according to the rupture that creates a present tense for the subject of the enunciation: eternity locates itself there through the name[54] resonating as first and last. The nominalization of the verb *to be* in its verbal forms of past, present, and future gives the ineffable name of God, YHWH.[55] This name is related to the meaning of Alpha and Omega, and to the future perfect of the prophetic utterance, that, through the present tense of enunciation, goes outside of time. For Joyce, this framework produces a "retrospective arrangement": memory is re-created in the event of the Word. This memory of an experienced past entails the attribution of meaning to this past—occurring by deferred action, or *après-coup,* as in the cutting-off point instituted by paradise lost.[56] Memory is thus projected, renewed, resuscitated: it becomes the production of an utterance, a dream, a piece of writing, in which the swallowing of the future by the present tense,[57] sustained by the backwards movement of retroactivity, is ultimately immobilized in the simultaneity of the two movements. The subject is engaged between the future and the past, between the not-yet-born and the already-dead, between the origin and the end. This heterogeneous vision is subjectivity itself, burning its candle at both ends, taken out of the course of time by a present enunciation or word.

The relation between the demand of the word (Stephen and the dead mother) and the Christly Word of eternal life demonstrates the capacity of symbolic discourse to parry the flow of futures into pasts, in what Augustine calls the immortality of the soul. The leap of *jouissance* outside time maintains two opposite terms together (Bloom and Stephen are "poles apart") as love accomplishes the non-synthetic union of Father and Son. For Joyce, the Trinitarian event plays itself out on the frontier between subject and object, comparable to a mystical swoon *into* symbolicity. This bliss of body and soul, of all and nothing, is in the letter: it is a form of sublimation. The encounter between Bloom and Stephen speaks for the night of being in which their desires and horrors bring them together. Joyce himself takes up position in the night, making it talk in the present enunciation—as if the mysterious, carnal, "non-logical" realm of femininity spread to include the unlimited temporality of writing in the *present.* The leap outside time dissolves past and future dimensions, holding them in the hollow of its body (according to Joycean fantasies);[58] hence the necessity of "Penelope" for Bloom's entry into eternity: "In the intense instant of imagination, when the mind,

Shelley says, is a fading coal, that which I was is that which I am and that which in possibility I may come to be" (194). The future and the past come together in the dimension of the imaginary, where memory and projection retain their verb tenses (their distance from the subject of the present), whereas the "intense instant of imagination" is closer to the realm of symbolicity. By sustaining paternity on one side and filiation on the other, this realm *creates* the present. "Ithaca" seems to confirm this interpretation. Before disappearing into the night (at the end of "Ithaca" Bloom goes to bed, "the childman weary, the manchild in the womb" [737]),[59] the catechismal voice remarks that Stephen hears the past in Bloom's Hebraic chant while Bloom sees the future in the person of Stephen.

The question of temporality is central to the Ulyssean micro-motif of the "retrospective arrangement." The expression is used by Kernan,[60] a character parallel to Bloom in his marginalized social position and another fictional phantom of Joyce's father. In "Wandering Rocks," Kernan thinks about history: "Times of the troubles. Must ask Ned Lambert to lend me those reminiscences of sir Jonah Barrington. When you look back on it all now in a kind of retrospective arrangement" (241). The evocation of death (accidents, Irish history, and past time recapitulated in the ballad celebrating the death of the Father: "*At the siege of Ross did my father fall*") focuses on its *remains,* on what is left over from it: dead bodies, the sweepings of America, money to be picked up, clothing, the blood of Emmet, even the "small gin" just consumed by Kernan himself. And then Kernan barely misses an important *passage:* "His Excellency! Too bad! Just missed that by a hair" (241). Thus Joyce displays a *missed present tense,* in which one no longer participates: the fallen instant rejoins the different remains of death in a "retrospective arrangement."

For Bloom, the death of the father is modulated by the emptiness of the filial position. His own detachment from religious worship (724) is disappointing to the father whose death becomes an obsession for him, masking his own death and his own paternal *lack* (the death of his name). This constitutes the failure of the future perfect, as suffered by Moses himself: "He died without having entered the land of promise. . . . And with a great future behind him" (143). In Stephen's proximity, Bloom takes up Kernan's expression: "He is young Leopold, as in a retrospective arrangement, a mirror within a mirror (hey, presto!), he beholdeth himself. . . . Now he is himself paternal and these about him might be his sons. . . . No, Leopold! Name and memory solace thee not" (413). Implicitly, a parallel is established between Bloom and Shakespeare, whose creation stemmed from the wound of his name and his memories—and his dead son: "Hamnet Shakespeare, who has died in Stratford that his namesake may live forever" (188). This vision (the Mallarméan "ressouvenir en avant") re-creates the past according to its trajectory toward the future and leaps outside time into the present.

In the present tense, time must burst its boundaries or go out of itself. Out of the past-future domain of Kernan's meditations, the "throwaway" works its way toward *jouissance:* "Elijah is coming" (240). The true, or revealed, present tense is sustained by a symbolicity anchored in absence (death itself and its integration in signs): its formulation is marked by the death of the father, rendered as the nomination that gives him life or resurrects him.

The access to the letter, running the Joycean gamut between biblical prophecy and Shakespeare (with a space between the two reserved for Dante), resolves, in *Ulysses,* the paternal and filial polarization. According to the unheard-of logic of the Trinity, Christ maintains himself in this knotty resolution: his surrender as victim seals the Father's eternity, and his own as well. Murder triggers resurrection. Desire surmounts mimetic violence (that makes of the sacrificial crisis an abyss of fallen bodies) in order to make the murder inflicted by the other into the *jouissance* of the Other: in the word. Through Hamlet, Shakespeare articulates the dimensions of speech that he incarnates: scandal, thwarted act, lust, and murder make Hamlet talk his way even into death. Thus he echoes his father, martyred by the desire of his brother Claudius. The act of murder designates the dead king as the agency of paternal power holding the keys to the other, i.e., the desired mother; and it is this very agency which consigns the holder of the keys to the symbolic region of the Other and of the authentic King. So it is that the spectral King Hamlet, whose death has an unmistakeable aura of exile, makes himself heard by Prince Hamlet.[61] It is the effect of the symbolic transmission of access to the Other, coming from the dead King's mouth, that calls forth in *Prince* Hamlet a new and subtle mastery of the word.

Magnificat: tongue and Trinity

The victim of the Passion is reborn, from his tragic fall, in the word that rhythmically marks the *absence* of the buried desiring body; the tomb is empty, the body is displaced, arranged in signs. "*Non hunc sed Barabbam!*"[62] The act of sparing Barabbas designates the figure who seems to disappear in the black smoke of desire's Passion, in sacrifice . . . *Giacomo Joyce.* Joyce saves (himself) from death with his Word of love; yet he is rejected by the other (the crowd, demoniacal and sinful: "she," the Jewish Virgin who says "No"). Once again the shadow of the object falls . . . on the page. The Resurrection operates through signs. Ever since the blood on the doorposts of Exodus 12:13, holocaust has been in the air: Christ takes on the sins of the world, in order to make of the generalized holocaust (from one desire to another) something else,[63] in order to make the desert flower.

Halfway between Stephen and Bloom, Giacomo points out, in his own way, the Trinitarian truth engaging one with the other, Son and Father, Stephen and Bloom. *Ulysses,* or the Summa Against Arius: "Is that then the divine substance wherein Father and Son are consubstantial? Where is poor dear Arius to try conclusions? Warring his life long on the contransmagnificandjewbangtantiality. Illstarred heresiarch" (38). All of the ecclesiastical history of the Trinity is recapitulated in "contransmagnificandjewbangtantiality." The Joycean experience of language shows through. The clashing of words against each other makes of the Trinitarian enunciation the meeting point of events, narratives, languages—thus indicating the path toward the *Wake.* In *contrans/tantiality,* the passage of the Word through carnal substance and, above all, the "divine substance" wherein Father and Son are consubstantial, can be heard: thus Augustine writes: "The word *homoousion,* accepted at the Council of Nicaea against the Arians, signifies that the three Persons are of one essence."[64] Stephen's words repeat the symbol or Nicene Creed, "the Son of God . . . consubstantial with the Father,"[65] and thereby invoke both the attack of Arius against the Trinity (i.e., his devaluation of the Son henceforth inferior to the Father) and the Catholic response, manifested in the adoption of the word *homoousios*.

But the relation (*contrans*) to substantiality implies not only consubstantiation but transsubstantiation as well, i.e., the specific term of the Eucharist. According to Saint Augustine, the Eucharist operates "transformations of matter" on bread and wine by means of "mystical prayer."[66] In Christian mystery,[67] "the invisible action of the Spirit of God," bread and wine become "body and blood of Christ." The term *transsubstantiation* enters into theological usage following the controversy between Bérenger and Lanfranc. Bérenger considered the Eucharist as a spiritual event without the material alteration of bread and wine, whereas Lanfranc maintained that the bread *is* the body of Christ.[68] The Church, of course, approved Lanfranc; transsubstantiation gained canonical acceptance in the Fourth Lateran Council.

According to Augustine,[69] speech is not of the order of the Eucharist: it is not the body of Christ. But it is through the effect of speech (the mystical prayer: the overturning of the Real by the Word) that the substantial transformation occurs.

At the center of the word, Joyce evokes the Incarnation in the womb of a Jewess: *magnificandjewbang*. The explosion of Christ's coming (Incarnation, Epiphany) produces a tumult among the Jews, and the uproar at the moment of the Crucifixion. *Magnificand* testifies to the relation between the Incarnation and language; it is the exaltation of divine instance in the Virgin's song: *Et ait Maria: Magnificat anima mea Dominum*, "And Mary said, My soul doth magnify the Lord" (Luke 1:46). Magnification, the enjoyment of the Holy Spirit, offers the gift of tongues.[70]

Beginning with Moses, the meaning of *jewbang* is articulated in the exiled tongue, bringing forth being from nonbeing (from the sacrificed, the object of expulsion): the "body" of the forbidden tongue gives the Mosaic Law, "*the tables of the Law, graven in the language of the outlaw*" (143).[71] The excluded language, outside of Law, creates it. The letter springs forth from the path of exile, where the only guide is . . . holder of the letter (the Judaic God, the Dantean Vergil, and, in "A Midsummer Night's Dream," the Shakespearean fairies—agents of metamorphosis). The pillar of the cloud guides Moses-Shakespeare: "A star by night, Stephen said, a pillar of the cloud by day" (210). The alternation of Law and out-law, woven in signs, is anticipated by Stephen, who designated it "FROM THE FATHERS" as implicit in the Catholic do-main of sin (and feminine flesh)—making Joyce speak its Au-gustinian love and horror[72] through the flesh that transforms him. The *jewbang* takes effect, above all, in the femininity that Joyce attributes not only to Bloom but to the entire Jewish people (the latter considered as the womb of Catholicism). Sin in Catholicism is an outlaw integrated in the Law (even into its apocalyptic measures) at the price of the word. According to Origen, in the early Church, prior to the institution of confession,[73] the *Dic ecclesiae*, the avowal of sins (*exomologein*), and conversion (allowing the reintegration into the commu-nity of excommunicated sinners) made it possible for peni-tence to "care for the wounds in the Church."[74] The passage of the *Confessions* quoted by Stephen subtly indicates the in-tegration of sin in the Law but immediately relegates it to non-being: "All that is, is good."[75] Stephen is caught between purity (being) and corruption in the labyrinth of sin. Desire and death cling together before the implacable Other: "It was revealed to me that those things are good which yet are cor-rupted which neither if they were supremely good nor unless they were good could be corrupted. Ah, curse you! That's Saint Augustine" (142). This is not yet the domain of the *felix culpa* that reverses penitence and recovers the overflow of sin in paschal joy resonant in *Finnegans Wake:* between the cor-poral punishment of Leviticus and Christian confession as such, the interval of penitence described above situates itself as half flesh, half word. Turmel cites a Judaic ritual adopted by the Church in the second century A.D.: at the beginning of the weekly *banquet,* the presiding individual makes a confession of sins in the name of all the participants.[76] If *felix culpa,* then along the lines of Bloom's *Copula felix* (483): sin and its reso-lution are subtended by a carnal weight of exile, absence, castration. By contrast, sin turns into *jouissance,* simultaneously eternal and punctual, rhythmically scanned by repetitions of Yes, in Molly's monologue, the counter-signature of Joyce's passport to eternity—in the form of the permutated *felix culpa* of *Finnegans Wake*.

Exile, sin, grace

The effect of the encounter is prolonged in the separation, in the Ulyssean space of exile (according to the masculine identity of Bloom and Stephen)—the feminine body of the Other, speaking in "Penelope." When Bloom disappears in the terminal point of "Ithaca" (a disappearance analogous to that of Stephen in the night), the point-encounter of the present tense, the seed of the Incarnation of the Word in Molly's womb, begins to speak: confession, desire, orality, sexuality, men with women, family, names, languages, music, love. Through the feminine angle (the pre-text of the flesh), Joyce catalogs sin and its overturning in the Dantean rose. This is the wake of the paschal night, ending with the flowering of Bloom.

Exile begins at the moment of separation, in Judaic terms. Joyce renders explicit his references to Exodus, commemorated by the Passover ordained by God (Exod. 12:17). In a ritual procession, Bloom and Stephen leave the house chanting Psalm 113, a Passover hymn that is part of the Hallel and is sung at the end of the *seder* meal: "Lighted Candle in Stick borne by BLOOM. Diaconal hat on Ashplant borne by STEPHEN. With what intonation *secreto* of what commemorative psalm? The 113th, *modus peregrinus: In exitu Israel de Egypto: domus Jacob de populo barbaro*" (698).

Several motifs or series of images in *Ulysses* seem to be knotted around this text: Judaic/Catholic, light/darkness, Moses/Christ, pillar of the cloud/star, exile/writing, Bloom/Stephen/Shakespeare. The displacement from the pillar of fire to the star marks the astronomical constellation of Shakespeare in a Christly context. The light in darkness (sparking a repetition of the Creation in the Prologue to the Gospel of Saint John) is taken up once more in the Catholic liturgy of Easter; the latter, through a series of semantic slides, shapes it into a coherent constellation focused on *lumen Christi*. The "benediction of the new fire" situates this light as that of desire and celebration, of the exit from Egypt, of grace. The paschal candle is blessed, the lamps are lit, the joys of Easter (*paschalibus gaudiis*) begin.

Psalm 113 is not unrelated to that which, from the place of the Other, founds exile and sets it in motion, just as Stephen's "parleyvoo" establishes the unconscious as the site of "*dessous troublants*," in "Circe." The circuit of exile seems to end in the space of femininity, the womb of Molly: "How did he elucidate the mystery of an invisible person, his wife Marion (Molly) Bloom, denoted by a visible splendid sign, a lamp?" (702).[77] This light indicates the visible/invisible presence ready to speak for the night of femininity, obscenity, and paschal joy.

In the past, newly baptized Christians sang Psalm 113 on Easter night, when they returned in thanksgiving to the baptistery of Lateran. (It is currently sung on Sundays.) Baptism is attached to the paschal celebration, and it is related to the darkened, then illuminated body of the Church—a divine maternal receptacle, linking the Incarnation to the paschal mystery that, in marking, *modus peregrinus*, the passage of Christ, seems to echo the gesture of the Incarnation itself in the birth of the *infantes* who have passed through baptism: "This new birth is prepared by a slow gestation in the womb of the Church, which gives birth, in the paschal night, to these living in divine life."[78]

The Judeo-Catholic liturgical signification indicated by Psalm 113 appears at key moments in the scriptural trajectory of Dante.[79] As Joyce situates the liturgical evocation of light, a sign of love and jubilation, at this juncture of *Ulysses*, the allusion to Dante's passage through language comes into play; the quotation of the psalm locates Stephen and Bloom with respect to canto II of the *Purgatorio*: "In exitu Israel de Aegypto" (II, 46). Vergil and the poet are explicitly described as pilgrims for the first time: "Noi siam peregrin come voi siete" (II, 63); it is Easter Sunday morning. The allusion to Dante reinforces Joyce's reference to Passover/Easter and to theology with respect to a conversion structured around the encounter of two characters in a relationship of paternity and filiation, and its scriptural consequences. In Dante's Epistle

XIII, he interprets the beginning of Psalm 113 according to the fourfold meaning of Scripture. *In exitu Israel* is invested with the Catholic letter—whose *passage* is *paschal.* The polysemic letter articulates the unsayable, the impossible or unspeakable, "the conversion of the soul leaving off mourning and the misery of sin for a state of grace" ["Si ad moralem sensum, significatur nobis conversio anime de luctu et miseria peccati ad statum gratie"]:[80] united, Bloom and Stephen become figures, absorbed into the poetic word of the Psalm.

Dante's scriptural presence, often felt in *Ulysses,* is spectacularly dramatized in "Oxen of the Sun." Stephen interprets the beginning of Saint Bernard's prayer in the *Paradiso:* "Vergine Madre, figlia del tuo figlio" (XXXIII, 5–6). As regards the fleshly confrontation between the Virgin and the Word, Stephen characterizes the feminine position as one of incest or ignorance-denegation: "Or she knew him . . . and was but creature of her creature, *vergine madre figlia di tuo figlio* or she knew him not and then stands she in the one denial or ignorance with Peter Piscator who lives in the house that Jack built"(391). The subversion of sin, turned into grace, allows access to the mother; this incest (knowledge, according to the Bible)[81] introduces flesh, the unspeakable dimension of mystery, and the jubilations of laughter and light into the Word (*fattore, fattura,* according to *Paradiso,* XXXIII, 5–6). This divine *jouissance* described by Dante is saturated with the Other's femininity. However, the successful incest that mingles the Word with the flesh designates, in the Son, the Father. The elision of the Oedipal conflict submits the flesh to the Word, but without the cut. The sole *jouissance* possible without castration is that of this Father making himself Son through a Virgin. There is neither sin nor mimetic desire. The potentially semiotic love of the mother does not threaten to take away the word (or speech, the symbolic dimension holding the Son back from incest) but (unlike Mrs. Dedalus) makes a gift of the word. For the Son, giving a child to the mother becomes the equivalent of giving oneself the mother as child, becoming the father of one's mother. Maternal eroticism must be mastered by symbolicity—*jouissance* and *knowledge,* mastery of incest. Stephen's hesitation or doubt, prior to the encounter with Bloom, is evidence of the distance (perceived as emptiness) separating him—and tragically so—from the Other.

Stephen is unable to bring himself into the world through the word (demanded of his mother, but not given by her): he needs Bloom. Molly's monologue is the word that Joyce brings into the world through a feminine mouth (doubled by the scandalous transsubstantiation of her menstrual flow into a stream of words). In the dis-graceful enunciation attributed to Molly (orality, narcissism, desire, betrayal), the vampire-like figure of femininity seems to shrink and disappear. Joyce overturns the prayer for the dying, replacing it with the joyous canticle of the quasi-virginal Molly remembering her first time with Bloom among the *roses* (rhododendrons or, etymologically, rose-trees) of Howth. This is the starting point of the path of "christian minstrelsy," of agony and song, taken in *Finnegans Wake*.

A successful incest: Stephen awaits a father to save himself from the guilt that puts Oedipus' eyes out, that leads him toward death, and Bloom desires a son in order to re-win and re-seduce his wife. With respect to women, Stephen is stymied. His dead mother, cause of desire and horror, emerges from the prayer of the dying, surrounded by the choir of virgins. She wears the bridal veil of virginity: assimilated into the body of the Church, her abjection is clothed in purity and she *condemns* Stephen's sin in the brothel: "Repent! O, the fire of hell!" (581). For Stephen, seduction constitutes the invasion of the abject other, the whore. The impossible love of the mother and the desire of the debauched feminine object[82]— mourning and horror—immobilize him in a proliferation of the imaginary that seems to hinder him from taking on flesh in the letter. The divorce between affect and sensuality[83] is supported by the force of repression. The child's denegation of the parents' sexual relations (the primal scene) splits femininity (impure, sexual) into the pure mother and the prostitute.[84] This is the underside of the "pure" adoration displayed in the Joycean depiction of mariolatry. The woman becomes the object of an interdiction: in her place, the divided structure imposes the *jouissance* of infernal and horrible sin, leading the subject to the total castration of death or . . .

the Church, eroticism concentrated entirely in a non-rapport, love of the Other. Through this polarization, Christianity recovers love and canalizes it into the path of flesh and the Word.[85]

On June 16, 1904, Bloom undoes the disjunction prostitute/virgin afflicting Stephen by offering him access to femininity, or to woman. By means of the "retrospective arrangement," Joyce constructs a fiction around the biographical kernel of the passage of the young man, Stephen, into the experienced Bloom. Prostitute and virgin come together: Gerty-Nausikaa holds to the perverse underclothing (the *dessous*, source of much Joycean delight) of the Virgin, Catholically wakened to obscenity. As for Molly, her fundamental obscenity annuls the split between whore and virgin, thereby revealing "woman" singular, according to Joyce. In *Ulysses* Joyce celebrates Shakespeare's "dark lady" and Dante's Beatrice in the ending of youth evoked by Stephen as well as Giacomo through Sweelink's song: "Youth Here Has End" (663).[86] *Giacomo Joyce* indicates the end of youth in the fact of assuming a stance in relation to women. The conclusion of Molly's monologue is focused on roses, introducing the resonance of Dante's "rosa sempiterna," the source of which is revealed as the Virgin. "Rosa mystica," wrote Joyce to Martha Fleischmann,[87] taking up the Litany of the Virgin, a favorite liturgical text of that ironic mariolater, Joyce himself.

Through Molly, the division between mother and prostitute is resolved. Her song of innocence and experience, in which the trajectory of Stephen-Bloom resonates through Blake's formulation, is witness to the seduction of the Fall and the mystical jubilation of the Virgin's love: "Ill go to Lambes . . . and get them to send us some flowers . . . shall I wear a white rose . . . Id love to have the whole place swimming in roses God of heaven . . . the sun shines for you he said the day we were lying among the rhododendrons on Howth head . . . the day I got him to propose to me yes first I gave him the bit of seedcake out of my mouth and it was leapyear like now yes 16 years ago my God after that long kiss I near lost my breath yes he said I was a flower of the mountain yes so we are flowers all a womans body yes . . . and I gave him all the pleasure I could leading him on till he asked me to say yes . . .

and the sea the sea crimson sometimes like fire and the glorious sunsets . . . and the rosegardens and the jessamine . . . where I was a Flower of the mountain yes when I put the rose in my hair . . . or shall I wear a red yes . . . so he could feel my breasts all perfume yes"(781–783).[88]

Joyce painstakingly disseminates the double or split identification of Eve/Mary throughout the monologue. Molly was born on September 8, the birthday of the Virgin ("mine was the 8th"); her matrilineal background is Jewish ("my being jewess looking after my mother"); but she vaguely participates in Catholic ritual ("I blessed myself and said a Hail Mary . . . make an act of contrition the candle I lit that evening in Whitefriars street chapel") (747, 771, 741). Molly often mentions roses, and the Virgin; she gives the "seedcake" (analogous to the *seedfruit*, Eve's apple) to Bloom. In a profusion of roses Molly gives herself to Bloom, and her final Yes, promising love and marriage, echoes the Virgin's Yes.[89] From paradise lost to paradise regained, from Adam to Christ: "The wound which Mary closed and anointed, that one who is so beautiful at her feet is she who opened it and pierced it" ("La piaga che Maria richiuse e unse, quella ch'è tanto bella da' suoi piedi è colei che l'aperse e che la punse" [*Paradiso*, XXXII, 4–6]). At the threshold of *Finnegans Wake*, the *felix culpa* is touched off. The stars moved by love that end the *Divina Commedia* and the Yes uttered by Molly come together in the point of the present tense, "Un punto solo,"[90] that answers the final question of "Ithaca": "Where? ●" (737).

The point of a present tense locating vision in the form of a retrospective arrangement echoes, through Molly, another feminine figure in Dante's poem, Francesca. Like Molly, her association with that specific *point* implies an ambivalence, or a doubling, of Eve's sin and Mary's purity; in canto V of the *Inferno*, Dante adumbrates an erotic version of the final "punto solo," in anticipated opposition to it—or in its reversed form. (Thus Stephen's allusions to Francesca when he quotes canto V in "Aeolus" prefigure an association linking her to Bloom's beloved and unfaithful Molly.) For Dante, the point ("ma solo un punto fu quel che ci vinse" [V, 132]) knots the dimensions of reading, courtly love, and *jouissance* within a temporality situated outside time—in the experience of an instant. Thus

Dante, the fictional poet listening to Francesca, *swoons*—disappearing into the fall of Paolo and Francesca as if into death ("com'io morisse" [V, 142]): as a point of retrospection, this paradoxical temporality situates the scriptural position of the poet.

June 16, 1904, marks the fictional encounter of Stephen and Bloom, concluding with the celebration torn from the past that can be heard in Molly's monologue: Joyce-Shakespeare, according to Joyce's personal mythical context, takes the floor. For Bloomsday is the day of Joyce's encounter with Nora, who *inspired* him, who *made him a man,* according to the love letters he wrote to her.[91] The point of the accomplishment of the past, perceived retrospectively, is opened to bear fictively the Joycean oeuvre beginning with this moment of 1904, the point of the present from which the present of the enunciation emerges.[92] The Stephen-Bloom encounter can be formulated as a "future perfect," the entry into the night of fiction. It arrests the fleeting course of time (painfully designated by Stephen: "Life is many days. This will end" [214])[93] in the creation of an event difficult to define or localize, a form of *jouissance* preliminary to the production of series and the loss of identities through fictional characters in *Finnegans Wake*.

Finnegans
Wake

4

Toward
Work in Progress

The *Portrait* presents the elaboration of a Catholic position in relation to the Word: the trajectory of a subject, of a fictional character, leads from the institution to theology. Within this trajectory, a double position is maintained; the artist wrestles with the priest, Lucifer with Christ, and these doubles work through the writing, or, rather, the scriptural identity of the individual character.

In *Ulysses,* the elaboration of the double position of the subject Stephen Dedalus is widened and deepened. The confrontation with the institution (*Non serviam*) reveals a new complexity in the failure of flight. Sin is explored—through mourning and horror, desire and death—theologically, eschatologically. The sin rejected in the *Portrait* as the domain of the institution is further taken into account, in *Ulysses,* on the level of the speaking subject. The passage here is from subjection to the institution to subjectivity in theology: thus one could describe the transition from the *Portrait of the Artist as a Young Man* to *Ulysses* as occurring in the sphere of the sacred. The consequence of this trajectory is a displacement on the level of writing. The *Portrait* is centered on the rupture or transcendence by the artist of the "nets" of institutionality. This break paradoxically allows him to become "the poet of his race"—thus the focus of vision on Stephen as the "portrait," the character. In *Ulysses,* the reader's attention is far more consistently focused on the invisible Ulysses (the Divine Nobody, Outis-Zeus) of language: styles, interior monologues, dialogues, as well as all the enunciations (often enigmatic) that are not identifiable, or that overflow the presumed identity of any single fictional character.

For the author on the verge of *Finnegans Wake*, the function of the fictional character would be to weaken the force of the enunciation to the advantage of the realistic enunciated declaration (the *énoncé*): the character as such sustains the *message*. The latter deprives the enunciation of its infinite resonance by classifying it, terminating it, putting it out of play. That is to say, the power of the decentered enunciation would be stabilized and thus lessened by the "rendering realistic" (or *vraisemblabilisation*)[1] invested (in the classical novel) in characters: the radiance of the enunciation, recorded in the form of anagrams that give rise to nominations, restores the "I" of the enunciation, whereas a character might have reduced the symbolic scope of the writing in question.

It is perhaps in this sense that we may note, with Joyce, the "finite" aspect of Stephen Dedalus *as a fictional character,*[2] and the great innovation of *Ulysses* with respect to the *Portrait,* language as "hero," at once center and decentering.[3] It is the subjectivity in theology that allows for the leap into language of *Ulysses*. The Judeo-Christian character of Bloom, in his paternity of the Word (in the enunciative force that, as we have seen, shelves the particulars of his character identity as such), brings Stephen into language and so into the world. The latter, in achieving filiation, swoons or fades into evanescence as a fictional character, thanks to Bloom's Trinitarian paternity: their passage across Dublin is that of Joyce across the Red Sea of language.

The approach of the Judaic enunciation—the symbolic, the truth, the Law, all the urgency of the power of speech that the Mosaic tradition called the five-fifths of the Law, or Torah— found the Catholic enunciation of the Word. (According to tradition, Moses is the author of the Pentateuch. He makes the Law into a prophetic enunciation, in which the *single* word of the transcendence is multiplied, divided, consumed, in the five-fifths of its utterance.) The Word, although the Word of the Father, nevertheless reintroduces the problem (the presence) of the flesh. He is the Word, *genitum non factum,* on the side of Judaic truth and, thus, far from pagan corporeality; and yet he has a mother. And it is through this fleshly element that the One God becomes a Triune God. The enjoyment of the powers of prophetic speech takes form in an incarnation, a resurrection. These mark the inclusion of sexuality, and of a *jouissance* of love, in the theological apparatus, thereby "humanizing" the Judaic formulation of the symbolic and fully situating its subjectivity. In recent times, Lacan has brought up the question of the Trinitarian RSI (the Real, the Symbolic, and the Imaginary), Catholically marking the imbrication of the One God with the maternal body through which one *passes,* taking on flesh—drives, rhythms, fantasies, representations, colors. The Word, says Saint Augustine, is the art of the Father:[4] one might say that the *symbolicity* that makes this *passage* through flesh (the expulsion from Egypt figures the symbolic birth into Catholicism) arrives at the Passover in languages, in tongues, as experienced by Joyce.

For Joyce this experience demands a particular position in regard to the community. The Jew who is Bloom/Christ/Stephen/Joyce says: *Non serviam.* This enunciation becomes the initiation into exile. "His exilicy" (*FW* 84.14), the exile, is he who makes choices, the heretic. But for Joyce, the heretical Jew and the heretical Catholic remain nonetheless Jew and Catholic. In *Ulysses,* it is Stephen who accuses Mulligan of heresy. Stephen with his *singular* Catholicism *of the exile* ("you have the cursed jesuit strain in you only it's injected the wrong way" [8]) defends the God of the Jews and the Trinity. In *Finnegans Wake* Joyce evokes the Judeo-Christian symbolic configuration on every page, and he does so in relation to his autobiographical and *scriptographical* enunciations; Judaic and Catholic symbolic discourse is at the heart of the Joycean experience *in* the voices of his writing.

Mulligan's heresy, condemned by Stephen, is that of pagan derision. But the institution accuses Stephen himself of heresy. The institution is often at a distance from *theological truth.* Theology demands a *via negativa,* a passage far from worldly and political powers. The more so, in that the label of heretic, attached to those who for one reason or another find themselves to be *singular* Jews or Catholics, leads to the production of writing. That is to say that the exile (the heretic), rejected by the order of the institution, gains access to the experience of theology. Moses, Christ, Saint Patrick—these are the privileged examples for Joyce: Stephen and Bloom are their fictional avatars. Without the *"outlaw,"* there are no *"tables of the Law"* (*U* 143). Shem is not "outlex" and "inlaw" for nothing (*FW* 169.3,4). Like Saint Patrick, Shem takes on his role of exile when he begins to write a *Confession* (a *Portrait of the Artist*) for himself.

The heresy of Joyce the Catholic is the assumption, in *Finnegans Wake,* of all possible symbolic positions in all religions, all sects. In the *Wake,* the religious scale is infinitely extended. The *Portrait* took up the question of Catholicism; *Ulysses* assimilated both Catholicism and Judaism; to monotheism the *Wake* adds the pagan religions of the East. Egypt plays an important role, first as the country of Judeo-Christian origins and of Passover, and second, as the origin of the cult of the Irish Druids.[5] Joyce told Arthur Power that the juxtaposition of the sacred and the obscene (responsible for the medieval characteristics of Irish symbolism) resulted from the fact that the Irish never accepted the *lex romana.*[6] The persistence of Irish paganism within the Catholic position produces Irish *heterogeneity,* or the sacred-comic duality. *Finnegans Wake* dramatizes not only this double position but the origin, or the creation, of Irish heterogeneity as well, i.e., the confrontation opposing Patrick to the Druids. The paschal conflict opposing the Irish Church to Rome is one of the consequences of the irreducible and singularly Irish heterogeneity; the opposition to England is another. The conflicts instigated by the double position of Ireland are deployed throughout *Finnegans Wake,* a text that seems ultimately to be an enigmatic incarnation of Irish heterogeneity.

On the one hand, Joyce makes a semblance of choosing *all* positions, of attributing the same significance to everything. The *Wake* gives the impression of being an encyclopedia of religions. Yet in fact Joyce privileges the Judeo-Christian position, and he explores it by working through the quasi-universal corpus of religious worship. By playing out—or outwitting—heresy, Joyce writes the truth of Catholicism through his progression through symbolic discourse. Thus, on the other hand, Joyce sets up a process of *dissolution*. The passage has a negative function, as chaos, dream, obscenity, parody. This dissolution or negativation manifests the *fragility* of truth, expressed by the Dedalian/Joycean symptom of doubt. Truth is re-created, through the Fall, through sin, through death. It bursts forth in an instant of bewilderment and illumination in which the Word is accomplice to the joke or *Witz.* Speaking joyce, his own language, Joyce makes the *jouissance* of the Judaic and Catholic truth his own. He telescopes theological, sacred symbolicity and Freudian, comic symbolicity in order to do this. For Joyce the Word functions according to *Witz:* language falls (lapses), jokes, dreams, in the nocturne of the *felix culpa.* Since the Fall, since the descent from the Tower of Babel, the enunciation is enigmatic,[7] infinitely *nocturnal:* the voyage leads from enigma to revelation, to the jubilation of the letter. The *jouissance* of the exile is in tongues.

Reading: the code of the Word

At every sentence the reader of *Finnegans Wake* is overwhelmed by the density of the text. The first fascination at the mosaic of languages eventually allows for the discovery of rhythms, intonations, motifs, "fictional characters" (or rather nominal entities), plays on words, allusions. After wandering through the labyrinth of laughter and tragedy, of beauty and scandal, the intoxicated reader identifies syntagmatic units, possibilities of meaning, clauses, sentences—a reduced narrational linearity—but only for an instant. The reader is taken up into an enormous weave, and after finding the narrative or linear thread, he follows it back toward the infinite variation of the mosaic. The *Wake* reader unravels his own reading at every moment; he gathers and disperses. His negative hollowing-out of the text, his Penelopean tapestry, slowly offers the keys to a pluralized reading.

The signifying plurality of the text spins any attempt at interpretation into a process of perpetual decentering. Each named element refers to its contrary, in an endless annulment: each seriously enunciated declaration is undermined by a burst of laughter, an error, a flight away from identity, making the speaking subject into an other. In this way, the *Wake* reading equivocates between *condensation* (the overdetermination of each word, or each letter: the overflow of historical, mythical, literary, religious, and biographical meanings that pass through the signifying and grammatical/graphical crossroads of languages) and *dissolution* (itself as multiple as the effects of condensation: the elements that create meaning are turned to their driven and nocturnal underside—sexuality, theology, parody. Their threads are unknotted, and, unbeknownst to themselves, they are spoken).

This dizzying effect of all and nothing, of an overflow and an abyss, is anchored in the signifying plurality itself. The words, enunciations, and languages themselves are the object of condensation-dissolution. Joyce says that he is engaged in putting the language to sleep;[8] one could say that he makes it *dream,* insofar as he submits it to primary elaboration. The immediate consequence of this is the subversion of univocal (or unequivocal) meaning. The signifier emerges in the dream: it is overdetermined, displaced, figurative; it is manipulated in a poetic form, and becomes the manifest content of the dream. On the other hand, this working-through of the signifier in Joyce's art exceeds the boundaries of univocal meaning in the domain of reading (writing). This explosion is produced at the very heart of the creation of meaning that is supposed to be univocal. In *Finnegans Wake,* a given signifier corresponds to several signifieds, in several languages, at the moment of its enunciation: a given conception of an object is encoded by several words, in several languages, at the same instant. Thus Freud's scheme in Appendix C of the *Papers on Metapsychology,*[9] in which he demonstrates that reading produces meaning only when thing-presentations and word-presentations are related by the sound of the signifier, becomes, for Joyce, a sort of wheel. The mediating instance of the signifier does not link a single thing-presentation to a single word-presentation but rather several thing-presentations to several word-presentations.

The mountain of the book that Joyce hollows from both sides, hoping to join the two paths in the middle,[10] can thus be seen as the enigmatic mountain of the signifier, allowing entry on one side through all phenomena (or thing-presentations) as such, and on the other, through the negativation, the absence, the dissolution of all phenomenality (of all things) in the inherent operation of language. Thus the *Wake* is the book of symbolicity as such; in this sense, we may interpret the inclusion of forty languages, several series of numbers and dates, and, above all, a multitude of proper names. This does not imply that Joyce is a linguist. He does not consume languages in the desire to codify them, but in the desire to make them his, to possess them. In order to create a passage through them of his artistic paternity, of his Word.[11] Joyce's linguistic experience can be read according to a theological dimension that constitutes it. The phrase "for the greeter glossary of code" solicits interpretation via the letters "Am.Dg." (*FW* 324.21–23) following it in the text: *Ad Majorem Dei Gloriam,* signing the act of writing with its Jesuit paraph.

The paschal constellation

In the words of Dom Gaspar Lefèbvre, Easter is "the culminating point of the life of the Church in its liturgical Cycle": "the Christian week, year and the entire Catholic religion gravitate around the mystery of Easter."[12] As we have seen, this Judeo-Christian event plays a focal role in *Ulysses;* a reading of the paschal celebration and of its formulation in the text of *Finnegans Wake* ought to render explicit the particularly Catholic approach to symbolicity manifest in Joyce's last great work. Given the Joycean strategy of condensation and dissolution, the analysis of the *Wake* is necessarily more problematic than that of earlier texts. The textual density of the *Wake* is such that the analysis must often ignore vast territories of meaning in the passages cited. It is to be hoped that the dual approach, through Joycean condensation as well as dissolution, partially compensates for this interpretive limitation by revealing some essential and often paradoxical aspects of the wake-process in language(s).

In *Finnegans Wake,* biblical and Trinitarian references abound. But the specificity of these references, as well as their *symbolic weight,* is often hidden by the symbolic depth or density established through the integration of references in the text. It is therefore necessary to unravel the anagrammatic strategy deployed by Joyce—who has worked the passage of the paschal event into the text. This passage takes the form of a dissemination: a constellation.

5

Easter
The Crucifixion

In *Finnegans Wake,* Book III, 3, "The third watch of Shaun," an investigator asks Yawn (who momentarily speaks with the voice of Saint Patrick) to explain to him why the Catholics have no *via crucis* leading directly to Heaven: "nor crime-slaved cruxway and no moorhens cry or mooner's plankgang there to lead us to hopenhaven" (478.15). But this "cruxway," enslaved by crimes, is also the path of purification (*crimes lavés*) leading to Heaven as a consequence of the Passion. The paschal context[1] is intimately linked with the main characters, or rather with what is said about them, since they hardly function as characters: Joyce seems to posit two anagrams, hce and alp, each of which figures a multiple subjectivity through a potential of infinite nomination. The infinity in question always operates from the starting point of a singularity—of role, utterance, act.[2]

At the conclusion of Book II, 3, "The scene in the pub," a series of enunciations criticizes Hce. The slanderers prepare to put him to death according to the Passion: "With easter greeding. Angus! Angus! Angus!" "And hike, here's the hearse and four horses with the interprovincial crucifixioners throwing lots inside"; "Tried mark, Easterlings. Sign, Soideric O'Cunnuc, Rix" (376.36, 377.24, 378.13). The threatening announcement of Easter is accompanied by liturgical allusions: the Sanctus of the Mass, assimilated in the paschal lamb

(Angus/*Agnus*), is enunciated in the pub itself, "the household of Hecech" (377.2). In the form of a fish, Hce is consumed by the Four (who are the Evangelists, in one of their many roles) in the Act of Thanksgiving. The liturgical enunciations of the "pure heart," "Let us give thanks to God," and "Amen" can be heard: "And thanking the fish, in core of them. To pass the grace for Gard sake! Ahmohn" (377.31). The specificity of the paschal reference is reinforced by the quotation of John 19:24, read on Holy Friday. The "crucifixioners throwing lots" are the four soldiers of whom it is written: "They parted my raiment among them and for my vestments they did cast lots." The Christly dramatization is anticipated by several indications of ritual: "Scapulars, beads, and a stump of a candle, Hubert was a Hunter, *chemins de la croixes* and Rosairette's egg, all the trimmings off the tree that she picked up" (376.5). This gathering of fragments of ritual, at a distance from the Christly instance, is situated in the ecclesiastical "she" of Alp (and perhaps old Kate as well). These scraps and objectified rituals of Christian worship are perhaps the fetishistic fragments of the ritual body of Hce himself, signed by the letter of the nursery rhyme: "Hubert was a Hunter." The accessories of the pluralized *via crucis* (*chemin de la croix*) indicate the *Christly* sacrifice of Hce as the object of ritualized commemoration. Marked by Easter ("Tried mark, Easterlings"), the commemoration is signed in the liturgy, from father ("Rix") to son: "Its segnet yores," its *signatures,* post (Shaun) and pen (Shem), "Poshtapengha" (377.28, .27).[3]

Joyce raises the banal daily existence of an ordinary family to the level of liturgical drama; he brings Christ's mystery down to the comic atmosphere of the pub. Ritual is presented in the form of objectified fragments, thus introducing the dimension of the body, or of flesh, at the site of symbolic discourse. Liturgy disengages itself from the Church in order to become subjective, singular, in the signature of Joycean writing.

The story of the Passion is at the core of the elaboration of Hce. At the beginning of the book, someone asks: "What then agentlike brought about that tragedy thundersday this municipal sin business?" (5.13). The Tenebrae of Holy Thursday ("tragedy thundersday") mark the mourning of ritual commemoration—the Last Supper, the Passion, the laying bare of the altars in memory of the fall of Christ into death. The "sin business" integrates the fall of Christ *qui tollis peccata mundi* into the Fall of Hce. Yet Hce like Adam, the first sinner, finds himself implicated (or inscribed: hechcE) in a primal scene: "he is ee and no counter he who will be ultimendly respunchable for the hubbub caused in Edenborough" (29.35). Joyce sets Hce in print as paradise lost as well as the innocent Christ in order to display the gamut of the Judeo-Christian treatment of sin. Henceforth Hce plays a central role in the Joycean integration of the problem of sin, in the discourse of the sacred as well as that of comedy.

Hce is guilty of Adamic sin even through his Christly suffering.[4] The primal scene, shrouded in obscurity, is the enunciative center of the book: it catalyzes and creates the endless talking about the thousand and one versions of the Fall.[5] This scene slips constantly into another, just as obscure, that marks the deferred action of the Fall and of culpability (with respect to the primal scene itself, localized in "prefall paradise peace" [30.27]). This second scene, Hce's encounter with the cad, seems to function as a screen for the primal scene. It locates Hce's fall in his speech, whereas the primal scene establishes the fall in terms of sexual scandal. The evangel (the gospel or good news of the New Testament) and the epistle of the Mass transmit the gossip, the narration, of Hce's Passion; the cad's wife confesses to "this overspoiled priest Mr Browne," "the gossiple so delivered in his epistolear" (38.25, .23). Thus the news is spread, "the substance of the tale of the evangelical busybozzy" (40.6).

It seems impossible to pinpoint the specific crime imputed to Hce. He seems to incarnate the slippage from guilt to innocence that makes Christ into a second Adam, and Adam into Eve's victim: "Guards were walking in (*pardonnez-leur, je vous en prie, eh?*) Montgomery Street. One voiced an opinion in which on either wide (*pardonnez!*), nodding, all the Finner Camps concurred (*je vous en prie, eh?*). It was the first woman, they said, souped him, that fatal wellesday" (58.25). Christ's words at the Crucifixion ("Père, pardonnez-leur; car ils ne savent ce qu'ils font")[6] recall the innocence of Hce, torn "limb from lamb" (58.7), betrayed by "the first woman." Hce is anagrammatically signed in the Adoration of the Cross on Good

Friday; his love and innocence are stressed by the Improperia: "Allwhichhole scrubs on scroll circuminiumluminatedhave encuoniams here and improperies there" (278.3).[7] The "hce" of illumination makes Hce into the subject of the four manuscript Gospels found in the Book of Kells.

In Alp's gathering of fragments, the allusion to Hce's dead body establishes the dimension of ritual: sin, attributed to femininity, is absorbed by the Church. Through the ills of sin and suffering that afflict the flesh, Joyce locates the possibility of assuming a position comparable to an incarnation in symbolicity. One could interpret the mariolatry of Stephen Dedalus in this light.[8] In the third chapter of the *Portrait,* Stephen reads aloud from the lesson of the Votive Mass of the Holy Virgin. While aware of his own duplicity, he nevertheless allows himself to be seduced by the "music" of the text, by the "glories" of the Virgin. Before her image, Stephen experiences the double *jouissance* of the sinner—the perverse love of the Law he transgresses and the love of femininity, the latter being the paradoxical representative of both the forbidden *jouissance* and the inviolable maternity protecting the sinner. In *Finnegans Wake,* this double position is underlined, through a parodic staging of Good Friday: "Eh jourd'weh! Oh jourd'woe! dosiriously it psalmodied. Guesturn's lothlied answring tomaronite's wail. Oasis, cedarous esaltarshoming Leafboughnoon! Oisis, coolpressus onmountof Sighing! Oasis, palmost esaltarshoming Gladdays! Oisis, phantastichal roseway anjerichol!" (470.13). It would seem that the exile and scandal of *Non serviam* give Joyce the liberty of pointing out, in parodic form, the double *jouissance* implicit in his own incarnation of the Word. The twenty-eight young girls "desiringly psalmodize" the lesson of the Virgin, the text that triggers Stephen's doubled jubilation. The "young man" pertinent to this part of the *Wake,* Shaun (Jaun), can achieve his "feat of passage" (473.15)—his access to the Word—only after the Maronite ritual (a dramatization, according to Joyce, of the burial of the body of Christ, among an assembly of girls dressed in white, with flowers and incense)[9] has marked with its virginal and feminine "music," with its dolorous *jouissance,* the being and destiny of the Word.

Thus, in the "geomatry lesson," the discovery of Alp's sex

elicits, on the part of Kevin (avatar or figure of Shaun, here recalled in his capacity as consumer), memory and desire focusing on the maternal breast: "to nibbleh ravenostonoriously ihs mum" (300.18).[10] There is an echo in this text of the body of the Virgin giving birth to *ihs*.[11] Christ's monogram (noted here *on paper;* "noland's browne jesus" [300.29], by the martyred writer Jerry, avatar or figure of Shem) is repeated a little later in the text concerning Jerry himself. It can be deciphered, thanks to Bloom's interpretation, in his own sacred-comic incarnation of the Christ: "O He Must Suffer!" (301.3).[12] This Bloomian formula is repeated in the context of Jaun's Passion: "(and how ill soufered!)" (454.24). The anagram his/ *ihs* signs the proper name of the incarnated Word while integrating within it the suffering of the Crucifixion.

In the *Wake*, the Incarnation becomes the Christmas gift offered by the mother, Alp: "a Christmas box apiece for aisch and iveryone of her childer" (209.27). This gift is sometimes assimilated in the Crucifixion: "a Rogerson Crusoe's Friday fast for Caducus Angelus Rubiconstein" (211.16). On the feminine side, suffering and *jouissance* emerge from the Incarnation and the Crucifixion for Mary Magdalene, presented at the moment of the Resurrection: "penteplenty of pity with lubilashings of lust for Olona Lena Magdalena" (211.7). The multiple nomination of Mary Magdalene (in Italian, Russian, and South American forms) may perhaps be read as a function of the *pente*—the Pentecost, when the gift of the Holy Spirit in the tongues of fire is heard by the subjects constituting the multitude, each in his *own language* (Acts 2:6). In the Alleluia of the Mass for Pentecost, mention is made of the fire of the Holy Spirit's love, filling hearts. This is the conclusion of the Crucifixion, anticipated by the proper name of Mary Magdalene.[13]

One of Alp's sons receives "a Congoswood cross on the back for Sunny Twimjim" (211.5). Here the crucifixion of Joyce, moving from the Jesuit school of Clongowes Wood College [14] toward his Word, is inseparable from the text. "Sunny Jim," the nickname given to Joyce during childhood,[15] indicates here the division of identities between Shaun and Shem as well as the role in the *Wake* of the encoded S. in the formula "J. J. and S.," John Jameson and Son (father, grandfather, and son:

John Joyce, son of James, and Joyce himself). Those who sign the "Nightletter" ("jake, jack and little sousoucie" [308.28]) are inscribed in the monogram of the whiskey constantly consumed at the *Wake*.[16]

The splitting of the role of Christ between Shem and Shaun and the autobiographical inclusions in the drama of the Crucifixion of the Word become manifest in the speech of Justius at the end of Book I, 7. Shaun-Justius directs his "Improperia"[17] at Shem, while relegating the Christly position to him: "you couldn't even pledge a crown of Thorne's to pawn a coat off Trevi's," "Bend down a stigmy till I!", "That a cross may crush me" (192.11, 193.17, .25). These images of Good Friday underline the sacred role of Shem, condemned by his fraternal enemy: "alternating the morosity of my delectations—a philtred love, trysting by tantrums, small peace in ppenmark—with sensibility, sponsibility, passibility and prostability"; . . . all that too with . . . accomplished women . . . consumed by amorous passion, struggling to possess themselves of your boosh, one son of Sorge for all daughters of Anguish" (189.4, .11).

Shaun notes the eroticism coloring the drama of Shem's crucifixion; his own fantasies and jealousy seem to motivate the sacrifice of Shem. The feminine entourage of Shem/Christ reproduces the tableau of the Eighth Station of the Way of the Cross, "Jesus consoles the daughters of Israel who follow him." The division of the brothers reveals the alternation of sinful *jouissance* ("morose delectation," according to Saint Thomas Aquinas)[18] and Christly suffering. This suffering is described as *sensibility*,[19] the capacity for sensation and emotion; as *sponsibility*, evocative of the Church as the bride of Christ (or, according to the analysis of the Latin *spondeo* by Benveniste, the notion of "garantir, répondre de quelque chose").[20] The concept of sponsibility is close to that of *sacramentum* (from *sacrare*, "declare as sacred") since it is the enunciation of the word that creates the state of being *sacer*.[21] Suffering leads to *prostability*, a Joycean construction echoing prostration, the liturgical attitude of lying down; in *Stephen Hero*, Stephen admires the strange theatricality of "the priests lying prostrate on the altar steps" in the Mass of the Presanctified.[22]

But it is the third term, *passibility*, that requires a specifically Catholic interpretation. It stems from *passible*, from the Latin *passibilis*, "capable of suffering or emotion." It is a term of theological usage, specifically connected with the Passion. Saint Thomas devotes several passages of the *Summa Theologica* to the question of the *passible*.[23] As concerns the soul of Christ, he remarks upon the problematic aspect of the *passible*, elsewhere identified with the corruption of sin.[24] How can one admit that the soul of Christ is passible without attributing sin to him? Saint Thomas manages this through an evocation of the *will* of Christ: "The soul of Christ, especially through divine power, could resist the passions and prevent their existence. But of his own will, Christ consented to suffer them, as much in his body as in his soul."[25] It is only where Christ is concerned that the suffering of the passible is distinguished from sin. And yet the *jouissance* of the Resurrection and of divine vision is, paradoxically, the consequence of the *lack* or *flaw* afflicting Christ, i.e., "his passible and mortal body": "Christ, because of his corporeal suffering, was led to beatitude and the glory of the body."[26] The *jouissance* attributed in the New Testament to Christ's love—that returns in the tongues of fire—is posited by Joyce through sin. He assumes a Christly position through sin's economy of suffering, transgression, and *jouissance*.

The *passibility* of Christ is the consequence of his love: "For the loue of the he was made man passyble and mortall; whiche was Immortall and Impassyble."[27] In Joyce's text, this love stands out in the parodization of the amorous passion of women gathered around Shem. The "boosh" they find so desirable entails not only the mouth (*la bouche*) of the sinner but also the *books* Shem has written, which seem to be, in the eyes of Shaun, "bosh"—devoid of meaning. Shaun noted the *passibility* of Shem as the Word. Through lack, meaning works its mystical path toward *jouissance:* "O you were excruciated, in honour bound to the cross of your own cruelfiction!" (192.17). All of Shaun's accusations revolve around Shem's sin as *relation* between carnal seduction (localized between Potiphar's wife and Joseph, in Genesis 39: "And Gay Socks jot it from Potapheu's wife" [193.20]) and verbal culpability (obscene writing on "defenseless paper" [189.9]). Thus Shem the *writer*, betrayed by his Judas-like brother, incarnates Christ: "Just a little judas tonic, my ghem of all jokes, to make you go green in the gazer" (193.9). Sin and holiness emerge in the drama of Good Friday according to *Finnegans Wake:* James Joyce disguised as the best of all jokes signs the Crucifixion with an X figuring his *jouissance*—or "joyance"—in names.

6

Holy Saturday

The night of the mystery

After the ecclesiastical dramatization of the Crucifixion Tenebrae, the Holy Saturday ceremonies take place. For Joyce,
this part of the Easter celebration was of particular importance. Jacques Mercanton writes: "He [Joyce] tells me that
Good Friday and Holy Saturday are the two days of the year
when he goes to Church, because of the liturgical ceremonies
that represent in their symbolic rites the oldest mysteries of
humanity."[1] On Holy Saturday in 1938, Joyce told him: "I saw
the rebirth of fire and water. Until next year. The rest is insignificant."[2] It is thus the *night* of Easter that most interests Joyce.
The vigil begins with the benediction of the new fire and the
paschal candle. It is followed by the reading of the prophecies, and then by the benediction of the baptismal fonts. Soon
afterward, at dawn, the Easter Mass announces the jubilation
of the Resurrection—the Gloria, the bells, and organs mark
the end of the vigil. And Joyce leaves the Church.

A consideration of this anecdote in relation to Joycean
writing allows for a greater understanding of the book of the
night that is *Finnegans Wake*. One might conceive of the "wake"
itself in terms of the Church vigil, of which Saint Augustine
writes: "During all this time while she moves through the centuries as in a night journey, her eyes fixed on the Holy Scriptures as on the lamps of the night, the Church watches until
the arrival of the Lord."[3] Joyce seems to follow the Augustin-

ian interpretation regarding Easter; it will become clear that this position originates in the old Philonian tradition. In a study of the Latin interpretation of Easter, Christine Mohrmann writes: "Several scholars have brought to light the fact that the oldest paschal celebration—as it took place during the nocturnal watch of Easter—brought together all the elements of the mystery of salvation. (. . . During long centuries the paschal vigil remains the night of the redemptive mystery, in all its plenitude, the knot itself of the entire Easter celebration."[4] Saint Augustine's sermon on the holy night explicitly draws the attention of the new Christians (the *infantes*) to the paschal watch: "Let us watch, then, my dear ones, for the burial of Christ was prolonged till this night, in order that in this very night the resurrection of the flesh that was mocked on the wood be accomplished. . . . But the watch of this night is so great that it could claim for itself, as proper name, the name common to all other watches. . . . Where life is, even there is the endless watch; to live is to hold vigil, and to hold vigil is to live."[5] For Joyce, the paschal celebration is concentrated in the watch as a "proper" name and a multiple one at the same time. Out of the wounds inflicted at the time of the Crucifixion comes this night—the preparation for and inclusion of the Resurrection. It would seem that crossing out the bearer of the Word as proper name would entail the loss of the power of speech. But the logic of Catholicism overturns this potentially apocalyptic silence. The eclipse of Christ fully reveals itself as the fall of the Other only at the moment of the watch, for the *Lumen Christi* indicates a new presence that can be qualified as *Trinitarian*. The jubilation of Holy Saturday bears witness to this new presence. The sacrifice, if indeed there has been what one would call a sacrifice, includes the voyage of the Word as a supplement, an overflow, the proffering of love by the possessor of languages—in the form of the Son. The wild jubilation that God the Father gives to the Jews at *simchat Torah,* impelling them to dance with the Bible in their arms, is given to Catholics on Holy Saturday through the resurgence of the Word and the love of the Holy Spirit. In Catholicism, the ineffable love of the Law is paradoxically elaborated in an ever more concentrated form in symbolicity—but also softening Judaic truth.

This softening of the truth occurs by way of the Redemption, i.e., a period of tenebrous silence from which one is born *infantes,* without speech: "Omai sarà più corta mia favella,/pur a quel ch'io ricordo, che d'un fante che bagni ancor la lingua a la mammella" (now will my speech fall more short, even in respect to that which I remember, than that of an infant who still bathes his tongue at the breast" [*Paradiso, XXXIII,* 106–108]). If meaning proliferates in Catholic *jouissance,* perhaps it only does so *after* this period spent without speech. This period is not Judaic: In Judaism, silence is symbolic. It is maintained in awe of the Holy Name (like the forbidden pronunciation of this name itself). Catholic silence is the silence of those who are in the process of being born into symbolicity, through the maternal body of the Church: "It is this hierarchical Church herself . . . that we call our mother. . . . She did not give birth to us in order to then abandon us and let us try our luck alone: she conserves us and keeps us together in her maternal breast. We do not stop living through her spirit, 'as the children enclosed in the womb of their mother live through the substance of their mother.' The true Catholic . . . loves to call her by the name of 'mother,' sprung forth from the heart of her first children, of which the texts of Christian antiquity show so much evidence. The true Catholic proclaims, with Saint Cyprian and Saint Augustine: 'He cannot have God as father, he who does not have the Church as mother.'"[6]

It is thus a voyage through darkness and silence, birth and death, that projects toward the Other those holding to the mystery (*sacramentum*) of the night of Easter. For Joyce this mystery is sustained in its nocturnal character. If the Joycean *jouissance* of the Resurrection does not linger, like that of Dante, over this particular moment of silence, it is perhaps because, for Joyce, *nothing* is visible except languages. They gave themselves to him, as when the fall of Babel became the intoxication of the Apostles at Pentecost. For Joyce as for certain others, this gift demands payment in the form of what he called, with San Juan de la Cruz, a "dark night."[7] Joyce submits language to the obscurity of its own night, where the eclipse of the signifying and the sexual Other is confronted with the meaning that is somewhere responsible for its banishment.[8] The enunciation multiplied beyond measure turns the *Wake* into a signifying labyrinth in which the mystery of the emergence of the Trinitarian divinity comes face to face with the inevitable comedy of the fall into desire. The Resurrection at the end can only be had at the price of its underside of spoken death. If the end of *Ulysses* shows the possibility of such a strategy—for, after all, the "resurrection" of Stephen could not have taken place prior to the apparition of death (inverted "nourishment," brought by the vampire) incarnated by his mother—the eventual disappearance of the characters as such in the incarnation of the voice can easily be understood as a consequence of the Resurrection.[9] It is not by chance that Joyce, in an enigmatic advertisement, sends us Hce, the omnipresent dead man, as an announcement of comedy and emergence, "comic and birthdays cards" (127.24).

The sexual drives implicated in the descent into the *dessous troublants* of night are confronted not only in death but also through the liturgical enunciation of the *felix culpa,* in the "Four O's" of the Exultet. This moment of jubilatory apostrophe, of intimate exclamation, gives to the sinner-become-subject— following the original sin that pulverized a hypothetical psychic unity—an "I" that locates its *jouissance* in the enunciation. This subject of the enunciation addresses the Other in the paradoxical formula of the oxymoron. The latter posits a rational impossibility, brushing the mystery of the *sacramentum,* that exceeds the boundaries of language with an overflow of reversed or overturned sin,[10] in which the subject manifests the relation of the Joycean artist to language through what Benveniste terms an "emotive discharge."[11]

According to Girard, Good Friday constitutes the symbolic cut of nonsacrificial sacrifice;[12] the sacrifice is monstrously gratuitous. Moreover, Christ as victim offers himself as already divine—indicating the gratuity of his sacrifice in another sense. That is to say that the sacrifice "normally" considered as a gift to the Other becomes simultaneously, in the Christly sacrifice, a gift of the Other giving himself to himself in the person of the Son. In other words, the sacrificial castration (of the other) slips toward an active dramatization of the drive . . . toward the Other.

The transition from Good Friday to Holy Saturday can be formulated in the slippage from the cut that makes sense as *loss,* tragic lack, to the cut as *border:* the happy night (*beata nox*) is specified as an approach toward *jouissance.* After the death, a re-beginning, a re-Genesis, and a re-Creation are woven through Christ and his renewed plenitude reflected in the overflow of the Exultet. Christ makes the journey through the drives of mortal flesh, conveyed in the following terms to that feminine figure of passionate desire, Mary Magdalene: "Touch me not; for I am not yet ascended to my father" (John 20:17). It is possible that the undoing of death (and, as we have seen, of "passibility") calls for the evidence of the driven flesh as it is offered on Holy Saturday, in symbolic form: the crucified body has become the paschal candle, the five wounds have become grains of incense. After the Passion of the Word, His Light is figured as the *jouissance* attributed to the Other; in this symbolization, the voyage of the body toward glory is underscored with an emotive overflow. Through this enig-matic representative of the beauty of the Word (inscribed as a cross, less as an imaginary object than as the support of the glory of eternity, marked Alpha and Omega),[13] Catholic sub-limation makes itself felt as love for the Other. The divinity solicits this love; the beauty of the Word, the "emotive dis-charge" of liturgy, ultimately originate in the passibility itself of Christ bound for "glory." This configuration brings to-gether the discourse of truth and its engagement of the pas-sibility that overflows its boundaries. Without Adam's Fall, there would be no Christly glory. Through this strategy, passibility is able to enjoy truth.

Et nox sicut dies illuminabitur

The liturgy of Holy Saturday, "whitest night mortal ever saw" (501.31), is constantly evoked in the *Wake.* In this book of the night, a wake from one end almost to the other, water and fire are constantly discussed. The references to the major fig-ures of Old Testament exposition of prophecy are constant, as are references to the narrative of the Creation, the first reading of the "Prophecies of Holy Saturday." The motif of the *felix culpa* is sustained from the beginning of the text till the dawn of the Resurrection in Book IV.

Finnegans Wake

The paschal candle in *Finnegans Wake* lights up the darkness: "when it so happen they were all sycamore and by the world forgot, since the phlegmish hoopicough, for all a possabled, after ete a bad cramp and johnny magories, and backscrat the poor bedsores and the farthing dip, their caschal pandle of magnegnousioum" (397.23). The subject of this passage is the Four as Evangelists, illuminated by the Irish version of the candle, the "caschal pandle"[14] that will be plunged in water ("dip") according to the benediction of new water. The Four, "Mat and Mar and Lu and Jo" (397.3), are ill, senile, moribund—and, above all, voyeurs. The dazzling light of the candle ("magnegnousioum") illuminates their entry into the dream that transforms their vision of the "passion" uniting Iseult and Tristan into a song; the sung parody focuses on the love of Iseult for them (and through them for the king, Mark): "sing a mamalujo" (398.4).

But the object of their vision, the fall of flesh (and into flesh), designated as "whoever the gulpable, and whatever the pulpous was" (396.23), only emphasizes their dying, animated by constant repetition on the level of the enunciation. They do not stop forgetting, repeating, contradicting, dying. The obscenity of death (the Catholic effect of the first sin) forms the abject background of their desire, incestuously displaced onto the young Iseult. Their impotence, the inevitable comedy of the paternal fall,[15] still allows them the scandal of the flesh on the (driven) level of vision. Their voyeurism, ironically illuminated by the light of Christ, sees in the avidly observed coupling of Tristan and Iseult (396) yet another version of the primal scene as dramatization of original sin. This vision through decay and the blackness of the flesh, "through their gangrene spentacles" (397.35), centers on the Christly position at least with respect to the *culpa* that must be overturned.[16] The presence in this text of the letter, illuminated by the candle, is no accident: "and read a letter or two every night . . . a capitaletter . . . on their old one page codex book of old year's eve 1132, M.M.L.J. old style" (397.27). The Irish-style gospel, here reduced to the punctuality of the letter, might perhaps contain a resonance of the Book of Kells, and in particular the illumination of its capital letters. If, in addition, the letter is that of Alp, we are coming very close to Hce's original sin. In any case, the paschal candle of the Four indicates, in the womb of the Church, the crossroad of death and grace that is constituted as *regeneration:* "the primal sacrament of baptism or the regeneration of all man by affusion of water" (606.10).

Elsewhere, several references situate the Holy Saturday ritual in the proximity of Alp and Shem. Shaun seems to denounce the incestuous desire that links Shem to their mother: he calls Shem "sonny douth-the-candle" (183.34). The candle dipped in baptismal water at the moment of the benediction is the figure of an explicit *fecundation* (etymologically: "to make fruitful"): the breath of the Holy Spirit enters into relation with the water. Shaun apparently interprets this ritual as an instance of sexual culpability, just as he attacks his brother at the instant of the geometrical revelation of the maternal genitals. Joyce integrates the ceremony in the *Wake* by relegating it to the "darkness of sin" that must be destroyed. His treatment of Catholicism implies an obscene *jouissance* wherever sin is supposed to surrender to the grace of the Holy Spirit.[17] *Jouissance* becomes divine in obscenity—i.e., precisely at the moment of the other *jouissance,* symbolic and amorous, that of the ardent fire emanating from the Other—in languages or tongues, driven by the Holy Spirit.

In this "wet place"[18] that was the wake, Joyce reveals what Lacan calls the obscene, spelled *eaubscène:*[19] writing and flesh come together as Shem the penman amorously writes the letter incarnating Alp, who will overturn Hce's original sin. But she does so by distributing among all her children the consequences of this original sin. Her letter simultaneously indicates and denies culpability; in language, Adam and Christ are linked together, sin and Word. The *jouissance* of the obscene gives form and flesh to beauty—henceforth irreducible to the emotive overflow that triggers its creation.

Thus attached to Alp, Shem is "that fenemine Parish Poser" (93.14), and "firewaterloover" (93.7), lover of the fire and water of paschal benediction, and of the whiskey signed J. J. and S. This love is active in the letter that is Alp's attempt to save Hce. Jerry, punished by Kevin for having geometrically lifted his mother's skirts, requests the sacramental candle in one version of the letter: "If you could me lendtill my pascol's

Finnegans Wake

kondyl. . . . With best apolojigs . . . and again begs guerdon for bistrispissing on your bunificence. . . . Blott" (302.3). The request for forgiveness makes itself heard with particular clarity at the moment of the Exultet, following the benediction of the paschal candle: the candle must "destroy the darkness of this night." The night become holy "cleanses faults."

Joyce himself observed that Alp gives to all her children "the ills flesh is heir to";[20] yet this punishment is still the "Christmas box" of the Incarnation, the transmission of passibility to the Word being born. Alp avenges Hce. His children have not stopped talking about his fall and the primal scene. Prior to opening Pandora's box, Alp adorns herself. Her preparations for seduction take the form of the paschal ceremony: "with leafmould she ushered round prunella isles and eslats dun, quincecunct, allover her little mary. Peeld gold of waxwork her jellybelly and her grains of incense. . . . A call to pay and light a taper . . . Anna Livia, oysterface, forth of her bassein came" (206.35–207.20). Alp becomes the paschal candle, her sex becomes the quincunx of the grains of incense. Her departure from the "bassein" figures the emergence of the candle from the water. In this representation of symbolic *jouissance,* provoked and fed by the first sin, Joyce seems to emphasize the carnal underside that reveals the fragility of salvation, practically drowned in the waves of sin and love. Alp overturns the first sin—by giving sin to her children; the generalized Fall operates according to paschal seduction, pre-text of jubilation.

The function of the letter as inscription of *jouissance* is part of the enigma of the name of the Father in *Finnegans Wake.* In Book I, 6, "Questions and Answers," the nomination of Hce makes of him a condensation of the Trinity, the God of Easter and, in particular, of the creator of the splendor of the paschal fire: "the flawhoolagh, the grasping one, the kindler of pascal fire" (128.33). Hce is at the same time Father, Son, and Holy Ghost. According to the liturgy, under the ruling majesty of the Father, the Son offers grace through the Holy Spirit: the Trinitarian event of Easter makes of Hce a tripartite triangular name. This name is not unrelated to the "trilitter" supposed to represent the feminine sex. This representation, however, takes the form of a triune symbol; the imaginary construction is constituted through the triangular letter. Through Hce, "the kindler of pascal fire" evokes Saint Patrick, at the site of the Holy Spirit, the giver of tongues. Patrick was the first paschal celebrant to confront the Druids, and in his *Confession* he writes of his experience of the mysterious *jouissance* of Catholic truth: no doubt, Joyce glimpsed in the figure of the Irish saint his *own* function as writer of the holy day of Easter.

Felix culpa

On Holy Saturday the "Eulogy of the paschal Night" is interrupted by the exclamation of the "Four O's." They end with the evocation of the "fortunate fall": "*O felix culpa, quae talem ac tantum meruit habere Redemptorem!*" (O happy fault which deserved to possess such and so great a Redeemer!). In the first chapter of the *Wake*, after the seduction of Jarl van Hoother by the Prankquean (also called Grace O'Malley,[21] i.e., grace out of evil, or *felix culpa!*), *O felix culpa* is uttered for the first time: "O foenix culprit! Ex nickylow malo comes mickelmassed bonum" (23.16). Joyce explicates this passage in a letter to H. Weaver: "*O felix culpa!* S. Augustine's famous phrase in praise of Adam's sin. Fortunate Fault! Without it the redeemer wd not have been born. Hence also for the antecedent sin of Lucifer without which Adam wd not have been created or able to fall."[22] (Contrary to Joyce's opinion, Saint Augustine was not the author of the *felix culpa*. However, he was not far from the source, since the *felix culpa* is attributed to Saint Ambrose.)[23]

Outside of paschal liturgy, the *felix culpa* is the object of allusions in several theological and literary works, of which the best known is surely *Paradise Lost*. If the first *felix culpa* in the *Wake* echoes the expression "Ex malo bonum fit,"[24] then one might legitimately attribute a Miltonian resonance to this passage.[25] In Book XII of *Paradise Lost,* the Archangel Michael ("mickelmassed") predicts the revelation of Christ. Adam utters the message of the *felix culpa* just prior to being led, with Eve, out of Paradise:

O goodness infinite, goodness immense!
That all this good of evil shall produce,
And evil turn to good; more wonderful
Then that which by creation first brought forth
Light out of darkness! full of doubt I stand,
Whether I should repent me now of sin
By mee done and occasiond, or rejoyce
Much more, that much more good thereof shall spring.[26]

The fact that the message of *felix culpa* is put into Adam's mouth reveals the wavering inherent in the Christian position. According to Kierkegaard, the first sin is "the qualitative leap of the individual":[27] looking ahead, one might call it *the leap into subjectivity*, noting that, for Milton, it is doubled by *a leap into the Word*, who undoes the knot of sin. The *jouissance* of sin conjured away by Milton, unlike the writers of the Catholic tradition) turns into infinite happiness—not without revealing, in Adam's hesitation, a certain mystery, impossible to define in rational terms, specific to the oxymoron. This rhetorical figure reproduces, in the *felix culpa*, the knot of sin: the repressed *jouissance* of transgression; the penitence of the guilty slipping from the body to speech;[28] and, finally, the sublimated form of *jouissance*, incommensurably surpassing the downfall of original sin.

The Catholic dogma of original sin entails a certain complicity between God and the transgressor of his interdiction. The latter reveals itself to be the cause of *jouissance; jouissance* itself, sublimated (distanced from its first and scandalous object, but without repression), nevertheless provides evidence for the necessity of transgression: "*O certe necessarium Adae peccatum, quod Cristi morte deletum est!*" (O truly needful sin of Adam, which was blotted out by the death of Christ!). It thus becomes easier to understand the confusion or wavering that Milton attributes to Adam. The oxymoron of the *felix culpa* is the figure of the overflow of an "emotive discharge" that itself seems to be contradictory—or doubled—in the framework of the first sinner; faced with the ambivalence expressed in "the happy fault," whose ineluctably irrational character was condemned by certain ecclesiastical authorities,[29] Adam is filled with *doubt*. The first scandalous desire (that which brought peccability into the human realm)[30] is already practically forgotten, consigned to the void: from this point on, doubt comes into being. According to Joyce (and Stephen), paternity and the Church are founded on the void, on uncertainty, on doubt (*U* 207); and Shem, the writer, is accused of being "of twosome twiminds": "you have reared your disunited kingdom on the vacuum of your own most intensely doubtful soul" (188.14, .6).

It is beginning with the Trinity, with paternity as a symbolic creation, that Adam's doubt simultaneously marks the loss of paradise, castration, exile, and the return of *jouissance* in redemption. For Milton's Adam, *felix culpa* brings out the overturning of original sin. After the interval of nonfelicity, of suffering, brought about by the Fall that dismissed the first *jouissance*, Adam "rejoyces." If, as observed by Arthur O. Lovejoy,[31] the paradox of the happy fault gives to Milton's poem the appearance of a *divine comedy*—i.e., according to Lovejoy, a story with a happy ending—we may perhaps interpret this divine comedy in a specifically Dantean sense. Milton's "rejoyce" brings out a Dantean *jouissance* (simultaneously more insistent, from a carnal point of view, and yet more sublimated than that of Milton) that returns in the writing of Joyce, whose name is written there for all to see.[32] The art of the *felix culpa* can be interpreted as the knot of passibility, enunciation, and nomination: it is revealed in the Joycean version of the *Divina Commedia*, specifically focused on the losing and regaining of paradise during Holy Saturday, the inscription of the heart of the paschal experience.

Joyce's "foenix culprit" resonates as Dublin's Phoenix Park (the Eden of *Finnegans Wake*), the site where Hce's drama of sin supposedly took place. The phoenix, the fabulous bird reborn from its own ashes, adds to Joyce's formula a medieval allusion to Christ's Resurrection.[33] Joyce's phoenix establishes a geographical link between Adam and Christ through Hce, thereby making of him a *guilty subject* of the Word.[34]

For Joyce, the fault rendered fortunate for the guilty subject (the "culprit") implies the sin of a man, probably Hce, with a woman, either a young Alp or his own daughter; feminine seduction and the paternal fall posit the question of original sin in the *Wake*. Starting with the subject Hce in his

Phoenix Park, we can ask the following question: What is the nature of the *culpa* that must be rendered *felix?* This question has been asked, throughout Catholic tradition, since the inception of the Church. Different responses have been formulated around the dogma of original sin. Before we explore Joyce's treatment of the *felix culpa,* a summary of the major points of this dogma—central in Joycean writing from *Stephen Hero* to *Finnegans Wake*—might be useful in order to assess its divinely comic status.

"sinsinsinning since the night of time" (505.9)

The first exposition of the doctrine of original sin is generally attributed to Paul in Romans 5–8. Adam is the figure of the "last Adam": "For if through the offence of one many be dead, much more the grace of God, and the gift by grace, *which is* by one man, Jesus Christ, hath abounded unto many" (Rom. 5:15). However, it has been observed that the Pauline doctrine concerns sin as such rather than original sin.[35] Tatian and his disciple Ireneus speak in terms of an original *downfall:* baptism introduces the Holy Spirit in us—the same Spirit that Adam and Eve had possessed before the Fall.[36] The before and after of the downfall seem to return to the Pauline opposition between "the law of God after the inward man" and "the law of sin which is in my members" (Rom. 7:22, 23): the law of the Spirit imposes itself as the antidote to the split resulting from human downfall.

For Tertullian, sin is corporeal, i.e., *irrational:* "Sed enim a diabolo immissio delicti, inrationale autem omne delictum" (it is the devil who introduced sin; but all that is irrational is sin).[37] Saint Hilary sharpens Tertullian's interpretation; his view of the irrational downfall is that it constitutes a capitulation to the empire of the body: "When we remember that the crime of our first father Adam exiled us from this Zion where life is without passion, without pain, without sin, that he *delivered us to this world* of disorder symbolized by Babylon, that he *delivered us to the body* prey to the disorder of vice, desire and passion, we justly proclaim ourselves as captives, in the spiritual sense."[38]

These interpretations emphasize the corporeal aspect of sin due to an initial division or split between the spirit and the body: this division is a consequence of the Fall. Irrationality itself is considered a manifestation of the body. As such, it is assimilated as sin, the animal element opposed to the spiritual element that will save us. The predominance of *denegation*[39] in such a construction seems to protect being, henceforth located in the spirit, victim of the body—and, originally, victim of Adam's body. The first man gave us mortality; we share his woes without sharing his culpability.[40]

Saint Augustine, "the Doctor of original sin and grace,"[41] slides the original downfall toward original *sin*.[42] Even as early as 397, long before the Pelagian controversy leading to his written defense of original sin, Augustine had formulated his famous doctrine of the *massa damnata*. First comes Adam's transgression; then, the powerlessness of fallen man[43] and the gratuitous occurrence of grace: "After the fall, all men formed nothing more than a mass infected by sin, and condemned to mortality, although God had only created what was good."[44] For Augustine, the cause of original sin is *concupiscence*. Fallen man "is led toward evil by the concupiscence that dominates him and seduces him with the attraction of something forbidden. . . . It is passion that impels him and he gives in to its victorious efforts. In order not to give way, and in order that the spirit of man be armed against cupidity, grace is necessary."[45] "Concupiscence . . . exists in us only because of sin."[46] Concupiscence is "shameful to men."[47] By linking culpability itself to concupiscence, Augustine eliminates the denegation of his predecessors, along with their blind optimism: the break between body and spirit gives way to the conscience of the individual who feels shame and whose weakness invokes the power of grace. Adam's offense as such establishes the Catholic in his double ardor, in his double *jouissance* of pardoned (grace-receiving) sinner. Beginning with Adam, Augustine makes of us desiring subjects. It is only through divine love, the symbolic gift coming from the Other, that the subject locked in the "animality" of desire becomes, miraculously, *sublime*.

Later, Saint Anselm rejects the Augustinian interpretation as being too physiological.[48] For Anselm, original sin consists of a deprivation of original justice: Adam "has become God's debtor."[49] Duns Scotus (and Occam as well) follows Anselm as regards the *carentia justitiae originalis debitae* and he eliminates the doctrine of concupiscence: "I say then that original sin is nothing more than the absence of the justice that we should have, and, if it is objected that concupiscence is original sin, I respond that concupiscence can be understood in several senses; but that in no sense is it a sin, given that *there is no sin in the sensitive part.*"[50]

Where Augustine uncovers a double and passible subject, Anselm and Duns Scotus find a subject burdened by the debt that founds the symbolic knot of Catholicism, at the source of the *felix culpa.* Augustinian sexual culpability is denied by Anselm and Duns Scotus in order to bring into relief a weakness not of the body but of the *will*—i.e., a relation to the Law. This debt must be paid off as language; the culpability that Augustine conceives from the point of view of the sinner is revised within the frame of a divine point of view. Original sin slips from the overflow of the drives (Augustine) to symbolic lack (Anselm). Joyce, like Freud, telescopes the two hypotheses, that of Augustine and that of Anselm: the subject of desire and the subject of the Symbolic are one. It is perhaps in this sense that Joyce's version of the fall of the Tower of Babel answers to the Fall of Adam. The paschal passage of the *felix culpa* overturns the fault and gains access to the *jouissance* in question; the subject must sublimate his desire, and displace his jubilation toward the Word. Joyce filters the enunciation of the *felix culpa* through the scandal of the flesh and the position of the sinner in the Symbolic dimension. Through the double *jouissance* of culpability and the grace that dispels it.

Adam's beautiful gift:[51] "O happy fault!"

On several occasions, Joyce posits the enunciation of the *felix culpa* as such, without "dissolving" it in the text, without personalizing it through the subjectivity specific to the *Wake.* At these points, the thematic importance of the *felix culpa* comes into relief. The two washerwomen mention Adam and Eve in the "garden of Erin" (203.1), at the site of the primal scene, when Alp seduces Hce (and vice versa): "O happy fault!" (202.34). At the beginning of Book II, 2, "Nightlessons," Joyce introduces the *felix culpa* into the text read and written by the children. The "original sun" (263.27) shines: the original *culpa* is imposed by "inkbottle authority" (263.24)—an indication of the symbolic relationship to interdiction and satisfaction that makes the fault a happy one: "O felicitous culpability" (263.29). The *felix culpa* translated into English (but maintaining the Latin signifiers) is described in the margin: "*Hearasay in paradox lust.*" Adam's heretical desire costs him his paradise. But this loss is countered by the transmission, in Milton's *Paradise Lost,* of Adam's paradoxical *felix culpa*—by hearsay.

The *felix culpa* that is the effect of the Word is performatively constituted in speech. The two opposed terms of the oxymoron come together in culpability itself in order to overturn the economy of the interdiction. Instead of punishment, *jouissance:* "When Adam Leftus and the devil took our hindmost, gegifting her with his painapple . . . while felixed is who culpas does" (246.28). At the beginning of Book I, 7, "Shem," a reprise of the "Ballat of Perce-Oreille" (175) (a parody of the four first paragraphs of the *Wake* itself) repeats the principal novelistic elements of *Finnegans Wake:* The Fall of Adam, Napoleon and Wellington, the fraternal enemies, Saint Patrick, Noah's Ark, Humpty Dumpty, Finnegan's Wake, the river and her daughters, the Four, the Twelve, and Perce-Oreille. This reprise is followed by the "fortunate fall": "O fortunous casualitas!" (175.29). The oxymoron of the *felix culpa,* subtly displaced from the narrative or novelistic dramatization, indicates the central working of *Finnegans Wake*—reconciling the brothers (Adam and Christ), uniting the Fall of the one and the Resurrection of the other. Joyce creates the world in the enunciation of the *felix culpa:* Shem and Shaun are united, the old Alp anticipates the arrival of the young Isabel, the fallen Hce awaits his own resurrection.

Joycean strategy utilizes the *felix culpa* as a mode of operation allowing for the union of contraries—theology and parody, or Christ and Lucifer—in the unbearable approach to negativity in language. The representation of Shaun includes, on the one hand, his Christly tracing of the *via crucis* and, on the other, his driven subjectivity, his *concupiscence.* Of course these two elements are presented simultaneously. The happy sin (in Chinese)[52] of "Fu Li's gulpa" (426.17) marks Shaun's *culpa* with a certain orality. In his sermon to the girls Shaun stresses original sin and its consequences: "A coil of cord, a colleen coy, a blush on a bush turned first man's laughter into wailful moither. O foolish cuppled! Ah, dice's error!" (433.28). David Hayman notes in this passage an allusion to the Mallarméan *coup de dès*,[53] the catastrophe/creation of Hce's coupling with Alp. This throw of the dice, the error of the first sin, turns Adam's laughter into tears. Shaun recites a list of interdictions ("Never . . .") directed at the young girls: he disguises *felix* as "foolish," and the *jouissance* that returns in the *felix culpa* is replaced by his own desire. At the core of the interdiction, Shaun betrays himself by attempting an incestuous seduction. The *felix culpa* emerges with respect to Shaun's carnal desires for the twenty-eight girls plus his sister: "If you want to be felixed come and be parked" (454.34).

On the one hand, the concupiscence of original sin is situated in feminine flesh. Having already written *Ulysses*, Joyce reintroduces the question of the horror produced by interdiction at the very heart of the cry of *felix culpa:* "Ahorror, he sayd . . . for finixed coulpure" (311.25). This horror is felt by the sons (like Stephen) faced with maternal sexuality since the first seduction: "since fillies calpered" (297.10). The mother ("our callback mother Gaudyanna" [294.28]) sings "consinuously" of this first "caper" (dance, ruse, trick) inscribed as Alp. The joy of grace (in Hebrew and Latin: "Gaudyanna"), presumably paschal, does not eliminate sin but rather *sublimates* it—since the *felix culpa*.[54] On the other hand, the feminine flesh evocative of horror assimilates the sacrificial presence of a dead body. Desire, the phallic failure (the fall into abjection), unite the mother Alp to Hce, who is put to death or undone by a fall into the permanent scandal of concupiscence. In Book II, 3, Butt tells the story of "Buckley and the Russian General," and the fall that is evoked through a sprinkling of allusions to the Crimean War[55] makes the *felix culpa* into a dead body, potentially identifiable (even at the site of his culpability) as an avatar of Hce: "It was Colporal Phailinx first" (346.36). It was corporeal failure first: Hce sacrificed by his "fellows" will be cut up like a Christly fish and eaten ("fellhellows . . . culponed"): "For we're all jollygame fellhellows which nobottle can deny! Here be trouts culponed for ye and salmons chined and sturgeons tranched" (569.26). The potentially homosexual scandal brought about by Hce at his fall arouses pity; at the least, the sacrificed Hce, like Bloom, pities himself: "Pity poor Haveth Childers Everywhere with Mudder!" "Away with him! Poor Felix Culapert!" (535.34, 536.8).

Hce's obvious phallic failure sets off discussions of the *origin*. The concupiscence of the first sin is the foundation of this enormous gossip, the liar's enunciation—intimate and inevitably deformed by its passage from subject to subject—that structures *Finnegans Wake*. It is this point of origin that engages all subjects in a movement of fall and resurrection, triggered by the first throw of the dice, the coupling of Hce and Alp. The *felix culpa* substitutes Christ for Adam, Mary for Eve—with the added implication of an incestuous success, as manifested by the Church. But in the beginning was the *culpa* of the first parents, Hce and Alp: "Which was the worst of them phaymix cupplerts?" (331.2).[56] Each subject enters into the crazy logic of the *felix culpa* through his or her own "fault"—his or her own portion of desire and *jouissance*, the heritage of original sin. Hce and Alp mark the beginning of this wild logic, the initiation of the concupiscence transmitted from the first man to all others. This transmission is effected symbolically, setting off an infinite seriation—procreation and paternity, a kind of Traducianism (a doctrine current in Augustine's time)[57] anagrammatically encoded as H C E and A L P. For Joyce, each subject is clearly linked to one or the other of these series. According to the dying/returning Alp, it is the *felix culpa* that links the first subjects to those who follow them: "Where once we led so many car couples have follied since" (623.21). The *culpa* rendered *felix* indicates the share of desire instrumental in the Creation (light out of darkness), recalling the famous "curve of an emotion"[58] integral to the Joycean vocation: "the charming details of light in dark are freshed from the feminiairity which breathes content. *O ferax cupla!* Ah, fairypair! The first exploder to make his ablations in these parks" (606.21). The principle of procreation, the point of origin, and the rupture posited by the first *jouissance* are revealed through this "fertile couple" (in Gaelic and Latin) of the *felix culpa*—a *fruitful* liaison between divinity and concupiscence. At the site of the fault, the *felix culpa* introduces the *fruit* of the Virgin's womb, the Word Incarnate.

Concupiscence brings the subject into the realm of his own decentering, or shows him riveted, through emotion, to the drives. The presupposed Law, cause of culpability, locates the sinner at a distance from transcendence, and inferior to it. The Anselmian *culpa* imposes a sacrificial relation (in which the inferiority of sacrifice rejoins the transcendence of divinity, according to Girard's analysis of the two faces of the sacred) between the original sinner and Christ—between passibility and the Word of the *felix culpa*. If one can legitimately evoke the question of the Christly Incarnation as regards writing, it is necessary to consider the *form*, the *beauty* of the Word, the emergence of the Incarnation as an Epiphany, in the liturgical sense, i.e., as the shining-forth of the mystery of the Incarnation. It is in this context that the nominative incarnation of the *felix culpa* through Hce can be formulated. In a list of his names[59] ("all abusive names he was called" [71.5]) Hce is named: "O'Phelim's Cutprice" (72.4). In this advertisement, evocative of the proverbial price of Parnell, betrayed by his people, Hce figures as the *cut* or sacrificed price of the martyred object at the interior of the enunciation of *O felix culpa*.

At the beginning of Book I, 5, "The Hen," Hce is named in a different list—but indirectly, through the title of the "Mamafesta," the letter written by Alp in order to save the *good name* of Hce: "Ophelia's Culpreints" (105.18). Ophelia's Prince Hamlet, Hce, offers the interlace of love and death, the heard injunction of paternity, the unbearable confrontation with murderous incest . . . and ultimate catastrophe. There will be no resurrection save that of the Word uttered by Hamlet, son of Shakespeare. It is in this symbolic region that the letter is titled *felix culpa*. And what if the letter was the text of *Finnegans Wake* itself, as Joyce so frequently hints? In Book I, 6, "Questions and Answers," number 3, someone asks for the title of □ (*Finnegans Wake* symbolized by Earwicker's pub),[60] but indicates that the title *is not* a whole series of names.

At this juncture, it is important to recall that Joyce asked his friends to guess the title of *Work in Progress* and that their erroneous responses, along with the guessing game itself, often reappear in the text.[61] Through this ritual, Joyce assumes the symbolic dimensions of the *enigma,* in order to guarantee a *reading* of his work. The ritual reveals the Catholic enigma of the *felix culpa* as a proper name: "not O'Faynix Coalprince" (139.35). This slyly denied title evokes the battle between Christ the phoenix and his adversary, the "Prince of Darkness."[62] Detached from novelistic elements (in this instance, from the title—"Finnegans Wake," like "Ulysses," imposes a structural unity on the text, a narrative architecture that filters something very different from the classical novel), the *felix culpa* provides these elements with a Catholic configuration, another signification, another proper name.

The status of the proper name posits the *felix culpa* as the *effect* of the Word. As a subject engendered in the form of the enunciation, infinitized as utterance, the Word undergoes its Incarnation and then its Passover in order to take charge of the original culpability. In other words, between culpability (*peccability,* according to Kierkegaard), locating the consequences of the drama of origins (and of the primal scene, i.e., the drama as perceived or fantasized by the subject whose *innocence* keeps him in the wings, until that point)[63] and its good fortune, the mediating Christ effects the passage of the Word. It follows, then, that the *felix culpa* allows for the leap of sin into the symbolic architecture, "synnbildising graters and things" (332.28). We have already seen the power of the proper name in this context, and its pluralization as an attempt to manifest the infinity of divine subjectivity. By substitution, all the names quoted by Pseudo-Denys the Areopagite become pseudonyms, proper names symbolically engendered and assumed. The subject overflows their individual boundaries; he wears them as the phoenix wears its body; he leaves them to put on others, as the phoenix dies in one incarnation and is reborn (resuscitated) in another. In the Joycean text this circuit occurs between Finnegan the phoenix and Hce, the infinite pseudonym: "whet between phoenix his calipers and that psourdonome sheath" (332.31).[64] This passage raises the question of the relation between Hce and Alp, the poetic multiplicity allowing Hce to go into hiding and to re-emerge, to make the passage or Passover/Easter: "Phoenix his calipers," *felix culpa.*

Toward the end of the night (Book III, 4, "The Fourth Watch of Shaun"), the nightmare of history (the permutations of the primal scene, set off by paternal desire) wakes Jerry: "O foetal sleep! Ah, fatal slip!" (563.10). The fatal slip in question is that of the Fall, represented on the level of the enunciation itself by . . . the *lapsus,* or slip of the tongue. The verbal parapraxis is inseparable from the *felix culpa* it inserts in the speech of Hce, who vainly tries to exonerate himself at the very moment he confesses himself to be the bearer of culpability rendered fortunate: "—Guilty but fellows culpows! It was felt by me sindeade. . . . I am ever incalpable . . . of unlifting upfallen girls" (363.20, .32).[65] Hce is the "dough-doughty doubleface" (363.21)—guilty and not guilty, sinner and redeemed. His language is ambivalent, constantly undermined by its double or opposite. Thus his sacred-comic position (actually composed of two double positions: that of the scapegoat, bearing unnameable abjection and become the signifying divinity, and that of non-sense from which sense or meaning emerges in the *Witz*) is made manifest through the Fall (or *lapsus*) recapitulated and rendered successful in the *felix culpa.*[66] The happy moment of the overturning of the fault is indicated in the letter at the end of the *Wake:* "O felicious coolpose!" (618.1). The paschal letter explores the oxymoron—sin and the Word, the irreconcilable contraries—and upends the heritage of death in the glory of the Resurrection. Toward the end of the *Wake,* the quintessence of Holy Saturday formed by the *felix culpa* is dramatized several times through allusions rather than enunciation. In the paschal letter, Alp defends Hce: "All men has done something. . . . We'll lave it" (621.32). What must be washed, Hce's sin, is concupiscence, according to Saint Augustine: "Honuphrius is a concupiscent exservicemajor who makes dishonest propositions to all" (572.21). Yet Hce as Christlike figure takes on the first sin and transforms it, according to the Pauline doctrine at the source of the *felix culpa,* at least as concerns the original *culpa.* In Book III, 3, Hce defends himself against accusations." Thanks to him, humanity, represented by the Twelve, "shall, in their second adams, all be made alive" (551.22). In other words (and still concerning Hce, in bed with Alp), "basal curse yet grace abunda" (577.15).[67] Despite the curse pronounced at the beginning, grace abounds.

In Joyce's *felix culpa,* Augustinian concupiscence (recalled by Kierkegaard, who establishes it as the origin of subjectivity) is inseparable from the relation to God that founds original sin according to Anselm and Duns Scotus. The "basal curse" situates the fault with respect to the Master. Hce's discourse as such, his "dishonest propositions," manifests his concupiscence. Culpability, linked to a primal *jouissance* (repressed by Milton but revealed by Joyce) must be paid for through language. Joyce represents the position of the subject cornered between flesh and symbolicity, between desire and debt: Hce and Alp "never learned the first day's lesson" (579.35); they never gave up the object of the interdiction. It is the revelation of the permanent scandal of sexuality that gives Joyce's writing its *modern* dimension; yet this revelation is at the heart of the Augustinian exposition of original sin. Having taken sinful *jouissance* to its limits—to ecstatic conversion—Augustine condemns it and overturns it in theological sublimation. But the power of this sublimation is rooted in the flesh: in the *City of God,*[68] the Doctor of original sin provides an extraordinary description of his anonymous *jouissance* of condemned sin. In Catholicism, *felicity* displaces this *jouissance* toward the sublimation of the *felix culpa*—the satisfaction of the Holy Spirit, even more powerful than that of the *culpa.* Having attributed the *felix culpa* to Augustine, Joyce underlines the power of the divine breath that goes beyond the fault of Eve and Adam, Alp and Hce: "for here the ruah of Ecclesiastes of Hippo outpuffs the writress of Havvah-ban-Annah" (38.29). The *ruah,* divine breath, is the deferred gift of the Word, whose paschal destiny brings about the *felix culpa.* The Word forms the knot of three threads: (1) *culpability,* the suffering and *jouissance* of the passible being, is the mark of the sacrificial economy positing interdiction and transgression; (2) *nomination:* the mark of the subject is pluralized and rendered infinite when the subject incarnates the instance of symbolicity; (3) *enunciation* as the subject's act of incarnation, the turn toward language of driven flesh: specifically rendered by Joyce, the incarnation of subjectivity focuses on that of the name.

The Word is offered in the triple instance of the *felix culpa*. Culpability is confronted or taken on, nomination is rendered infinite, enunciation is illuminated.

Exodus

Sacrifice, name, enunciation: the Trinitarian dimension of Easter relays that of Passover. Catholicism records the doubling of the Christly *beata nox* in the first *vere beata nox*—the night of the paschal lamb, the pillar of light, the passage across the Red Sea. In the liturgy of Holy Saturday, the Christly "reality" of the paschal night is supported by the Judaic "figures" of the Exodus. Christian ritual is grafted onto Judaic symbolicity. Having taken it upon himself in *Ulysses* to restore Judaic paternity to its place, in *Finnegans Wake* Joyce continues the dramatic revelation of the Judaic quality of Catholicism. Joyce's personalized paschal night emphasizes the symbolic domain of Judaism.

In the liturgy of Holy Saturday, the Exodus is repeated through the eulogy of the paschal night, the benedictions of new fire and water, the recitation of biblical prophecies. Holy Saturday is constructed in four movements: the annual holiday, the rememoration of the Christly Passover, the Judaic Passover night, and the night when God brought the Hebrews out of Egypt. This fourfold symbolic structure is double since it is both Judaic and Catholic. The Christ or "true Lamb" duplicates the first lamb of the original Passover; Catholic remembering repeats that ordained by God to Moses. In *Finnegans Wake,* Joyce preserves the double structure organized around Bloom and Stephen in *Ulysses.* As we have seen, *Wake* characters are unfolded in an extensive multiplication, and their roles overlap in a perpetual slippage: the unfolding or doubling of Judaism within Catholicism comes through elsewhere, not in the characters but in the Joycean relation to writing.

In the course of the paschal night, Joyce inserts in the text of the *Wake* several allusions to Passover—the central, essential experience of Judaism—by way of references to *Ulysses*. In Book III, 3, someone tells the story of Hce's fall for the thousandth time; but this time it is told according to Bloom's Christlike expulsion in "Cyclops": "He was allaughed? And then baited? The whole gammat?—Loonacied! Marterdyed!! Madwakemiherculossed!!! Judascessed!!!! Pairaskivvymenaced!!!!! Luredogged!!!!!! And, needatellye, faulscrescendied!!!!!!!" (492.3). The beginning of the Greek alphabet (the tongue of the New Testament) indicates the Christly dimension of the character being laughed at, baited, etc.—running the sacrificial gamut, echoing the Citizen's speech against Bloom. The "gammat" that follows summarizes the days of Holy Week: madness, martyrdom, the watch, the betrayal by Judas, the *paraskeuê* (the Judaic Sabbath eve, particularly Good Friday), the day of the Lord (Saturday, in Danish), and the Sunday (in Russian) of the Resurrection (in Old Church Slavonic).

This passage is followed by a question regarding Alp (the *delta* continuing the Greek alphabet): "his daintree diva . . . singing him henpecked" (492.9). She resembles Molly Bloom, the "diva," wife of a Jew. The evocation of the Red Sea ("the Crasnian Sea" [492.10]) underlines the Judaic rememoration of Passover. Alp begins to defend Hce, for whom she is having a letter written. Outis ("nobody"), menaced by the Citizen in "Cyclops," is thrown out at the moment he reveals his Christly truth: "Our Outis cuts his thruth. Arkaway now!" (493.26). Like Noah in the ark, the expelled Hce is simultaneously Hce the redemptor, the man of God. In order to stress the resemblance between Hce and Bloom, the two Christlike figures of Moses, and the importance of the link between Judaism and Catholicism generating the text of *Ulysses*, Joyce recapitulates the Judeo-Catholic context of "Lotuseaters" in Alp's defense of Hce. Allusions to the Ulyssean context include the lotus ("padham"), "slow poisoning," and "family drugger" (492.23, .16, .21). The references to the seductions of the Church recall Bloom's reflections during the mass, notably regarding confession and mariolatry ("laxative tendency to mary" [492.31]), the confession of the adulterous wife ("especially with him being forbidden fruit and certified by his sexular clergy" [492.31]), the seductive powers of priests and liturgical chant ("with a basketful of priesters crossing the singor-geous to aroint him" [492.33]). Bloom concludes this chapter with the anticipation of the bath and the Christly cup of the Judaic Passover: *This is my body.* Hce as well is seated in his lotus garden/receptacle: "When he was sitting him hump-backed in dry dryfilthyheat to his trinidads pinslers" (492.29). Three, three, and three, plus the German *Dreifaltigkeit:* Hce like Bloom is seated in his Christly function, in the *Trinity.*

In Book II, 4, "Mamalujo," the Four Evangelists tell the history of Ireland. They evoke Noah ("nomads flood," "after the wreak of Wormans' Noe" [386.28, 387.21]) prior to an explicit reference to Exodus: "and then there was the drown-ing of Pharoah and all his pedestrians and they were all com-pletely drowned into the sea, the red sea, and then poor Mer-kin Cornyngwham, the official out of the castle on pension, when he was completely drowned off Erin Isles . . . in the red sea" (387.25). The Four take a sinister pleasure in the telling of various deaths. As at certain key moments of *Ulysses,* the double focus on Judaism and Christianity is itself based on a twofold opposition, Egypt vs. Israel and England ("the castle") vs. Ireland. The oblique reminder of the paschal victory ("O truly blessed night, which despoiled the Egyptians and en-riched the Hebrews!") integrates the novelistic, structural, and biographical contexts of *Ulysses* in the *Wake.* First, Martin Cunningham, who according to Bloom is foundering in mar-ital woes,[69] is compared to Pharoah's Egyptians. Everyone around Bloom (and Stephen) seems to be engulfed, like Ulys-ses' sailors, in corporeality, repetition, the real. From book to book, Joyce poses the question of death (of the *world,* for Catholics)[70] from which one must escape: paternity and filia-tion, through the symbolic body of *Ulysses,* point toward the only possible strategy, the only solution. Ulysses' difficulties during the Odyssey provide the structural reference: one ex-ample of this is the old sailor in "Eumaeus" (the disguised Ulysses, *pseudangelos*). After the ordeal, Ulysses remembers the sand in the Red Sea . . .[71] more like Moses than Ulysses, in fact. The drowning of the Egyptians lends its resonance to the opening of *Ulysses* with its drowned corpse, who echoes, in turn, the biographical element of the character of Martin Cunningham.[72] Through the parodic meditations of the Four, the representatives of death, Joyce indicates the knots that tighten around his paschal inscription.

Elsewhere, Joyce establishes the resonances of Passover in the intonation of Psalm 113: "Ay, and untuoning his culothone in an exitous erseroyal. *Deo Jupto*" (353.17). This passage of Book II, 3, concerns the murder of the Russian General (associated with Hce) committed by Buckley, an Irish soldier (Butt). The General's dignity is destroyed by abjection. In John Joyce's scatological story, Buckley shoots the General only when the latter wipes himself with a clump of (Irish) earth.[73] The disgusted Buckley makes a sacrifice of the Father Hce ("His Cumbulent Embulence" [352.32]). If the General resembles Bloom on trial in "Circe" (*U* 460) in his *abject* appearance, that resemblance may be due to his *Trinitarian* character, invoked by Taff: "Trisseme, the mangoat! and the name of the Most Marsiful, the Aweghost, the Gragious One!" (353.2). Like Bloom, the Russian General finds his symbolic roots in Judaism. Elsewhere in the *Wake,* he is named with the anniversary of the Creation, the festival of the New Year, Rosh Hashanah: "between his bulchritudes and the roshashanaral" (340.27). His intonation of Psalm 113 underlines the Judaic presence of Passover and celebrates divine mastery (the theme of the psalm) at the very moment of the Christlike sacrifice. According to Joyce, Jew and Catholic come together at the moment of the paschal experience in a doubled exit, a doubled *jouissance:* "With what intonation *secreto* of what commemorative psalm? The 113th, *modus peregrinus. In exitu Israel de Egypto: domus Jacob de populo barbaro*" (*U* 698). Father and Son, Bloom and Stephen, share the Passover of their encounter and immediately separate: the invocation establishes the paternity without which there is no creation. Filiation is situated in the reception or transmission of paternity—through which pass symbolicity, grace, and what the Judaic tradition terms the creative Word.[74] Joyce allows his text to pivot between Judaism and Catholicism, between the scriptures of *Ulysses* and *Finnegans Wake.* Psalm 113 marks the emergence of the Word in the space between the two, the Passover of James Joyce, celebrating scatologically, parodically, *In exitu Israel de Egypto* or his own confrontation with paternity, exile, and language.

For Joyce, the Exodus profiled in Psalm 113 establishes the

Catholic liaison between the first Easter, the biblical Passover, and the ceremony of the paschal night, the festival of the *Lumen Christi*. Yet the Judeo-Catholic doubling of the paschal experience is fully introduced into *Finnegans Wake* through the staging of the proper name. Beginning with the trial of the original sinner and the Christly trajectory supposed to take up the burden of original sin, the name of Hce resounds everywhere in scandal, sacrifice, and death—but also in symbolic creation, in paternity. In Book III, 1, "The First Watch of Shaun," his name follows the paschal path of the *Father:* Shaun claims that his paschal path is as old "as Nelson his trifulgurayous pillar" (422.30).[75] The pillar of fire of the Hebrews has become a triple *fulguration* thanks to a Trinitarian presence ("tryone, tryon and triune" [422.2.6]). Shaun attempts to remember the beginning, the first sin of Hce motivating Shem's complicity with his mother: "Then mem and hem and the jacquejack. All about Wucherer and righting his name for him" (422.33). Signed hce (in "Wu*che*rer"), the paternal usurer is the subject of the famous letter, in which his reputation must be put to rights through the writing of his name—his salvation.

The W of Hce's name echoes the W of Shakespeare, astronomically inscribed, for Stephen, in the skies of *Ulysses*. Joyce, the artist of the proper name,[76] is himself the "Wucherer" (the paternal usurer) demanding payment in tongues, appropriating names, discourses, and *jouissances* for himself—and, like Shem, signatures as well—all of them forbidden. Shem signs himself Hce, as plagiarizer and writer at the same time; he thus usurps a proper name he is supposed to save. Shem's filial ambivalence regarding Hce reveals him to be an "ambitrickster" (423.6). The salvation and the putting to death tend to run together, thanks to the Judaic and Catholic doubling of Passover/Easter. Shaun describes Shem's language: "the idioglossary he invented uder hicks hyssop! Hock!" (423.9). Shem has invented a private, personal language—the tongue of *Finnegans Wake,* one would think. No doubt he invented it under his hat—become "hyssop," recalling the Sunday antiphon of *Asperges me,* as well as its paschal context: "Thou shalt sprinkle me with hyssop, O Lord, and I shall be cleansed." Moses, at the moment of Passover, instructs the Ancients of

Israel: "And ye shall take a bunch of hyssop, and dip *it* in the blood that *is* in the bason, and strike the lintel and the two side posts with the blood that *is* in the bason; and none of you shall go out at the door of his house until the morning" (Exod. 12:22). Shem thus takes charge of Hce's purification through language. The *Asperges me* prepares the "sacrifice" within the Mass: *Hoc est enim corpus meum* becomes "Hock!" Shem's apparent ambivalence seems to touch on the Oedipal relation of son to father but without altering the arrangement of divine paternity that makes a *resurrection* out of *sacrifice*. This symbolic apparatus makes death into a life of grace through the reification of this trajectory in the ceremony of the Eucharist. The knot of sin, death, and *grace* (the supremely symbolic gift, love passing through the word) is, for Joyce, the scriptural center of Catholicism. This *scriptural* knot, demonstrating the relation of the writer to his paschal paternity, is at the heart of *Finnegans Wake*.

Joyce often alludes to Exodus 12, and particularly to the markings of blood on the doorposts. These marks are signifiers offered to the Exterminating Angel in order that the Passover take place, i.e., in order that the Angel *spare* the Israelites by *limping around* them or *skipping over* them, in order that he *leap*.[77] These marks initiate the slippage from sacrifice to writing; they trigger a *leap* outside death, or a leap *into* the symbolic relation characterizing Judaism. The monotheistic subject locates himself here, leaving behind him the multiple gods of Egyptian civilization. Concerning this rupture, Freud points out, in paganism, the traces of an incestuous satisfaction attributed to the mother-child dyad; but in Judaism he finds wandering, exile, the search for a very different truth.[78] The subject renounces forever the delights of incest and invests in paschal marks—*signatures* shining like candles in the dark night of the Exterminating Angel's limping, leaping, dancing passage. The white page, the unsigned lintel, attract death to the Egyptian side, inadequate to the symbolic task imposed by the divine gaze. Where nothing is written . . .

This ritual recorded in the text of Exodus brings out the symbolic weight of Mosaic religion. It reveals the privileged position of the paschal event, textualizing the definitive rupture of Judaism with neighboring forms of religion. In it resonates the effect, the meaning, of the name *Pesah,* Passover, crucial with respect to the eventual role played by the holiday and the theological interpretation later attributed to it. The divine ruse of paschal writing is played out in comic form in Book I, 7, "Shem." In the midst of the bloody nightmare of history, while everyone religiously and joyously celebrates war ("chanting the Gillooly chorus, from the Monster Book of Paltryattic Puetrie, *O pura e pia bella!*" [178.16]), Shem is frightened. He addresses the God of emptiness ("as he prayed to the cloud Incertitude" [178.31]). His telescope becomes the revolver destined to sacrifice him as a scapegoat: "he got the charm of his optical life . . . blinking down the barrel of an irregular revolver . . . handled by an unknown quarreler who, supposedly, had been told off to shade and shoot shy Shem" (179.1). Shem the "baalamb" (178.13) is caught in sacrificial ambivalence. He is put to death and spared, sacrificed and expelled like Moses[79] or Noah ("noahs and cul verts agush with tears of joy," "finding out for himself . . . whether true conciliation was forging ahead or falling back after the celestious intemperance" [178.12, .32]), submitted to divine will and separated from the community at the moment of the sacrificial crisis. Shem the victim (like Noah, or Joyce himself) anxiously awaits the end of the storm, the rainbow sign of divine approbation, "the sevenspan *ponte dei colori*" (178.24).

Shem's attempt to avoid sacrifice (to be spared) brings him closer to the Judaic point of view depicted in Exodus: "After the thorough fright he got that bloody, Swithun's day, though every doorpost in muchtried Lucalizod was smeared with generous erstborn gore" (178.8). At the paschal moment, Shem takes up the Judaic position. The blood of the paschal lamb corresponds to the blood of the firstborn Egyptians in order to underline the relation between the symbolic marks and the "true" sacrifice (the putting to death of the firstborn) that occurs in their absence. These symbolic marks of the paschal sacrifice should be read according to the scriptural position they imply. In this instance, this position is assumed by the character of Shem the penman. He reveals the Mosaic trajectory through negativity within the scriptural enterprise.

Moses traces the path of the Jews through the sacrificial crisis of the Egyptians—across the waters of the Red Sea, the figure of death. The *wake* of Moses designates the passage of the Jews through Egyptian corporeality;[80] the Mosaic mastery of the sea is miraculous insofar as the divine triumph over the *real* dimension presents itself as the greatest possible *jouissance* of the *true*. It is in this sense that one can interpret the equation Wake = Resurrection—the assimilation of the Irish ballad of "Finnegan's Wake" in the Wake of *Finnegan*—who then becomes the proper name of the equation. Truth turns death into resurrection. The sacrificial ambivalence opening out toward this particular truth indicates Shem's relation to language. He has been put to death and saved—elsewhere, "outlex" and "inlaw" (169.15, .16)—like Moses, presented halfway between the divine Law and the outlaw of the Egyptians (*U* 142). The paschal reference of the *Wake* is preceded by the declaration of Shem's desire: "he would wipe alley english spooker, multaphoniaksically spuking, off the face of the erse" (178.6). The passage of Moses through the sea that destroys the Egyptian army is comparable to the passage or "wake" cleared by Shem through the "body" of the English language. This negative passage prepares the symbolic incarnation. The oxymoron of the symbolic incarnation is an attempt to approximate the sacrifice of the old language, the unheeded language of others, reduced to its communicative function. It is transformed by the cunning ear of the writer who attempts to resuscitate it. Since the writer does so in his or her own mouth and proper name, its form resembles an incarnation. Of course, given the proportions of Joyce's symbolic demands, this new tongue hardly resembles the old one, vanished from the symbolic surface like the Egyptians. Shem's sonorous enunciation of multiple tongues and voices ("multaphoniaksically spuking") dismisses English words with all the phantoms (spooks) of the old language—the dated utterances caught in the network of the nightmare of history. Mosaic and Mallarméan, Shem seeks the new word, the promised word.

In Book I, 3, "The Goat" (62—64), Hce's masked aggressor takes on the identity of the cad. Joyce filters his own scriptural presence through the aggressor/cad via Shem and his paschal writing.[81] In the midst of attempts to establish the truth about Hce, his original sin, and the attack against him, the aggressor is quoted. He admits to having drunk too much in a series of Dublin pubs: "the wretch's statement that, muttering Irish, he had had had o'gloriously a'lot too much hanguest or hoshoe fine to drink" (63.21). The figuration of Alpha-Omega (o'a' . . . hanguest/hoshoe),[82] the pub called "the Holy Lamb," and the allusion to the (Catholic and Joycean) Annunciation[83] place the double paschal context. The aggressor attempts to justify himself through lies, one version of the Joycean writing of fiction: "Yet how lamely hobbles the hoy of his then pseudo-jocax axplanation how, according to his own story, he . . . was merely trying to open zozimus a bottlop stoub" (63.30). The fiction embroidered around the opening of a bottle of stout,[84] supposed to motivate the violent gestures of the aggressor (against Hce?), slips toward the context of Exodus. Sounds become "babel," tongues and scriptures, the marks on the doorposts and lintels at the time of the first Passover: "This battering babel allower the door and sideposts, he always said, was not in the very remotests like the belzey babble of a bottle of boose" (64.9). Someone named Maurice Behan gives evidence against the aggressor by saying that his "babel" was either musical or volcanic (64.13–15). These noises do not remind him of the devilry of alcohol ("belzey babble"): it is a "nooningless knockturn" (64.15), a nocturne bereft of meaning and light—i.e., *Finnegans Wake*—written like the paschal markings of the Israelites. But, first, the "nooningless knockturn" is the attempt to know the truth according to Maurice Behan, after which the text of the *Wake* starts up again: Alp's rain, the mud, the two washerwomen: "be the chandeleure of the Rejaneyjailey they were all night wasching the walters of" (64.19). The chandelier of a Roman jail is also the *Chandeleur* (Candlemas) of the *Regina Coeli*, or the birth of the mariolatrous paschal lamb James Joyce, on February 2, the day of the purification of the Virgin and of the presentation of Christ in the Temple. Annunciation becomes enunciation in the Passover of *Finnegans Wake*.

At the end of Book III, 3, "The Third Watch of Shaun," Hce himself evokes the context of the Exodus. Joyce layers his text with allusions to the mass, monotheistic (Judaic, Christian, Islamic) mysticism, and Passover/Easter. Hce enumerates the geographical and architectural sites, including the

Seven Wonders of the World, constructed by him for Alp. He explicitly names the biblical Passover, and states that no blood has been spilled since then: "I did spread before my Livvy, where Lord street lolls and ladies linger . . . but never a blid had bledded or bludded since long agore when the whole blighty acre was bladey well pessovered" (553.4). The consonantal sequence *bld* occurs four times (five if "blighty" is included) in the phrase concerning Passover; Joyce seems to formulate a Semitic rendering of the word *blood,* presented as a three-letter root. The paschal blood (like that of Abel) is thus heard, rendered sonorous without being completely readable in the English of the sentence. As we have seen, Joyce tends to combine the blood of the lamb and that of the Egyptians in order to bring out the ambivalence specific to the paschal experience of death and life. Passover spares the Hebrews, thanks to the blood become proto-scripture, and sheds the blood of the Egyptians, who have made no marks. Hce seems to take the position of the *spared:* he is on the Judaic side of the paschal story. For him, Passover is the object of rememoration; like the father of the Jewish family, he must say: "The Lord intervened for me, when I came out of Egypt."[85] Thus, on the level of the enunciation, he allies himself with Moses; he delivers the explanation of the paschal ritual to the community. The ritual is combined with its future rememoration, with the sparing from sacrifice, and with a symbolic identity crystallized in the name of Passover itself. Elsewhere, the stuttering of Hce[86] recalls the flawed language of Moses, who complains that he speaks heavily (Exod. 4:10). This flaw is a symptom of the *Ineffable Name:* held at the throat by the unspeakable, Hce repeats himself, thereby putting his own utterance to death. Through this mutilation, guilt and the Fall resonate: they recapitulate Hce's position in relation to the Other.

Starting with "Passover," Hce gains access to his paternity, to his *symbolic creation.* The signs of blood are marked on the wonders built by Hce, the Ibsenesque architect of towers, *Bygmester Solness,* the Masterbuilder.[87] *Bygmester* Hce builds churches more than anything else: "my stavekirks . . . arked for covennanters and shinners' rifuge: descent from above on us, Hagiasofia of Astralia . . . Hams, circuitize! Shemites, retrace!: . . . hereround is't holied!" (552.3). Hce evokes Judaic Law—the Ark of the Covenant (as well as the Ark of the synagogue and that of Noah).[88] But the litanies of Notre-Dame de Lorette describe the Virgin as the Ark of the Alliance and the Refuge of Sinners. Hce's ritual invocation of the Holy Spirit seems to take the feminized, ecclesiastical form of the Mosque Hagia Sophia, or Holy Wisdom. Hce points out the circuit, the circular wandering, of Ham; giving orders from his paternal position, Hce takes on the voice of Noah after his intoxication and Ham's transgression (Gen. 9:22). Just as Noah blesses Shem by the Name he bears, Hce ordains the *tracing in names* (*shemot*) to *Shem*. Like Noah, Hce transmits his paternity to Shem through the *regere fines* ("tracing borders in straight lines").[89] From Hce to Shem, the *rex* is the great priest who maps out the limits of consecrated space: "Operation whose magical character is visible: it is a question of marking the limits of interior and exterior, the kingdom of the sacred and the kingdom of the profane." "This tracery is effected by the individual invested with the very highest powers, the *rex*."[90]

When he constructs Alp's cathedrals, Hce asks Shem to provide the sacred tracery; when he declares "hereround is't holied," the tracing has been accomplished and construction begins. In order to underline the symbolic aspect of his creation, Hce describes the seduction of Alp in scriptural terms: "with fairskin book and ruling rod, vein of my vergin page, her chastener ever" (552.36). Sexual mastery (*h . . . c . . . e . . .*) takes place in writing on the virgin page. Hce boasts of having given her anagram to Alp, in the gift of *alp*habets. But the formula is ambivalent, and it is possible that Alp, matrix of writing and source of alphabets and languages, teaches Hce the Greek and Irish alphabets: "I did learn my little ana countrymouse in alphabeater cameltemper, from alderbirk to tannenyou" (553.2). (*Alpha, beta, gamma, delta: ailm, beth, teithne, ur.*) Starting with the desire that links them together, their relation to writing is complementary, double, reciprocal: "When the waves give up yours the soil may for me" (624.3), says Alp of the letter Hce awaits. On the other hand, it is from Hce's earth that Alp awaits the resurrection of the letter addressed to her: "I wrote me hopes and buried the page when I heard

Thy voice" (624.4). Hce's letter was dictated by Alp. The letter Alp self-addresses was written according to the call of Hce. At their crossing: Shem the Penman, *rex* by his father, the incestuous favorite of his mother, "a child of Maam, Festy King" (85.23), according to his brother Shaun.

Ecclesiastical creation slides toward scriptural creation, thanks to the dimensions of the paschal event: "her paddypalace on the crossknoll with massgo bell, sixton clashclosh-uant, duominous . . . doom adimdim adoom adimadim: . . . gospelly pewmillieu, christous pewmillieu" (532.23). Hce Christ (Hoke or *Hoc Est*) restores, for Alp, Saint Patrick's Cathedral, the source of the bells that can be heard ringing. And the paschal Kyrie can be heard as well, in Old Slavonic, following the litanies of Holy Saturday. The Resurrection is announced and again the bells ring. The Catholic Easter is named soon after the mention of the Passover: "the eiligh ediculous Pas-sivucant (glorietta's inexcellsiored!): for irkdays and for follie-days till the comple anniums of calendarias, gregoromaios and gypsyjuliennes" (553.14). The Easter festival is composed of *passivus* and *vocans;* [91] the body and its language—suffering and the call, nomination, *vocation*—make themselves heard in the doubled, Catholic Passover. The paschal Kyrie and Gloria mark the turning point of Holy Saturday and the beginning of the Resurrection celebration. The references to the calendar and to those who reformed it focus the speech on a *symbolic point,* the anniversary (in Spanish: *cumpleaños*) of the Resurrection. This is the point where time stops, to emerge anew, from the beginning until the "comple anniums," the end of time. The Apocalypse and eternity are inscribed in *the Alpha and the Omega,* in the Word that grafts eschatology onto the alphabet, "from alder birk to tannenyou."

The Catholic experience is sustained by the Judaic Passover; for Joyce, "Passivucant" echoes "pessovered" preceding it. In a paschal letter, Athanasius recalls the key moment of the Exodus and of Passover in order to focus on the paschal significance of the New Testament: "But now that we eat the Word (the *Logos*) of the Father and sign the lintels of our hearts with the blood of the New Testament, we proclaim the grace given to us by the Redemptor."[92] Joyce delivers the specifically

Judaic meaning of the Catholic metaphor as employed by
Athanasius. At the same time, he gives an explicit account of
that signature in question, through the subject-writer or
"Penman" of *Finnegans Wake*.

7

Paschal Time
The Calendar

The *punctual* aspect of the paschal experience, the anticipated return of a "retrospective arrangement," brings forth the historical moment of the Resurrection and inserts it, displaces it, through the effect of a future perfect that telescopes the centuries, toward the immediate future of the celebrants of Holy Saturday. The experience relived, repeated in the ritual frame, gains cyclic access to the privileged *punctum* of the Resurrection, which took place once and for all time. In this respect, the liturgical cycle is but a ruse, a means of symbolically regulating time and distancing it from natural time. The proof of this is the organization of the liturgical cycle around the Dantean *punto solo,* the "leap" recorded in Exodus (echoed by the Kierkegaardian leap into subjectivity) that becomes, in Catholicism, the day of Easter. It would seem, then, that this punctual aspect of Catholicism must have caused, at least in part, the controversies about the date of the paschal celebration. In his "comple anniums of calendarias," Hce introduces the question of this date in *Finnegans Wake* at the threshold of his resurrection in Book IV. Joyce's investment in the paschal *punctum* emerges in his evocation of the date as such in the *Wake* and in his version of two paschal controversies, woven into the text.

Joyce often evokes the Resurrection *punctum* in a subtle fashion, without naming it, in order to allow it to *pass* into his own language, in order to make it *spring forth* from this language. In his sermon (Book III, 2), Jaun remarks: "Out with lent! Clap hands postilium! Fastintide is by" (453.36). If Lent and the pre-Easter fast are over, then it is the day of Easter itself, named in Book I, 3, as the "peoplade's eggday" (69.28) according to the folk custom of eating eggs to celebrate Easter.[1] Hce is hidden away in order to spare him from sacrifice. His risk is described as "tempting gracious providence by a stroll on the peoplade's eggday, unused as he was yet to being freely clodded" (69.28). The Resurrection that becomes operative beginning with Hce's death is simultaneously the consequence of the (Judaic) paschal preservation or sparing. Elsewhere, Joyce continues to telescope the two moments (sacrifice and sparing, or death and resurrection). In the same chapter (Book I, 3), the meeting between Buckley and the Russian General that will end in the General's death is described as the day of Easter: "the same snot ob the dunhill, fully several yearschaums riper, encountered by the General on that redletter morning or maynoon jovesday" (50.30). Buckley here resembles the cad. The "redletter morning" is tinted with the General's blood and with the Adamic sin[2] of Hce. This sin leads to Christ's victory: "redletter man" is slang for a Roman Catholic.[3] But the central meaning of this locution is related to the ecclesiastical calendar. The *Oxford English Dictionary* (OED) defines *red letter* as "a letter made with red ink, or with some red pigment, esp. as used in ecclesiastical calendars to indicate saints' days and church festivals." A "red letter day" is "a saint's day or church festival indicated in the calendar by red letters; hence, any memorable, fortunate or specially happy day." From an ecclesiastical point of view, the primary "red letter day" would be Easter. It is in this context that "that red mass I was looking at" (304.7)—annotated "*Catastrophe and Anabasis*" (304.L26) in "Nightlessons" (Book II, 2)—can be interpreted as the upheaval of the Fall and the ascension inherent in Christly Resurrection.

In *Finnegans Wake,* the "red letter day" seems to recapitulate the condemnation to death and the act of sparing, the passion and the resurrection—of Hce the Father, and of his Christlike son and his double. The confusion between "post" and "pen-man" in the Joycean Trinitarian configuration displays the enigma itself of the double paschal position in Judaism as in Catholicism. On the other hand, the pathway of the living Word (Shaun) merges with a symbolic position in writing (Shem) in the famous *letter,* the defense of Hce by Alp. It is then this letter that organizes the unity of the Trinity: through the name of the Father Hce, the anaphoric name of *Hoc est. . . .*[4] The letter delivered by Shaun gives evidence of his murderous hatred for his brother, and his paschal sacrifice: "I'll try and collect my extraprofessional postages owing to me by Thaddeus Kellesque Squire, dr, for nondesirable printed matter. Great pains off him I'll take and that'll be your redletter calendar, window machree! I'll knock it out of him!" (456.29). This hatred turns to the passion of the Father ("I'd be tempted rigidly to become a passionate father" [457.6]) and in Book III, 3, Shaun delivers his hatred impossibly transformed into love of the Father, thanks to the letter, written by Shem, announcing the "red letter day" of Hce's resurrection: "Detter for you, Mr Nobru. Toot toot! Better for you, Mr Anol! This is the way we. Of a redtetterday morning" (490.26). The hidden "L" of the letter passes through the "delta" of Alp and the symbolic *debt* to the "B" of "better"— the best of the letter; from Adam to Christ, through the "t" of the Crucifixion ("tettetter") to the morning of the Resurrection.

At the moment of the Resurrection—"through strength towards joyance, adyatants, where he gets up" (598.24), "the regenerations of the incarnations" (600.9)—Hce's festival is celebrated: "his feist a ferial for curdnal communial, so be who would celibrate the holy mystery upon or that the pirigrim from Mainylands beatend, the calmleaved hutcaged by that look wholse glaum is sure he means bisnisgels to empalmover. A naked yogpriest, clothed of sundust, his oakey doaked with frondest leoves, offrand to the ewon of her owen" (600.34). Hce's paschal "feist" or "ferial" (his "Feiste Sonntag") begins with the *body* (*feist,* in German, means corpulent) and the blood of "communial" (Communion); the references to palm trees and the offering (in French: *l'offrande*) evoke the paschal rememoration of the Judaic festival of Sukkoth (Tabernacles) and the benediction of the branches (*rameaux*) on Palm Sunday, anticipating Easter. The site mentioned in this sequence is appropriate to the celebration of the Holy Mystery. The city of Alp/Isolde/Isis that emerges is, according to the churches named, Dublin. Paschal time begins with the first of the Glorious Mysteries, the Resurrection, here celebrated by a pilgrim: "One of the most striking and original features of Irish Christianity is the love of wandering, *peregrinatio,* which was interpreted in both its literal and its figurative sense." Concerning Irish saints: "Their special ideal was defined as 'seeking the place of one's resurrection,' which is the kind of motive Adamnan had in mind when he tells us that St Columbia left Ireland for Britain: '*pro Christo peregrinari volens enavigavit.*'"[5] This Irish point of view is in perfect agreement with the configuration of *Finnegans Wake.* Irish wandering recalls its Judaic counterpart that makes Bloom, Hce, and Joyce himself into Mosaic and Christlike figures, paternal and filial figures. If Joyce's wandering ceases, give or take a few pages, at this moment of return to Dublin in the writing of Hce's resurrection, it is because in "the whole clangalied" (601.9), the ringing of Dublin bells, resonates the end of his long night: "*Sicut campanulae petalliferentes* they coroll in caroll round Botany Bay. S. Wilhelmina's, S. Gardenia's, S. Phibia's, S. Veslandrua's." (601.16). Proust's *jeunes filles* have metamorphosed into the rainbow girls, the churches, the bells announcing the jubilation of the Resurrection. This metamorphosis is woven through a series of feminized Church names. Joyce answers his own question: "Euh! Thaet is seu whaet shaell one naeme it!" (601.30). How can this particular jubilation be named, if not in the superfluity of vowels and the overflow of names sounding this other resurrection, this other peregrination leading to *jouissance* in Joycean writing: visible, and above all resonant, it is the moment when the paschal *point* surges forth in the musicalized joy of the Resurrection.

The doubling of paschal signification is resolved at the moment of the Resurrection, knotting the Fall and the Ascension together. This moment locates the crossing of measured time with the atemporality of eschatology. The date chosen for the Easter holiday, the calculation of this date, and its traditions are inseparable from a position within Catholicism. In *Finnegans Wake,* the question of this date is all the more relevant since, from beginning to end, time is a major topic of discussion. Hce often announces the time while preparing to close the pub; in the deferred primal scene, the cad triggers Hce's feelings of guilt by asking him the time; and Shem, in all his major avatars, is anxious to find out what time it is. Yet in spite of this precision, there is a certain vagueness about the date of Easter. In Book I, 7, "Shem," Shaun tells his brother: "You were bred, fostered and fattened from holy childhood up in this two easter island on the piejaw of hilarious heaven and roaring the other place" (188.9). The "two easter island" is Ireland, divided between Heaven and Hell, the Catholic institution and its condemnation. In the following chapter, "Anna Livia Plurabelle," Alp gives gifts to her children: "a niester egg with a twicedated shell and a dynamight right for Pavl the Curate" (210.35). Here again, the paschal festival is divided: the Easter egg has two dates and the negation introduced in it ("niester" rather than "an/easter") manifests the "No" of the controversy—as well as the refusal of the institution, unwilling to accept Irish resistance.

In the seventh century, Roman missionaries[6] discovered that, because of Ireland's century-long isolation, the Irish methods for calculating the date of the Easter holiday had long since fallen out of use on the Continent. Easter was not celebrated on the same day in Rome and in Ireland. Between 629 and 636, the south gave in to pressure, but the north of Ireland held out against the Roman practice for a longer period. The question was an important one, underpinning that of faith itself. Despite a great deal of direct communication with Rome, it was only in 696 at the Synod of Birr that the north capitulated before Roman authority. It is interesting to note that the monastery founded by Saint Columcille at Iona, later transferred to Kells, remained faithful to the Irish Church throughout the paschal controversy.[7]

Joyce is manifestly conscious of the problem of calculating the Easter celebration date, at the heart of the controversy. In Book I, 6, Hce seems to incarnate Christ: "he can get on as early as the twentysecond of Mars but occasionally he doesn't come off before Virgintiquinque Germinal" (134.12). Here encoded in French, according to the French revolutionary calendar, is the day of the Resurrection, situated between March 22 and April 25.[8] At the beginning of *Finnegans Wake*, in Book I, 2, "The Ballad," Joyce inserts the most explicit allusion to the Irish position in the controversies with Rome. Among the Dubliners ("liffeyside people" [42.25]) there can be found "a particularist prebendary pondering on the roman easter, the tonsure question and greek uniates" (43.12). Greek Uniates accept Catholic authority, including that of the Pope, while maintaining the use of their own liturgy, with the result that they are halfway between submission to Rome and the schismatic position of the Church that conserves its individual character. In this sense, they are comparable to the Celtic Church prior to the disciplinary controversies, especially to the organization of Iona. One of these controversies took up the question of Celtic tonsure, attributed by the partisans of Roman usage to Simon Magus;[9] it is true that the Druids wore the tonsure, and no doubt Rome wanted to attenuate Irish individualism via the condemnation of Celtic tonsure. In the Joycean text, the Dubliner pondering these questions is a Celtic particularist, a salaried ecclesiastic who is a partisan of the Irish Church, especially regarding the paschal controversy, or "the roman easter."[10] Why does Joyce stress this division?

According to Dom Gougaud, the Council of Arles in 314 and that of Nicea in 325 prepared the paschal controversy. In the first, it was decided that Easter should be celebrated on the same day all over the world. In the second, "It was declared that Easter should be celebrated in the whole universe on the same Sunday, but never on the same day as the Jews."[11] The coincidence of the Judaic Passover and the Resurrection was possible according to the Celtic calculation; and the dissidents claimed they took their Passover from Saint John.[12] In this, they repeated the Quarto-Deciman position of the twelfth-century controversy:[13] the Asiatic Church, following Saint John, celebrated the Christian Passover on the same day as the Jewish holiday, the fourteenth day of the moon of the month of Nissan. A letter by Ireneus narrates the conflict opposing Polycarp, partisan of the practice "of John and of the other Apostles with whom he had lived,"[14] to Pope Anicet. It is possible that Joyce alludes to these circumstances shortly before the Resurrection sequence ("his feist a ferial," etc.) when he names Polycarp: "Polycarp pool . . . whereinn once we lave

'tis alve and vale . . . the regenerations of the incarnations"
(600.5). Elsewhere, Joyce names the three protagonists of the
controversy: "For ancients link with presents as the human
chain extends, have done, do and will agian as John Polycarp
and Irenews eye-to-eye ayewitnessed" (254.8). The witness
named here possibly refers to Polycarp's position with respect
to John, and seems to echo Ireneus' letter. The face-to-face
"ayewitnessed"[15] gives evidence of personal experience and
faith, whence the affirmation of an enormous ecstatic Yes, recalling the end of *Ulysses:* "Oyes! Oyeses! Oyesesyeses!" (604.22).
John, Polycarp, Ireneus: the past, the present of the enunciation, and the future—of a paschal form of writing, always
"news" in the eschatological dimension through which Joyce
filters his Trinitarian Yes.

Forming a backdrop to the paschal controversy opposing
the Irish Church to the Roman *unitas catholica,* the Quarto-
Deciman controversy opposes evangelical tradition to the Roman Catholic institution. The latter demands homogeneity,
unity. It feels threatened by the Celtic tradition and above all
by the truth to which John and his followers bear witness—
the paschal truth founding the Christly dimension, the Passover "of the Lord." The Church attempts to dissociate itself
from the Judaic Passover. According to Turmel, this attempt
explains the radical change that takes place in the domain of
ritual. He locates this internal alteration of the Christian Passover around the year 140 A.D.: "Until then the ritual consisted
in eating the paschal lamb with unleavened bread, and it was
celebrated on the day of the full moon in Spring: it had thus
preserved its Jewish character. After this date it was given the
resurrection of Christ as its object, and it was celebrated on
the Sunday following the full moon, in such a way as to destroy all its links to Judaism."[16]

Behind the conflicts of calculation, tradition, community,
lies the kernel of the inadmissible, the repressed: Judaism.
The gaze displaced toward the Resurrection alone is no longer
willing to envision the expulsion, the wandering, the cut between Jew and Egyptian, and, beyond, the Passover of the
Father: through Moses, divine paternity, the beginning of
writing and prophetic speech, knot the Jewish people to the
Law written with the hand of God. For the entire truth of

Judaism takes root, paradoxically enough, in the departure from Egypt, with rupture as the object of rememoration, the principal subjective position: in the wake of the Law, the paternity that holds good, the voice calling in the desert. The dimension of emptiness constitutive of the Symbolic founds the structure of Judaism (and of paternity) such that the Catholic institution does not want to hear about it. And Joyce who, more than any other, lived the Judaic position of the Irishman, takes up this position on the level of his Catholic experience itself. He writes the drama of the doubled position of his Ireland—Celtic, Quarto-Deciman, and Judaic as well as Catholic, apostolic, and Roman. According to paschal legislation (councils, synods, etc.), Rome refuses to acknowledge its symbolic origin (the Father and "his" people). Judaic paternity returns in the form of the Irish Church and bears with it a second symbolic position that threatens the homogeneity legislated by Rome. The Irish *double*, according to the institutional view, emerges from the abyss. It operates a problematic anamnesis, with respect to the Judaism that Rome would rather forget. It is hardly surprising that the Irish Church (like the partisans of the Quarto-Deciman tradition before her) is accused of demoniacal qualities and threatened with excommunication. Between Roman authority and Judaic paternity, Ireland is "this two easter island" caught between Heaven and Hell: between "easter" and "niester." This double position, maintaining the dismissed and forbidden truth as well as the institutional authority, echoes the *Witz*, structured by meaning in uncomfortable intimacy with non-sense. The heterogeneity of the double symbolic position, in which the production of meaning is supported by the *rupture* of univocity—by a revelation of the decentering of the subject— juxtaposes the Judeo-Catholic form of the sacred and the joke. It is in the space of the encounter between theology and the Freudian *Witz* that Joyce pursues in the *Wake* the venture of *Ulysses:* the merging of the sacred and the comic, through the doubled position appropriate to each of the two domains. The Jew repressed by Catholicism encounters the Catholic through paternity, and within an Irish context. The *Witz* brings together, on sacred territory—Judaic and Catholic, according to Joyce—the Jewish joke (Bloom's humor and Freud's precious collection of jokes in *The Joke and Its Relation to the Unconscious*)[17] and the comic tradition of Ireland. The resulting effect of "bewilderment and illumination"[18] traces the crossing, sexual and sacred, demoniacal and divine, from which a text issues forth:[19] *Finnegans Wake.* And a language of proper names: joyce.

8

The Resurrection

Although Joyce's allusions to the date (and the controversies) of Easter often do not explicitly name the Resurrection in order to bring into relief the Judaic/Irish resonance of the Passover, the specifically Catholic dimension of Easter is nevertheless sustained elsewhere in the *Wake*. The punctual event of the Resurrection is presented through its performative nomination as well as in the scriptural experience rooted, for Joyce, in the slippage of Holy Saturday—the wake through negativity: death, night, silence. The paschal stake of the Resurrection is posited from the beginning of the *Wake*, in Book I, 2, "The Ballad": "And not all the king's men nor his horses Will resurrect his corpus For there's no true speill . . . That's able to raise a Cain" (47.29). This conclusion of the chapter (and of the "Ballad of Persse O' Reilly") places Hce at the crossing of the nursery rhyme of Humpty Dumpty and the song of Resurrection: "and the canto was chantied there chorussed and christened where by the old tollgate, Saint Annona's Street and Church" (44.5). Humpty Dumpty, the broken egg, is the comical homologue of the Easter egg, whose fall ("the fallth of hampty damp" [619.8]) through negativity brings about the Resurrection. Because of denegation, the Resurrection presents itself as impossible: all the king's horses and all the king's men cannot bring about the Resurrection of the Christly body so essential to Christian worship. But since the Resurrection does take place in Book IV of the *Wake*, the denegation must be read otherwise. For the Resurrection of Christ is neither animal nor human. This Resurrection comes

128

from elsewhere. Far from reglueing the pieces of a body in which "being" is invested, it reveals the location *elsewhere* of being, its disengagement from the body—a position recapitulated in the *passage* itself of Easter and in the leap into celebration and jubilation founding its meaning. The Resurrection of the "corpus" takes its force from the Other, for whom the body is rather insignificant when compared to the radiant body of Christ. Christ multiplies his *passage* in the infinity of transsubstantiation, forever engaging the symbolic power of God in the crossing of perceived substances (bread and wine) by the Word in its essentially paschal form (the body and blood of Christ). This passage marks with its signature the overflow of the substances by the gift of this singular subjectivity; a symbolic gift (the Word) and a gift filled with miraculous love (grace): the Eucharist. The Resurrection is the proof and even the logical conclusion of this eucharistic grace becoming, in turn, the rite of rememoration of the singular event of the Resurrection. The unfolding of the paschal event overturns the original Fall and takes upon itself the weight of the culpability that made of Adam the first subject: "the corruptible lay quick . . . the common or ere-in-garden castaway in red resurrection to condemn so they might convince him . . . Humpheres Cheops Exarchas, of their proper sins" (62.18).

Hce is simultaneously Adam and Christ (the second Adam). Although he bears the culpability of others as scapegoat, he is still personally guilty. Contrary to Christly purity, Hce as *father* has tainted all of humanity and dragged it down in his fall: "The great fall of the offwall entailed . . . the pftjschute of Finnegan" (3.30), "he's such a grandfallar" (29.6), "He was fafafather of all schemes for to bother us" (45.15). Since his fall into culpability, Hce's symptom has made him "fafafather": he stutters. This defect, the object of scorn, wounds Hce in his paternity itself, and constitutes the Joycean dramatization of the compulsion to repetition. Where repression condemns the subject to repetition without rememoration, Hce subjected to his condemned and repressed concupiscence repeats not an act but a syllable. He breaks his words into fractions as his desiring body was broken into pieces at the moment of his sacrifice: "they have torn him limb from lamb" (58.7). On the subject of the primal scene, equally repressed,

he stutters his protests of innocence just as other voices tirelessly and serially repeat the questions, interpretations, and
hypotheses of what happened between Hce and Alp (or the
girls) at the moment of this originating scene. The compulsion to repetition is demoniacal because of its automatism and
because of what it reveals, little by little, in *Finnegans Wake:*
the fall of Hce into desire. The domain of concupiscence, of
sin, coincides with that of death: Joyce displays, through Hce,
the two sides of the Catholic experience, the Fall into the
kingdom of the devil and the divine Resurrection, the profane and the sacred. Joyce successfully brings the two together in his representation of the multiple subject Hce, particularly in Book IV. The ambivalence of the Ballad as regards
the Resurrection—does it take place or not?—brings out the
necessary doubling of Joyce's Catholic position and, at the same
time, the path must be cleared through the negativity founding symbolic *jouissance:* the underground of sublimation.
Jouissance is sustained by the position maintaining even unto
death the opening toward the Other: Job takes this role upon
himself, and Joyce echoes his text in "Oxen of the Sun" (*U*
383) as in the first love letter to Martha Fleischmann.[1] Job
enunciates his position in pain and mourning: "Naked came
I out of my mother's womb, and naked shall I return thither:
the LORD gave, and the LORD hath taken away; blessed be
the name of the LORD" (Job 1:21). Hurt in his paternity by
the adversary (Satan, the cad, etc.), Hce takes on the role of
Job: his resurrection, like Job's victory, is the effect of a resurgence through pain and mourning of this same paternity, with
its element of *impossible* experience with respect to substance
or to nature. One of Hce's names bears witness to this impossibility, including an echo of the paschal egg: "Hatches Cocks'
Eggs" (71.27).

The experience of the return or the effects of paternity
established by the Resurrection implies a miraculous springing-forth, a *revelation,* a *vision.* (As shown by Mary Magdalene,
the Resurrection is audible and visible, if not completely tangible.) In Book I, 4, "The Lion," an avatar of Shaun ("an eye,
ear, nose and throat witness" [86.32]—a doctor resembling
Gogarty-Mulligan) is questioned about the lion, Hce: "As to
his religion, if any? It was the see-you-Sunday sort. Exactly

what he meant by a pederast prig? Bejacob's, just a gent who prayed his lent" (89.13). These prayers precede the Resurrection. The displacement of the holy day of the week—from Saturday, the Jewish Sabbath, to Sunday (the day when Christians see each other in church) marks the attempt at differentiation on the part of Christians, and thus the break with Judaic customs. On the other hand, the answer to the question of "Religion?" (to which Joyce, at Trieste, answers: "Senza")[2] describes the man in question as a "Sunday Catholic." This Catholicism so lightly taken, presented in a comic manner, allows a glimpse of a more serious dimension, manifested through a visual element—"*see*-you-Sunday sort"—in which the three s's act as an oblique reminder of "filiu*s* et *s*piritu *s*ancti": Hce's Catholicism. This description evokes the fulgurant vision of the resuscitated and luminous Christ. This light assimilates pagan sun worship, but nonetheless it represents a Catholic symbol of the light produced by the emergence of truth in its most beautiful and truest form: the Word.

The Catholic *vision* is underlined elsewhere regarding the Resurrection. In the question on Finn MacCool (Book I, 6, "Questions and Answers"), the enigma of Hce's identity is uttered: "the *w*eibduck *w*ill *w*ail bitternly over the *rotter's resurrection*: loses weight in the *moon night* but *girds girder* by the *sundawn*" (138.34; author's italics). Joyce focuses on Hce's resurrection as the pivot between nocturnal negativity and the eclipse of substance and the day of Easter, allowing the resurgence of substance with the light that renders a *vision* of it possible. At the same time, the displacement of the Judaic Saturday toward the Christian Sunday manifests itself through an allusion to another transition[3]—that of the moon, strategically crucial in the religion of Semitic nomads[4] (and leaving traces in Judaism), to the pagan-Christian sun. As "sundawn," it signals the Resurrection. The Resurrection takes on a comic tone, since its subject is a "rotter" (189.18), the slang term for a disagreeable person, with overtones of decay, non-sense, the "bosh" associated with the passible character of Shem in Book I, 7. From a stylistic point of view, this passage is remarkable for its alliteration, the repetition of consonants suggesting a "root language."[5] The alliteration evokes the roots of Hebrew (and other Semitic tongues) and thus the *origin* of Catholicism in the Old Testament; on the other hand, it alludes to the alliteration of Anglo-Saxon poetry at the origin of the English language. Hce's individual language can also be heard here. The series of repeated consonants seem evocative of his stuttering; the defect that marks his paternity with its *original* aspect. Hce, or the roots of the Resurrection: points of origin and forms of language are transformed at the privileged moment, encoded by the opposition of moon and sun, of invisible and visible. The latter, thanks to the *Lumen Christi,* has become a *vision.*

The Resurrection is *announced* in the *Wake* as it is in Catholicism—by the return of the bells after their silent trajectory. In the liturgy, following the mourning of Holy Week, the Gloria, bells, and organs put this jubilation into music. In the "Clangalied" sequence of Book IV, the girls' voices celebrating Kevin are compared to the ringing bells of Dublin churches (whose names are feminized by Joyce, in order to underline the metaphorization). The meaning of this "clangalied" is further explicated in Book III, 4 ("the Fourth Watch of Shaun"), not far from the staging of the Resurrection in Book IV. The Resurrection is invoked; Hce is called by several of his names and the joyous ringing of bells is anticipated: "Mbv! The annamation of evabusies, the livlianess of her laughings, such as a plurity of bells!" (568.4). "Me amble duty to your grace's majers! Arise, sir Pompkey Dompkey! Ear! Ear! Weakear!" (568.25). "Carilloners will ring their gluckspeels. Rng rng! Rng rng! S. Presbutt-in-the-North, S. Mark Underloop, S. Lorenz-by-the-Toolechest, . . . (*etc.*)" (569.4). "How chimant in effect! Alla tinaling pealabells! So a many of churches one cannot pray own's prayers. 'Tis holyyears day!" (569.11). The invocation to Earwicker/Humpty Dumpty (Hce) passes through the ear that names him (*Ear*wicker) and that becomes the imperative of listening: "(H)ear!" The focus of the liturgical cycle ("holyyears day") will be marked by the call of feminine voices, and thus the calling of Alp's voice—animated, laughing, a "plurity of bells." These are still the bells of Dublin churches inscribing Alp with her sacred monogram, BVM ("Mbv"). As the Virgin, she combines the wife and daughters of Hce, the voices of bells, the churches, and the ultimate feminine presence infinitized by the Church. The "liquid"[6] presence of Alp is transmitted in onomatopoetic English: the L's and R's sound the bells of the Resurrection ("Carilloners . . . ring . . . gluckspeels. Rng rng! Rng rng! . . . chimant . . . tingaling pealabells").

Weaving into this music is the cockcrow, signal of the end of the nocturnal vigil, announcement of the new day; enunciation and song, the Joycean cockcrow becomes a voice of jubilation at the dawn of the Resurrection. It is heard above all in Book IV, celebrating the Resurrection that takes place there: "Conk a dook he'll doo" (595.30), "kirikirikiring" (612.11), "Cockalooralooraloomenos" (615.8), "Ericoricori coricome huntsome" (623.1). Violent, musical, repetitive, the cockcrow signs its last form Ech. Returning, it welcomes the last speech of the book—that it has itself rendered possible— when Alp's apostrophe marks the creation/dissolution of a feminine discourse as the end of the night or as the threshold between night and day. Joyce talks out his singular femininity: maternal incest with the dying mother; rape, desire, and maternity; paternal incest with the daughter locked in his own image. He constitutes his last instance of resurrection and of paternity by taking sexual scandal and culpability to their limits. Out of them he bodies forth a voice whose word vacillates between desire and disappearance, between identity and the *swoon* that overflows its boundaries: the infinitized voice of the subject caught between birth and death, creation and undoing. Alp or Job speaks through a woman's body: "When I came down out of me mother" (627.8), "And it's old and old . . . I go back to you, my cold father" (627.36), "My leaves have drifted from me" (628.6), "Take. . . . Given!" (628.14), "We might call on the Old Lord," "His is house of laws" (623.11). ("Naked came I out of my mother's womb, and naked shall I return thither: the LORD gave, and the LORD hath taken away; blessed be the name of the LORD.")

The very beginning of Book IV names the Resurrection by way of reference to the visual phenomena of the light of day and the auditory "daylight" produced in the calls, cries, and ringing bells: "Array! Surrection! Eireweeker to the wohld bludyn word. O rally, O rally, O rally! Phlenxty, O rally! . . . Haze sea east to Osseania. Here! Here! . . . Calling all danes to dawn. . . . The eversower of the seeds of light . . . Pu Nuseht, lord of risings . . . speaketh" (593.14). "Array Surrection" proceeds orally ("calling . . . O rally . . . speaketh"), through the call to Hce—Eireweeker, Phlenxty (the phoenix?), Haze sea east (= Hce). The sun (the suN uP), god of risings, god of dawns, is also the God of the bewildering and luminous Word—the creator of puns: *PuN useth.*[7] The conjunction of nominative permutations of Hce and the Resurrection gives a Joycean version of the Resurrection: it passes through the ear—in French: *perce l'oreille,* or Persse O' Reilly. Hce is the fiction incarnate pierced by its Christly trajectory. Persse O'Reilly, or how Joyce takes possession of Christian truth. The Resurrection (beginning with the future perfect of death) makes of James A. Joyce, scripturally signed, a "radiant body"[8] offered up in the dream, or in the apocalyptic vision, or in the prophetic revelation, that is *Finnegans Wake.*

The *Wake* text circulates a certain number of names and symbols associated with the Resurrection: the eggs, the cockcrow, the phoenix, the bells, the opposition between night and day. These images unveil the status of Catholicism in the Joycean experience. They accentuate the intimate link between the Christly trajectory and Joyce's vision. *Finnegans Wake* is a paschal book, not in the sense of thematic unity but rather in the sense of an interpretation of the symbolic enterprise. Since any interpretation is partial, especially with respect to a book of the proportions of the *Wake,* one cannot totalize *one* reading, one possible weave, one series of signifying networks. Judeo-Christianity, however, and particularly its paschal episodes play a fundamental role in Joyce's work—they leave an imprint on the symbolic organization of the writing: vision and hearing (Shaun and Shem); sacrifice and resurrection (Hce); sin, life, letters (Alp). From the doubled Passover emerge the elements, the figures, the series of nominative positions of Joycean eschatology. The performative of the Resurrection is supported by the negative dimensions of the Fall, of death, etc. The ambivalence of the "Wake" (death and waking) and of the *Wake* (i.e., of the text of countless oppositions—thematic, syntactic, etymological, etc.) is profoundly *paschal* in this sense. Perhaps this explains why Joyce so heavily emphasizes Holy Saturday, with its telescoping of mourning and festivity. The *oxymoron* crystallizes the paschal experience, and, with it, the writing of Joyce.

The oxymoron of the *felix culpa* filtered through the song of "Finnegan's Wake" introduces the paschal couple, death, and resurrection: "your phumeral's a roselixion" (346.13). Joyce makes the passage through death into a resurrection that resonates as an elixir, the eucharistic quintessence leading to eternity (the elixir of long life) and the heavenly rose of Dante's vision toward the end of the *Paradiso*. Joyce moves from the ardent flowering of the *Portrait* through the Marian roses of Molly Bloom toward the Dantean "roselixion." His trajectory always indicates a double position—drive and sublimation, decline and an "other" *jouissance*—within Catholicism. Love and languages, the scriptural rose opens before Joyce and names his resurrection in *Finnegans Wake*.

In Book IV, this double position is integrated in the revelation of the Resurrection.[9] The sinner's profane terror and the sacred jubilation are intimately mingled; the eclipse and the emergence of a divine presence make the subjective experience of the Resurrection into a radical separation from what took place before it, a cut and a re-beginning: "Endee he sendee. Diu! The has goning at gone, the is coming to come. . . . Doom is the faste" (598.9). The "he" who sent the End gave the Law and the splendor of the Last Judgment (*le faste*) that is also the fast of the paschal watch ended at the moment of the cockcrow. The disappearance/appearance (the *symbolic* function) of the apostrophized God (who is partially castrated of his name, like Osiris bereft of his sex) reveals the intermediary status of the Joycean position, its interlace of a doubled disappearance ("goning at gone") followed by a doubled appearance ("coming to come") marking the subject's loss and *jouissance*. Loss and *jouissance* are recorded in the tongue-become-text, or in the textualized fiction of the language created by Joyce. The lost e's of *God* (Dieu) and *Thee* are found in "Endee he sendee," the letter He sends at the end. What would this eschatological end be, stemming from the Resurrection, if not the "the" whose subtle breath ends the letter Joyce sends to us, *Finnegans Wake*? Only a few pages before this final "the," here figured as a form of address to the Other, Alp announces to Hce the arrival of the phoenix that he is no longer and that he will be again: "It's Phoenix, dear. And the flame is, hear! . . . Since the lausafire has lost and the book of the depth is. Closed. Come! Step out of your shell!" (621.1) Lucifer's failure indicates the revelation to come as *jouissance*. The book of the deep and the dead is closing. Divine victory embraces Satan's failure in the book ending with the Resurrection. Like the Bible, ending with the vision of the Apocalypse, beyond which there is neither death nor night; or like the *Divina Commedia*, concluding with the vision of paradise. The end of the negative dimension is the end of the text. The path of symbolic *jouissance* stops there, having said its last "Yes," having uttered its last breath: "the."

Joyce renders explicit the paschal and eschatological weight of his writing through the character of Shem. The latter represents, often via parody, the writer as Joyce conceived of himself—including biographical elements, desires, and acts of writing—in his relation to the letter, and to languages. Shem is dramatized most frequently by Shaun. At the end of Book I, 7, "Shem," a confrontation between the twins takes place through the double monologue opposing Justius to Mercius. The whirlwind of fraternal identities seems to be focused on the Word; Shaun's position, his jealousy, may be interpreted as the desire to write rather than to deliver the letter. For if Shaun incarnates (in a parodic representation, of course) the Christ of the Passion and the founder of the Church, it is still Shem who incarnates the Word. Shaun-Justius utters a series of bitter reproaches (more *Improperia*, perhaps) against his Christly twin crucified on the cross of fiction: "to let you have your Sarday spree and holinight sleep (fame would come to you twixt a sleep and a wake) and leave to lie till Paraskivee and the cockcock crows for Danmark" (192.19). "Do you hear what I'm seeing, hammet?" (193.10). Holy Saturday is the privileged moment of Shem's activity, as indicated by the holiday intoxication and sleep mentioned here. Between the sleep and the wake—between Christ's descent from the cross and his Resurrection, the heterogeneity of Holy Saturday operates a slippage. Shem here resembles Joyce, with his nights of alcohol and writing. Renown came to him between the publication of *Ulysses* and the writing of *Finnegans Wake*, between Molly's sleep and the wake of Finnegan.

Shaun assigns to Shem's Christly voyage a particular temporal sequence. After Good Friday, he intends to leave his brother in bed until the *Parascève* (Good Friday, the death or sleep of Christ) followed by the cockcrow of the Resurrection, the "wake." Shem will not wake up till Good Friday of the following year—or perhaps never: Shaun could then retrieve the Christly role he desires and estimates wrongly usurped from him by his brother. Shaun leaves Shem *to lie:* to create lies, fictions, plagiarized signatures, scriptures.

According to the time/space division opposing them, Shem hears where Shaun sees: "Do you hear what I'm seeing, hammet?" Shaun in Book III resembles the Watch who see the specter of the king at the beginning of *Hamlet*. The specter only makes himself *heard* by Hamlet. This hearing or transmission of a voice going beyond all limits to make itself heard founds paternity. Shem-Hamlet, through the utterance of Mercius, will describe the meaning of this paternity given by Hce, as well as the consequences of the unique power of hearing that is his. Joyce himself, following Hamlet and formulating Shem, acts as the subject of paternity, through the symbolic transmission of a voice according to the terms attributed to Stephen Dedalus: "A mystical estate, an apostolic succession" (*U* 207). Joyce told Eugene Jolas: "I hear my father talking to me. I wonder where he is."[10] He wrote to Harriet Weaver: "It seems to me his voice has somehow got into my body or throat. Lately, more than ever."[11] In *Finnegans Wake,* Joyce stages the two structural possibilities of paternal transmission. As resuscitated creator, Hce is invested with paternity. But for Hce dead, the transmission has already occurred (like that from John to William Shakespeare, according to Stephen [*U* 207])—as seen in the monologue of Mercius. Regarding verbal, Catholic paternity (opposed to temporal paternity, Shaun's worldly or military power), the transmission takes place for Shem ("hammet"[12]) the penman.

In his monologue, Shem-Mercius explicates paternity and its transmission according to a specifically Wakeian framework incorporating a Trinitarian model: "now ere the compline hour of being alone athands itself and a puff or so before we yield our spiritus to the wind, for (though that royal one has not yet drunk a gouttelette from his consummation . . . and the public house proprietor have not budged a millimetre and all that has been done has yet to be done and done again, when's day's woe, and lo, you're doomed, joyday dawns and, la, you dominate)" (194.4). In parentheses, Shem adumbrates the artist's detachment, maintained with relation to the narrative elements of *Finnegans Wake* (and, in particular, to those of BookI,2, concluding with a sung commentary: the latter bears Shem's mark as well, including the characteristic distance imposed by aesthetic creation). Shem refers to Hce in his pub as king and in the entire series awaiting them in Joyce's tongue. The generalized sacrifice for which Shaun is responsible will be countered by the final gesture of Mercius, when he points the wand. If Shaun is the adversary, the purveyor of death, Shem is the purveyor of Resurrection.

At the same time, the sacrifice of Shem ordained by Justius-Shaun puts Shem in the Christlike position; the moment of his eclipse anchors him in the Trinitarian model and in the fiction of the *Wake* (beginning with the song of "Finnegan's Wake"). The configurations of Shaun and Shem unite in that of Hce-Finnegan, victim/transmitter of death and resurrection—Catholic and Irish, true and comic. Shem alludes to Hce's last supper, the cup and the Christly consumption. The Crucifixion takes place the day "when"—the day of time, or temporal preparation of the Resurrection point. This "woe" of time lasts until the dawn of the day of the Resurrection: "joyday dawns." The present tense of Shem-Mercius' enunciation anticipates . . ."the compline hour," the last hour of the divine rite. This hour marks the liturgical entry into night and the final hour of the life of Christ. The remarks of Mercius seem to be partly based on John 19:28–30, i.e., the accomplishment of the Scriptures, the "consummation" of Christ (the vinegar he is given to drink) and his death. This passage ends with the last word of Christ: "*Consummatum est. Et inclinato capite tradidit spiritum.*" The "consummation" of the "royal one" clearly refers to the Johannine context, following "and a puff or so before we yield our spiritus to the wind," alluding to the giving up of the "*spiritum.*" But the words *puff, spiritus,* and *wind* seem to translate in three different ways the Hebrew *ruah*—the creating Spirit, at the source of languages—art, according to Joyce. Shem at the edge of death is the *Word:* which means that he will make death into a path of pilgrimage ending in the *Resurrection,* i.e., a sublime *jouissance* uncompromised by any quirk of nature (chance, uncertainty), corporeality, or sinful drive. The Resurrection entails a permanent state of grace, an unlimited gift of tongues, a beginning without end. At this Judeo-Catholic juncture, Joyce announces art: the gift of tongues.

Shem's monologue alludes to that other death omnipresent in Joyce's writing—that of the mother, fictionalized as the mother of Stephen Dedalus: "to me unseen blusher in an obscene coalhole . . . dweller in the downandoutermost where voice only of the dead may come, because ye left from me, because ye laughed on me, because, O me lonly son, ye are forgetting me!, that our turfbrown mummy is acoming, alpilla, beltilla, ciltilla, deltilla, running with her tidings, old the news of the great big world" (194.17). Shem situates himself in the blackness of obscenity, perhaps in a Dantean *Inferno* filled with the voices of the dead. Like Stephen in "Circe," he is in the realm of fantasy and vision, sexuality, and apocalypse. At the beginning of *Ulysses,* maternal death raises questions of love, sin, creation, and the Trinity; these questions are drawn together by Stephen's experience of the Catholic and scriptural problematic. In *Finnegans Wake,* this problematic founds the role of Shem: here Joyce leaves behind the blank-paged anticipation of Stephen in order to stage a portrait of the young artist *who writes—Ulysses,* and even *Finnegans Wake.*

In *Ulysses,* the knot of flesh, sin, love, and creation allows Stephen to bring forth his (anticipated) writing as the intermediary between abject death and holy ritual. Its starting point is the prayer for the dying that haunts him throughout Bloomsday: *Liliata rutilantium te confessorum turma circumdet: iubilantium te virginum chorus excipiat.* This prayer is anagrammatized twice in Book I, 3, "The Goat." Reference is made to Hce and two girls responsible for his fall: "(the consummatory pairs of provocatives, of which remained provokingly but two, the ones he fell for, *Lili and Tutu, cork'em!*) . . . (you ruad that before, soaky" (52.1; author's italics). The page is covered with allusions to Communion, bottles of stout, pregnancy, and the Incarnation: the focus is on Christ's consumation and the *ruah*. Joyce writes: you already read that—in *Ulysses:* the prayer has become the intermediary between death and grace in Hce's fall and the writing of *Finnegans Wake*.

A few pages later, Shem's writing is interpreted as an illumination from the Book of Kells. The subject is "the coffin, a triumph of the illusionist's art" (66.28); there is an establishment selling "funeral requisites" (66.34). In the text, someone asks why the latter are necessary, and is answered: "Because the *flash brides* or *bride* in their *lily* boleros . . . and your upright grooms . . . what else in this mortal world, now ours, when meet there night, mid their nackt, me there naket, made their nought the hour strikes, would bring them rightcame back in the flesh" (66.36, author's italics). *Liliata* ("lily") *rutilantium* ("flash") *virginum* ("brides" or "bride"): in this symbolic context, the rotting Mrs. Dedalus appeared, dressed like a bride, to the "mortal world" of "Circe." Stephen here encounters night, his own nudity as nocturnal subject, and apocalyptic negativity at the end of time: "made their nought the hour strikes." Through this nocturnal scripture, moreover, he encounters the Resurretion as such: "Would bring them rightcame back in the flesh." The prayer-become-writing (by Stephen/Shem) leads to the Resurrection figured, in *Ulysses,* through the vision of the mother. In the *Wake*, this progression is rendered explicit, in part because the No uttered in response to the institution no longer comes into play between Stephen/Shem and the mother as in *Ulysses*. The refusal now takes place between Shem and Shaun. On the other hand, it is through Shem that Joyce reveals the enterprise of his own writing; rather than reinventing the mother's visibility, he resuscitates her in the enunciation itself, that of Shem-Mercius: "because ye left from me, because ye laughed on me, because, O my lonly son, ye are forgetting me!" The speaking voice here seems to be that of Alp, interrupting the monologue that precedes and follows the three "because" clauses of her speech.[13] Or, rather, it is Shem who recovers or intercepts the feminine enunciation of his mother and makes it heard in his own words—just as the innumerable anecdotes of "gossipaceous Anna Livia" (195.4) become the "tales" that Shem puts into serial form in the *Wake*. Shem's letter-work, the illuminations of the Book of Kells-become-writing—his *style*—finds its origin (the cause of its being: "because") in the alphabet offered by Alp: "that our turfbrown mummy is acoming, alpilla, beltilla, ciltilla, deltilla, running with her tidings." The tide is composed of news, or words—she (*illa*), the *alp*habet, the letter (a, b, c, d). Shem makes her talk, operating the Resurrection of the Word: "he lifts the lifewand and the dumb speak" (195.5). In *Finnegans Wake*, Joyce intercepts *paternal transmission* (Fall and Resurrection, comic and sacred) in the intersection of love and the symbolic. The eroticizing of the letter, the feminine (maternal) enunciation, seem to be close to the nocturnal language that Joyce wants to make his own in style, in "joyce," as it is spoken since the scripture of Molly's illuminated and illuminating voice. Her monologue announces the Resurrection of the *Wake:* in the middle of the night, she ends her enunciation in a shower of roses, colors, sunrays become her own illumination: "The sun shines for you" (*U* 782). Of course, in this illumination of the Resurrection, it is Joyce himself who comes into focus, having become an illumination in his own words: "scribings scrawled on eggs" (615.10), or paschal writing. The case rests with his treatment of folklore concerning the sun of the Resurrection.[14] In *Ulysses*, Molly alludes to the superstitions of Mrs. Rubio: "All her miracles of the saints and her black blessed virgin with the silver dress and the sun dancing 3 times on Easter Sunday' (*U* 759). But in *Finnegans Wake*, it is Joyce himself, "Jambs," who writes (himself into) the Catholic dance of the sun—the paschal *jouissance* of the Word. The fifty-two-year-old Joyce ("trippudiating round the aria with his fifty-two heirs of age!" [513.22]) in the process of writing *Finnegans Wake* sees himself as the Christly sun mentioned by Dante at the end of the *Divina Commedia*, the end of the *Paradiso:* "Dawncing the kniejinsky choreopiscopally like an easter sun round the colander, the vice!" (513.11). The dance of writing—paschal *jouissance*—marks this day of Resurrection as a Joycean festival.

For after all, the Resurrection in *Finnegans Wake* takes place under Joyce's ("Borsalino") hat: "in the bonze age of anteproresurrectionism to entrust their easter neapearrance to Borsaiolini's house of hatcraft" (483.10). In the call "Array! Sur-rection!" of Book IV, Joyce sounds the biblical call in which he heard the beauty of the English language, its suppleness and power;[15] *arise,* or *be resurrected.* Alp foreshadows her en-counter with Hce at the end of the text: "To scand the aris-ing" (623.26).[16] Language and letter, she rhythmically scans this Resurrection in which Joyce says to Hce, Word and flesh, *arise in me.* Joyce says to languages, and especially to English: arise in my language, give me this day the gift of tongues that I might scan the Resurrection where it occurs—in the wet place of the "wake," in the driven tracings of language. This joy in tongues—"joyance," "joyicity" (598.25, 414.23)—brings the festivities of dance and, especially, song into the excla-mations of joy (*io,* the exclamation point)[17] or the intonations of exclamation that saturate the text, particularly Book IV. The exclamation point translates the call of the Resurrection into rising intonation, musical *crescendo.* This call is presented in *Finnegans Wake* as the end of *passage,* the paschal experi-ence: the spoken wake leading from the mourning and grief of death to the joyful clamor of Resurrection.

9

Name, Meaning, and Time
The Paschal Enunciation

In *Finnegans Wake,* paschal symbolism becomes the vehicle for the Judeo-Catholic meaning that saturates the text. Moreover, religious discourse enters into the domain of the textual subject; it becomes a personalized utterance. In this text—Joyce's recovery[1] or capture of the words, voices, languages surrounding him—the symbolic systems themselves are presented in the form of enunciations. The paschal festival is read and heard in the act of enunciation that gives voice to the original consecration. In Book III, 4, voyeurs (the washerwomen?) describe the last act of intercourse between Hce and Alp; it is a tragicomic failure, an unconsummated prelude to the successful and true consummation of Book IV. The following enigmatic remark is made: "We're parring all Oogster till the empsyseas run googlie" (584.8). The reference to Hce (the egg) or, rather, to his paternity is named as "Easter"; the reference to Alp recalls the sea, now emptied. At this moment (584–585) the cockcrow is heard, as if to indicate the departure from death and the entry into the revealed and apocalyptic world: into the Joycean re-writing of the text of the Revelation. In this world according to the Resurrection, all will have made the Christly voyage through carnal death toward the "arising" in the flesh of the Scriptures, in symbolicity—the radiant body of the Word: "wuck to doodledoo," "Cocorico!" "Echolo choree choroh choree cho-

ree chorico!" (584.22–585.4). This song to come (of "shan-
tyqueer," "cock of the morgans" [584.21, .25]) inspires Joyce's
listening ear: "Echo," "Echolo." The song delivers Hce intact,
resuscitated in the joy of Easter morning, anagrammatized
and signed Ech. The increasingly joyous enunciation foreshadows that which will become the final book of the *Wake*.

Hce is again central to the unfolding of the paschal enunciation in Book II, 3, "The Scene in the Pub," and particularly
in the story of the Norwegian captain. The latter is an avatar
of Hce: "Howe cools Eavybrolly!" (315.20). He seems to wish
a happy Easter to the Dubliners around him: "With a good
eastering and a good westering" (315.26). The specifically
paschal tenor of this enunciation is partially hidden by the
reference to the opposition of east and west. However, the
latter manifests itself as internal to the paschal event. In the
Wake (and even since the writing of "The Dead") east and west
encode birth and death—paschal heterogeneity, recapitulated in the liturgy of Holy Saturday. In the text of the *Wake*,
the split Hce is simultaneously the Norwegian captain and the
innkeeper, or "the shop's housebound" (the ship's husband)
in conflict with him: "And he got and gave the ekspedient for
Hombreyhambrey wilcomer what's the good word. He made
the sign on the feaster. Cloth be laid!" (317.6, .9). The Easter
enunciation includes the "good news," that of the *Verbum* ("the
good word"), as it slips toward the sign of the Cross: *verba et
mystica signa crucis.*[2] This signature is signed in communion,
whose first instance, the Last Supper, founds the intermediary regions between Judaism and Christianity: the Last Supper is both Passover and Easter. In addition, Joyce's "Easter"
become "feaster" recalls the essential quality of Passover, the
feast par excellence.[3] Joyce stresses the split in the paschal
celebration, scanning the text with a repetition, a movement
of opening and closing; the Judeo-Christian split paradoxically founds the unity of Joyce's paschal moment. In this sense,
Hce's doubles seem to merge at the end of the sequence of
the Norwegian captain. Bruno's Hermetic principle of multiplicity moving toward unity is formulated on the level of the
Joycean enunciation and then in Joycean *nomination*, insofar
as the latter maintains series of oppositions and divisions by
integrating them within the proper names that are the core

of *Wake* symbolicity. Meaning, dispersed according to these oppositions, is ultimately guaranteed only by the name as proper name. The presence of Passover/Easter as the signature of the Judeo-Christian subject is anchored in the enunciations of the *name* of the paschal holiday. The Joycean enunciation is an elaboration of the proper name.

The name of the holiday is assimilated into Hce's name at several points of the text. The Judeo-Catholic dimension of the sacred lends itself to the subject of the name: the latter becomes the subject of paternity. Here Hce finds his tongue, his voice and the possibility of invoking God: "You invoiced him last Eatster so he ought to give us hockockles and everything" (623.7). The paschal invocation revolves around this divine paternal gift of the *name*. It is the symbolic nourishment ("Eatster") of a God whose offering to Hce is described as "*hockockles and everything*," i.e., his own *invocation*. Its ritual repetition maintains the sacred-comic relation constituting the text. Starting with "hce," the Father makes a gift to Hce of his name as proper, or singular. Alp says: "His is house of laws" (623.11).

The condensation of Hce's name with the name of Easter is rendered explicit on three occasions. In Book III, 3, Yawn names his father: "—Hunkalus Childared Easterheld" (480.20). This passage alludes to the Irish converted by Saint Patrick.[4] Hce is present as a pagan father become Christian. At the same time, he is the father threatening his sons,[5] the Dubliner (Scandinavian pagan and, like Saint Patrick, Gallic Christian). The uncle-child-hero of Easter surely has some affinities with the triple Catholic nomination: in the Name of . . . Hce. At the beginning of Book III, 4, this Trinitarian Dubliner is related to the Virgin, the daughter Isabel, and the married/widowed wife. The litany of Our Lady of Lorette can be heard: "Saint Holy and Saint Ivory," "tocher of davy's, tocher of ivileagh" (556.3, 557.10). Isabel is a nun, a saint, a widow: "on Holiday, Christmas, Easter mornings" (557.8). Hce, in his erotic context, is as Catholic as ever. The cycle of Christ, the paschal holiday, and the divine birth are represented at the crossroad of *desire* and the *proper name*. Whence the poetic liturgy of the litany of Our Lady of Lorette, well loved by Joyce. At the origin: the *Incarnation*. At the end of Book III, 4, allusion is made to "our all honoured Christmastyde easteredman" (590.21). The Catholic cycle is explicit. It begins at Christmas and ends at Easter, as the trajectory leading from the Incarnation to the Resurrection. This passage insists on the *past* of Hce: he is honour*ed*, christmas*tyde*, easter*ed*. Hce is dead; he only exists in the form of a past participle. This is the last page before the IV of the Resurrection.

Easter is the proper name attached to the subject of paternity, Hce. So begins his paschal identity. His fate is intimately linked to the name of Easter, overflowing the boundaries of his own name. In the passages just discussed here, the two names are inseparable. Hce becomes the paschal subject; in the final book of the *Wake*, Hce emerges as the *present tense* of Easter.

Given this extraordinary merging of the Name of the Father Hce—or of the Nomination of the Father, starting with the monogram HCE—with Passover/Easter as the proper name of the Judaic and Christian festival—of the Trinitarian experience of symbolicity—we may pose the question of the meaning of this Passover in *Finnegans Wake*. In a sense, this question has already been asked since it threads its way through the confrontation of the Joycean text with the Judaic and Catholic texts. But the integration of Judeo-Christian paschal meaning in the *Wake* occurs not only on the level of biblical and theological discourse, but also on the level of names themselves. For Joyce, Passover/Easter is the proper name as a symbol (or a condensation) of eschatology.

The paschal name

The name of Passover, *pesah,* is of uncertain etymological origin. Several hypotheses have been proposed: "to spare," "to limp around something," no doubt referring to the gesture of the Exterminating Angel in Exodus 12:13. In biblical Hebrew, *pesah* becomes a ritual dance ("to hop," "to leap"). Two forms are found in Egyptian: pa-śh', "the memory," and P'sh, "the blow."[6] These attempts at etymological explanation seem to confirm the meaning of the text of Exodus. The divine event, the leap of the plague of destruction, allow mortal violence to be sidetracked. Jubilation is the consequence of this act of sparing, as is the divine commandment of rememoration.

The leap, the act of "passing over" that spares the Israelites thanks to the blood become symbol, is the first element of the meaning of Passover/Easter. This leap is remembered each year in ritual joy, "a feast to the Lord" (Exod. 12:14). The second element of the celebration, the one that traditionally defines or identifies Passover, is the lamb ("the passover"; Exod. 12:21) sacrificed and eaten according to prescribed ritual. According to H. Haag, the ritual repetition of this element is a "memorial," a "sacramental representation":[7] Jewish ritual is replaced in Christian worship by the Eucharist (the memorial of the Passion). The third element of the meaning of Passover can be read as the "leap," the "blow," the "passing beyond," that constitute the going out of Egypt. According to the biblical text, the death that strikes the Egyptians (but spares the Hebrews, because of the signs marking their dwellings— thus the "passover") motivates the expulsion of the Hebrews. The latter represent the power of *death*, expelled during the *night* by the Egyptians. This night is celebrated as vigil or wake: "It *is* a night to be much observed unto the LORD for bringing them out from the land of Egypt: this *is* that night of the LORD to be observed of all the children of Israel in their generations" (Exod. 12:42). Forever after.

The holy wake is the trajectory through death. One enters into wandering as into a journey through the symbolic: the OED gives one definition of *passage* as the entry into a violent and amorous relation—into the holy Word, beyond any terrain or country. For the Jew, henceforth, the only "proper" (specific) place will be the enunciation, in the past, future, *present*, of Passover: "The Lord intervened for me, when *I* went out of Egypt."[8] According to the Mishna, the celebration of the going out of Egypt is elaborated around the utterance of this sentence. It is in this sense a second "passover," passage above/around. The interval of a leap constitutes itself in the departure from the country of death, i.e., paganism. In the departure from the *world*, since Judeo-Christianity rejects it in favor of symbolic sublimation. The negation of the world, its figuration: a passage, the path cleared by words. The narrow opening into the otherwise "impassible" or impossible domain of the real. This experience of passage, of the departure from Egypt, resonates once again in the Catholic liturgy of Holy Saturday. It is the tracing of the Resurrection, interpreted from a negative angle, beginning with the abyss of death.

The three elements of paschal celebration, its ritual repetition, arrange themselves according to two significations: the passover to be eaten and the Passover as leap, departure, *passage*. This last signification is the heart of the meaning and the name of Passover/Easter; it determines the vocation of Israel. The passover to be eaten was originally a pre-Israelite ritual practiced by nomadic shepherds. In the text of Exodus, it becomes a Hebrew sacrament and allows for a narrative transition toward the elements of passage: the animal blood become proto-scripture or cross creates Judaic immunity to the tenth plague, thanks to the leap (Passover) of the Angel. This Passover is accomplished in the departure from Egypt that leads the Hebrews toward the symbolic relation with God, i.e., the Law. The Passover takes on the name of *passage*.

According to Christine Mohrmann,[9] the Catholic interpretation, Easter, is split into two positions. One of these we may interpret as originating in the pre-Israelite passover sacrifice (that will become a Hebrew sacrament, but within a symbolic structure rendered *other* in the terms of the vocation of Israel). The other position focuses on the passage of the Angel and the Exodus. Thus Passover/Easter (*pascha*) is interpreted as either *Passion* or *Resurrection*. The two positions are elaborated according to two etymologies: *pascha* can be read as a proper name that is divided or split. Its symbolic identity produces either the subject of sacrifice or passion (*passio, pati*)— i.e., a subject who disappears—or the subject of passage (*transitus*), who emerges in the enunciation of an *I*, through death. Emergence, appearance, revelation, accomplishment: Resurrection.

Philo of Alexandria advocates and transmits the ancient Judaic tradition; he interprets Passover as passage (Exod. 12) and refers to the passage from Egypt.[10] Augustine rejects *passio* in favor of *transitus*.[11] He refers to John 13:1, the explication of the Judaic etymology: "Now before the feast of the passover, when Jesus knew that his hour was come that he should depart out of this world unto the Father." Augustine writes, "It is thus the passage from this mortal life to another immortal life . . . that is represented in the passion and the resurrection of the Lord."[12] Augustine's emphasis on the paschal watch on Holy Saturday seems to confirm this interpretation. The *transitus* brings out the synthetic aspect of Passover, combining death and life, sadness and joy, Fall and Resurrection. The nocturnal, negative aspect of "transition" or *passage*—of the paschal wake—reveals the mystery of Passover. It is the accomplishment of the negation of the world, operated within the discourse of the subject. In Christ's passage from death to life, the subject sees its *own* singular passage from death to life. The mystical experience of the sacrament affects the subject who locates within it his *I*, his enunciation. His or her singular speech: a Revelation.

Joyce clearly follows the Philonian and Augustinian tradition. Only in Book II,4, "Mamalujo," does he name Passover as a Passion. Since the four Evangelists are the focus of this sequence, perhaps Joyce names the Passover as Passion in order to underline the relation between the *Wake* and the text of the Gospels (cf. the Book of Kells, particularly its dramatization of the Passion). But elsewhere in *Finnegans Wake*, i.e., outside the specifically evangelical context associated with "Mamalujo," Joyce writes the name of Easter as *passage*.

The Passion of the Four is located halfway between the sacred history of holy Scripture and the sexual scandals preserved as folklore and myth: "the subject being their passion grand" (394.24). Hce is present as "Earl Hoovedsoon's choosing" (394.27). The latter mixes his sexuality/paternity and his specifically Irish geography with the call of Judaic monotheism, the Shema: "wherebejubers in the pancosmic urge the allimmanence of that which Itself is Itself Alone (hear, O hear Caller Errin!)" (394.32). Hce, the Jew who is Christ, asks the question of the Trinity as a continuation of Jewish monotheism through the Passion: "perilwhitened passionplanting pugnoplangent intuitions of reunited selfdom . . . in the higher dimissional selfless Allself" (394.35). Joyce parodies religious discourse, especially that of theosophy. Nevertheless, he stages Passover as the Passion through the text of the Gospels: "fall-

ing over all synopticals and a panegyric and repeating themselves" (394.5). Joyce insists on the Passover named Passion as
concerns the role of the writer (Mamalujoyce?) captured, en-
tranced, between holiness and abjection, between sacred and
comic: the Passion of *Giacomo Joyce,* like that of the Four, wav-
ers between the symbolicity of the Christ's Passion and the
amorous passion of both the young man (his suffering/*jouissance*) and the incestuous, betrayed father[13] (King Mark, the
Four themselves). The intercourse of Tristan and Isolde,
watched by the Four, is encoded as *passion:* "the twooned to-
gethered, and giving the mhost phassionable wheathers"
(396.24).

The name of Passover/Easter briefly presents itself in the
Wake as the Passion: it sets off the paschal and Christian experience whose accomplishment is on the order of a *passage*.
As seen in *Giacomo Joyce,* desire maintained in a certain context makes a detour around pleasure and gives way before
sublimated *jouissance,* before the path of writing: the OED
defines *pass* as *to work a path, to cross, to go beyond, to pronounce.*
The passage in question recalls the *Wake* text and its beginnings in "Penelope," characterized by Joyce as *passport for eternity,* or *passage* (an undefined part of a speech, text, or musical
composition: a digression or remark [OED]). Molly's monologue—all digression, all enunciation, without beginning or
end—is the prelude to the indefinable writing of *Finnegans
Wake:* speech, music, paschal text.

The passage of the Word. Its crossing, *transitus,* or paschal
act, is implicated in a series of references to the passage of
Christ. In the staging of Shem's crucifixion (Book I, 7) Shaun
remarks: "(let him pass, pleasegoodjesusalem, in a bundle of
straw" (192.35). The passage and birth of Christ are named
in combination. In the following chapter, "Alp," the washerwomen gossip about the sexual relations between Hce and
Alp: "O, tell me all I want to hear, how loft she was lift a
laddery dextro! . . . Letting on she didn't care . . . him man in
passession, the proxenete!" (198.15). Hce in position pos-
sesses and *passes.* The confirmation of his passage rests with
the paschal antiphon joyously sung by Stephen at the entrance to "Circe,"[14] where his own passage occurs: "*a latere
dextro.*" At the end of Book III, 1, Shem confirms the pro-

foundly paschal sense of passage when he says: "thou are passing hence, mine bruder, able Shaun" (427.18). On the following page, a series of allusions to Shaun's return ends the chapter. Shaun's passage leads to his resurrection, in his Christly eschatology ("your own escapology" [428.21]): "Tis well we know you were loth to leave us . . . but . . . when the natural morning of your nocturne blankmerges into the national morning of golden sunup . . . you will shiff across the Moylend sea and round up in your own escapology some canonisator's day or other, sack on back, alack!" (428.14). The Resurrection of Book IV ("Pu nuseth, lord of risings . . . speaketh" [593.35]) is evoked in the morning of "golden sunup." The passage or Passover of eschatological return— cleared path, circuit, flow of time (OED)—gathers all of *Finnegans Wake* in its nets. This first Passover is unfolded by Shem (Shaun's double) in the form of Dave the Dancekerl, left in Shaun's place when the latter departs.

Dave has undergone "a blindfold passage by the 4.32" (462.35), echoing the paschal arrival of Saint Patrick in the year 432—a date that appears often in the *Wake* as the mark of the first celebration of Easter in Ireland. History and legend have made this date into the supreme moment of Christian *passage*. Patrick's opposition to the Druids is itself an act of passage: *transgression* of pagan interdictions, *exchange of communication, exchange of blows,*[15] *the tracing of a path* until then impassable. The paschal word *passes from the mouth; it is spoken,* once and for all time. This is the *transitus,* the conversion of Ireland. Passover composes a series: Moses, Christ, Saint Patrick . . .

And Joyce. Through the anonymous name of "Work in Progress," Joyce will inscribe the passage taken by his own Word. "Work in Progress" is the name of *Joycean passage* worked through writing since the arpeggioed "Yes" of Penelope. From this point on, the passage in question is a passage through nomination. The ersatz title of *Work in Progress* is nonetheless a true title, since it recovers writing as a *passage toward the absent name.* According to biographical evidence, Joyce directed his entourage toward the enigma of this absent name. The dénouement of this nomination is staged as a *revelation: Finnegans Wake,* name and writing, the wake of Passover/Easter.

This revelation is heard by a Catholic ear. In Book I, 2, "The Ballad," Hce's sin is discussed in church: "to ear the passon," in "his law language" (39.24). Joyce includes here another dimension of the verb *to pass: to discharge, pronounce, say legally* (OED). This passage from ear to mouth is repeated in Book III, 2, when Shem again describes Shaun's Christly itinerary: "your feat of passage" (473.14). But the passage in question is that of "Work in Progress" (or "Wip," as Joyce signs it monogrammatically in his correspondence) and therefore that of the Word as experienced by Shem in the writing of the letter/*Finnegans Wake*. Posited as the writer, Shem—the Irish form of James—is (logically enough, where Joyce himself is concerned) the Shem of Hebrew, "name." He addresses his brother, literally sending him off, in order that he deliver his Letter: "Brave footsore Haun! Work your progress! . . . The silent cock shall crow at last. . . . morroweth whereon every past shall full fost sleep. Amain" (473.20). The final *amen* of this invocation discloses the liturgical context of the "feat of passage" that is "Work in Progress." Shem aims at the eschatological point at which passage reveals the slippage toward a present tense, a paschal time (like that of cockcrow) that will put the past to sleep: it is the anticipated point of the Resurrection, the waking of time as present time, the "pressant" (221.17).

In Book I, 3, "The Goat," Osti-Fosti, potential avatar of Shem and presumed composer of the ballad, is the writer of "this Eyrawyggla saga" (48.28). He apparently writes "Work in Progress" as *passage:* "(he began Tuonisonian but worked his passage up as far as the we-all-hang-together Animandovites)" (48.34). The passage appears in writing as the displacement from the one to the multiple—a quintessentially Joycean strategy leading him from the simple lyrical voice of *Chamber Music* to the musical score of unlimited voices in *Finnegans Wake*. In Book III, 4, the "future present" of Book IV is anticipated: "A progress shall be made in walk, ney?" (567.20). Shaun's voyage unfolds negatively. The text undoes the weave of time,[16] parodies the Word and its expulsion from this world: it slips toward the negative progress of passage. Death and the first paschal celebration are assimilated into "Work in Progress," the place-marker of the *name* of passage:

Passover/Easter.[17] Joyce brings together the negative passage through English ("inplayn unglish" [609.15]) and the bursting of paschal celebration outside the Druidic interdiction. Passage is *transgression, going beyond, death, tracing, exchange of communication* (OED). The *pronounced* or *spoken* word of the paschal enunciation indicates the entwinement of language (communication, text, love, and violence) with death (the flow of time). The latter forms a "passing away," the passage elsewhere of the disappearing subject, who slips into passage, in order not to be swallowed up by the blank spaces of silence.

Joyce evokes the passage or work "in Progress" just as Saint Patrick has lit the paschal fire before he fights against the Druids. Their battle will end in Patrick's victory, and thus the spontaneous conversion of Ireland. On the threshold of the paschal entry into Judeo-Catholic symbolicity (Patrick being the figure of Moses and Christ),[18] someone asks: "who ever they wolk in process?" (609.31).[19] The answer indicates Patrick's identity: "the Chrystanthemlander . . . moveyovering the cabrattlefield of slaine" (609.32). Patrick is here assimilated as the person working a passage through death in writing: the slain, the ritual flowers of death, and the Passover of the Angel moving over the terrain of violent death, as well as the mention of Cabra, refer to "Tilly."[20] In this poem, Joyce obliquely inscribes the mourning at his mother's death. This passage of "Work in Progress" recalls his beginnings, the first attempts to confront death and its silence; it is thus his own passage that Joyce writes in *Finnegans Wake*. His commentary is explicit in Book IV: "the week of wakes is out and over; . . . the Phoenican wakes. Passing. One. We are passing. Two. From sleep we are passing. Three. Into the wikeawades warld from sleep we are passing. Four. Come, hours, be ours!" (608.30). Beginning with the present participle of Passover/Easter, we are projected into the Resurrection. Out of sleep, out of night, Joyce inserts the hidden title of the book: *Phoenican(s) wake*. We wake to the name as such, to the name as passage through the figures I, II, III, IV, here named, of Joyce's final text. This miniature summary of *Finnegans Wake* ends in the call to time—the *jouissance* of time as the present tense of Easter: the opening of the instant.

It is in this instant that passage is offered as *accomplishment, realization, production, issue* (OED). Yet the negative dimension turns accomplishment into disappearance, death, itself interpreted as a passage. Thus at the end of the book of the Resurrection (Book IV), Alp undergoes a passage, in the simultaneity of her accomplishment and her disappearance: "I am passing out. O bitter ending! I'll slip away before they're up" (627.34). The slipping of passage is offered as a *consummation* at the end of the *Wake*. Alp continues: "We pass through grass behush the bush to. Whish! . . . Take. Bussoftlhee, mememormee! . . . Lps. The keys to. Given!" (268.12). In consummation, a *transmission:* "Take." "Given!" The kiss of Arrah na Pogue has often been mentioned at this juncture; she gives the key to the prison gate. In another framework, it seems that the oral transmission taking place in Alp's enunciation is Joyce's gift of his language, his name, his paschal presence. In the accomplishment of the instant, in the scriptural/eschatological consummation of time, something works its passage; language, moving through the night of all tongues and all enunciations, is engaged. This language is lost and found again—at the end, when time stops at the instant of accomplishment: "For here the holy language. Soons to come. To pausse" (246.14). This is echoed at the beginning of Book IV: "A flasch and, rasch, it shall come to pasch" (594.16). Here passage and *pascha* are explicitly united in writing, starting with the instant of fulguration that identifies them as consummation and transmission. Father Boyle has observed in this sentence a fragmentary quotation of Hopkins' poem, "That Nature Is a Heraclitean Fire and of the Comfort of the Resurrection."[21] Joyce's *passage* takes up the transmission of the infinity of the Word to the ephemeral poet, as Hopkins sees it: "In a flash, at a trumpet crash, I am all at once what Christ is."[22] Hopkins's poor Jack fades away, swoons into the passage that makes him Christ, "immortal diamond." Joyce condenses this fulgurant transmission in the "pasch." In Book III, 4, he writes: "Take. And take. Vellicate nyche! Be ones as wes for gives for gives now the hour of passings sembles quick with quelled. Adieu" (563.34). The gift of the Word takes place in the pardon of sins (give, forgive, take) at the paschal hour (in Serbian: *Vellicate nyche,* i.e., Easter).[23] In the leap of the instant, accomplishment and consummation *to God:* "Adieu."

Since this passage is focused on the twins Jacob and Esau, "Jerkoff and Eatsup" (563.24), the enunciation of the transmission ("Take . . .") could allude to the paternal benediction received by Jacob in Genesis 27. This benediction confirms Genesis 25:23, the statement of God's preference for Jacob. According to Genesis 27:36, the name of *Ya 'aqob* alludes to the fact that Jacob supplants (*'aqab*) his brother. Isaac's benediction is thus halfway between the nomination of "Jacob" and his new nomination as "Israel." In his analysis of the wrestling with the Angel, Barthes notes the relation of benediction and nomination: he remarks that the episode when Jacob becomes Israel "functions like *the creation of a multiple tracing.*"[24] This multiple tracing signs passage in names: Joyce's Take/ Give, so close to Job's message (1:21) announcing the tenor of all benediction, arrives at that of the name of God. The accomplishment of Job ("Blessed is the name of the LORD") is behind Joyce's "Adieu." The passage of the text woven in names is offered as the paschal accomplishment. It operates in the liquid voyage through the language Alp offers to Hce—multiple and exotic enunciations, stories and fictions become sites of passage. Of a *Work in Progress:* "I will tell you all sorts of makeup things, strangerous. And show to every simple story-place we pass. . . . That'll be some kingly work in progress" (625.5).

10

The Passage
toward Pentecost

From the first leap of *pesah*, the beginning of the wandering of the Jews, the paschal celebration can be read as a heterogeneous nocturnal passage. The language of *pascha* makes its biblical entrance into infinity by passing toward eschatology—i.e., the visionary, prophetical dimension created by the apocalyptical break with the temporal world. The apocalypse (like the Four Last Things) relates the speaking subject to God: the rupture with the temporal element has infinite consequences. Fifty days after Passover/Easter, the Pentecost establishes the return of the Holy Spirit as God's gift to man. Thus, the intransitive passage, rather than ending, culminates in a *passing on*, a transmission. This passage gives Pentecost its specific symbolic dimension, crowning the paschal cycle.

A condensation of multiple meanings is knotted in the Judaic Pentecost, giving rise to many names: the Festival of the Fiftieth Day, the Harvest Festival, the Feast of Weeks, the Day of First Fruits.[1] The paschal period concludes with Pentecost. During the Judaic adaptation of pre-Israelite ritual, the Pentecost became the anniversary marking the gift of the Law on Mount Sinai. In the apocryphal *Book of Jubilees* as well as in the biblical Book of Chronicles (2, 15:15), Pentecost is associated with the Alliance of Mount Sinai. After the second century A.D., official Judaism viewed Pentecost as the festival of the giving of the Law.[2] Pentecost celebrates a key moment in

156

the vocation of Israel, and thus confirms the consequences anticipated at the moment of departure from Egypt: in the Zohar, the time between Passover and the Pentecost forms "the courting days of the bridegroom Israel with the bride Torah."

According to rabbinical commentaries and apocryphal writings, Pentecost is identified as the festival of revelation. The liturgical staging of this revelation emphasizes the gift of the Law through the voice of God: his word is multiplied and disseminated in a plurality of tongues. Rabbinical literature recalls a tradition stating that when God gave the Law on Mount Sinai, his voice was heard by all nations, dividing itself into as many languages as there were peoples to hear it. According to Rabbi Johanan: "Each word coming out of the month of the Almighty was apportioned into 70 tongues, such that each people heard the divine commandment in its own tongue."[3] Philo Judaeus relates a midrashic tradition concerning the Revelation on Mount Sinai: "To their surprise, a voice was heard coming from the fire flowing from the sky: the flame became words articulated in the language familiar to the hearers, and what was said was so clear and distinct that they seemed to see it rather than hear it."[4] The voice heard on Mount Sinai becomes visible at Pentecost. The midrash describes the Revelation in the form of the tongues of flame. The voice aflame with infinite language, the luminous word, becomes a dream-image, a multiple illumination—in which language unfolds as kaleidoscopic theophany, as mystical vision. According to the remarks of Philo Judaeus, the articulation and clarity of the spoken word exceed the invisibility of hearing. But what is visible voice? An illumination of darkness: the jubilation of the ineffable *Verbum* is heard by the subject's infinite ear. Language singular has become the infinite plurality of languages as sublimated enjoyment, *jouissance*, is displaced toward visibility—the flames in which God's appearance is vocalized, the written creation of the Word in fire: divine signatures. It is written in the Zohar, the Book of Splendor, that the word in its infinite dimensions shines with a holy light.[5] The mysteries of the letter and of signification resonate in the mystical word.

As described in Acts 2, the Christian Pentecost appropriates the tongues of flame, the descent of the Holy Spirit, and the plurality of tongues. Luke knew Philo's midrash. Delcor quotes Elbogen in the *Supplément au Dictionnaire de la Bible:* "The festival of Weeks was surely known as festival of Revelation, and the effusion of the Holy Spirit in the Acts of the Apostles is merely a return to the Old Revelation."[6] The New Testament Pentecost takes place on the same day as the Jewish holiday of thanksgiving: fifty days after the Redemption, the evangelical harvest is reaped. The gift of the New Law repeats the gift of the Law on Mount Sinai. The Church begins in Jerusalem the apostolate anticipated by Christ. Pentecost concludes the Easter cycle: it is second only to the Resurrection in liturgical importance. Its liturgy overflows with joyous exclamations, hallelujahs, evocations of light and the Holy Spirit.

Tertullian says that Pentecost records God's *exaltation* and "the paschal gift of Christ."[7] Hippolytus distinguishes Easter as the remembrance of *immolation* from Pentecost as the mystery of *exaltation* (related to the Ascension).[8] Patristic tradition admits the link between the two celebrations of Pentecost but preserves the primacy of Christian tradition by relegating the Judaic Pentecost to the status of *figure.* In 385, the Pope Siricius writes: "The gift of the Law is (the figure of) that of evangelical predication. For it is on the same day, that of the Pentecost, that the Law was given and the Holy Spirit descended on the disciples in order that they take on authority and know how to preach the evangelical law."[9]

Formerly, Pentecost was celebrated as a night watch. Tertullian writes that the object of the Pentecost is parousia;[10] the Second Coming of Christ operates as message, gift, excess of love, and an overflow of language singular into languages plural. Pentecost was sometimes dramatized in the early Church: masses of roses were spilled down from the vault during the Sequence; a dove flew, a trumpet was sounded as a reminder of the shofar on Sinai and the great noise marking the descent of the Holy Spirit on the Apostles.[11] Pentecost is the *presence* of the Word, reunited with the Father: this presence is transmitted through the tongues of fire. The form taken by the Holy Spirit is the pluralized gift of languages.

In Joyce's writing, the transmission of tongues in the gift

of grace assures the symbolic dimension of *passage*. Pentecost is the symbolic core of the Joycean reading of Judeo-Christian tradition; as the culmination of Passover/Easter, it enables him to engage in the plurality of tongues. Thus Joyce begins to talk in tongues that have somehow become his own, without losing their communicability or conventions of signification. Consonants and vowels, constant solidity and the flow of signifiers, mountain languages and river languages of Hce and Alp, engender all the languages summoned to *Finnegans Wake*. For Joyce, language as meaning and language as music are coupled in the heterogeneity of "soundsense": "between his voyous and her consinnantes! . . . Are we speachin d'anglas landadge or are you spraking sea Djoytsch?" (485.10). The Joycean answer to the question is: both of those languages and many others, perhaps up to the seventy languages of God. But also, beginning with the ground of English, Joyce's Judaic wandering through what was previously an *impasse,* the Red Sea of languages, leads him toward a personalized multiple language spoken in tongues, *given:* "spraking sea Djoytsch," speaking Joyce.

Joyce's Pentecost is anchored in Judaic symbolism. At the end of Book II, 1, the nightfall of "The Mime" chapter, the dramatization dissolves and the utterances of daylight fall silent before the moon, the vigil, the lamps. This nightfall indicates the entry into Judaism; Joyce marks a return to nocturnal language with two pages of allusions to Jewish holiday and liturgy (244–245). this chapter is compared to a *fable* (thus recalling the principal sketches forming the structure of the *Wake*)[12] with Judaic resonances: "And now with robby brerfox's fishy fable lissaned out, the threads simwht toran and knots in its antargumends" (245.9). This fable answers certain religious questions discussed by the "pesciolines in Liffeyetta's bowl" (245.11)—including the procession/position of the Holy Spirit: "the poissission of the hoghly course" (245.13). Hce's family and pub are mentioned: "A's the sign. . . . Where Chavvyout Chacer calls the cup" (245.35). Joyce subtly integrates his symbols and proper names in the text—he makes of it a smooth (in French: *lisse*) surface, like the fable heard from beginning to end ("lissaned out"). The threads are torn and knotted: the text is a woven net of knotted threads, a fishnet to catch names with. Simchat Torah, the Rejoicing of the Law, is the Jewish holiday related to Pentecost, Shavuoth[13] ("Chavvyout"). Joyce names himself as Torah, Law, and text, the reading of which ends and begins again on this holiday. The gift of the Law to Moses is the object of festivity. Joyce displaces this celebration toward his own gift of tongues in the allusion to the Targum, Aramaic translations of the Torah, poetic variations on the Holy Text.[14] The Targumim recall the pentecostal division of tongues, the gift of the Torah itself: "The Talmud states that every commandment that issued from God's mouth in the Revelation on Mount Sinai was divided and could be heard in all seventy languages."[15]

The fable in question seems to resemble the Torah—and *Finnegans Wake*. Joyce's writing, like the Kabbalists' reading of Torah, is a weave of names, a living network of the different names of God. Joyce articulates the transmission of the Pentecost, and its mystical revelation. The latter is perhaps encoded in the "A's the sign" before the name of Shavuoth. The Aleph (containing the essence of the alphabet and all of language)[16] begins the first commandment: and yet it is merely a movement of the larynx preceding a vowel at the beginning of a word. While answering a question asked in (and since) the Talmud, Rabbi Mendel of Rymanow specified that the community of Israel heard only the Aleph at the moment of the revelation; but the Aleph escapes the ear and only signs the "I" of the transmission ("(" followed by "YHWH"), the shifter of sacred discourse. In the Aleph, Israel hears nothing: nothing other than the speech act itself, the instance of *transmission* to the prophet. It is thus Moses who interpreted the voice of God.[17] "A's the sign" would indicate the gift of the Law as a mystical revelation: the divine message gives rise to a listening ear, an interpretation, an entry into languages.

In Book I, 4, the Jewish context of the Pentecost is named as "Yuddanfest" (82.36), i.e., *Judenfest*. It is then doubled by its Christian repetition, or rather *tripled* in the J. J. and S. desired by the cad: "Which at very first wind of gay gay and whiskwigs wick's ears pricked up, the starving gunman" (83.5). As described in Acts, the Pentecost is a Trinitarian production; Joyce's position in the eucharistic formula of John Jameson and Son is displaced toward Shem. The latter pronounces a series of names of the pubs where he will spend the money given to him by Hce. The shofar or ram's horn is sounded ("might ramify up his Sheofon" [83.8]) in a comical celebration of the Revelation on Mount Sinai. Shem's *jouissance* or mystical enjoyment goes beyond the affirmative meaning of a single language: he is heard "remarxing in languidoily, seemingly much more highly pleased than tongue could tell" (83.15). He speaks in tongues: "in the Nichtian glossery which purveys aprioric roots for aposteriorious tongues this is nat language at any sinse of the world" (83.10). The tongues of fire sent to the Apostles after the Resurrection are "aposteriorious"; the "aprioric roots" of the *Verbum*, the Hebraic roots of Shem's "root language," become infinite, eucharistically divided into the seventy tongues of the Revelation (424.17).

"Nichtian glossery" and "nat language" indicate Shem's refusal of the community of messages, that of institutions, and the community's negative reply to him: like the mocking witnesses described in the account of the Apostles' Pentecost (Acts 2), the community in the person of Shaun excludes Shem's "root language" from its dictionary.[18] But Shem's strategy of negativity is operative in his *nocturnal* language. Here Joyce stresses a dual liturgical reference, from the pillar of fire in the desert and the light of Exodus to the night watch of both Holy Saturday and the Pentecost ("daylit dielate night of nights" [83.27]), and from the Revelation on Mount Sinai until the triple hallelujah uttered at Pentecost as at the Resurrection ("hillelulia, killelulia, allenalaw" [83.34]). The Judeo-Catholic vision is summarized in this Latin exclamation derived from the Hebrew "praise Yahweh," uttered with greatest frequency during the paschal period. The text records the negativity of a language in *passage*, its confrontation with the "sins of the world." The Jews break with paganism and expel themselves from Egypt. Then they enter a symbolic night, as the Holy Name calls them to the Torah—night language in any sense of God's Word. (In the Targumim, God is called "Word," *Memra*.)[19] The word of the Other world, without end. Joyce played on this in *Ulysses* when the slippage from word to world, through a slip of the pen, bore with it the darkness of sexuality, as far as Bloom's passage was concerned.[20] In the *Wake*, the Word bursts forth from darkness (sins of the world) in Shem's discourse. The liturgical *peccata mundi* are taken up by the passage of Christ as *Verbum;* they cling to the underside of language as the gift of tongues. The *culpa* is "*culpa*" only in language: if language is engaged to render it *felix,* a nearly impassible path must first be taken, a trajectory of passage. Shem's strategy of negativity goes in this direction.

On the one hand, this strategy consists in dissolving what Christians call the *world* (flesh, death, abjection: the pleasure principle as creator of scraps, left-over detritus) in tongues. The enterprise of nocturnal language is the confrontation opposing symbolicity to the sin that, as interdiction, posits it (*sinse*) and then as the repressed, overflows its boundaries with the drives.[21] On the other hand, the strategy consists in dissolving the particular language (English, in the case of Joyce or Shem) in the multiplicity of languages: English becomes a series of enunciations that are undermined, pulverized, and pluralized by the lexical and syntactic presence of other languages. English as such begins to disappear into fragments. Its apparent unity has been invaded. In the gaps, in the spaces between fragments, the writer's self-inscription takes on the heterogeneity of the *felix culpa,* the sublime *jouissance* of the overturning of sin through grace. The speaking "I" of the enunciation overflows meaning and springs forth from it: *jaillissement,*[22] according to the Church Fathers. And the ear hearing the transmission divides itself into tongues that have become the voices of multiple "I"'s speaking at Pentecost. Joyce intercepts multiplicity as hearing, as enunciation, as writing . . . in order to dissolve his language. Eclipsed, it will spring forth as the gift of tongues. Nocturnal language is a *mosaic* of the Word: a space in which luminous bursts of languages work their passage into writing.[23] The spectacles of vision become the visionary eyes of theology looking through the illuminated representation of the Bible; Shem, like Joyce himself, wears "semicoloured stained glasses" (463.14).

During his Christly itinerary, Shaun specifies the Judeo-Christian liturgical context of Pentecost and the relation of its *passage* to the sins that must be absorbed. His sermon alludes to the Mass ("introit," "offrand," "cofarreating," "uttering mass," "offertory," "what's the first sing to be sung?" "for the over of lithurgy," "the sinkts in the colander" [432.5, .9, .11, .12, .17, .29, .32, .36]), to the Last Supper ("Manducare Monday," "in china dominos," "good friday" [433.6, .7, .12]), to Easter ("pasqualines" [432.30]), to the Madonna ("Here she's, is a bell, that's wares in heaven, virgin white . . . vikissy mannona," "hailies fingringmaries" [433.3, 435.30]), and to the *felix culpa* ("O foolish cuppled! Ah, dice's error!" [433.30]). This staging of Catholicism is organized around the central event of the Pentecost: "what a lawful day it was, there and then, for a consommation with an effusion" (432.13). Shaun seems to announce the paternal transmission of the Law: "the ten commandments" (433.11). This transmission is anticipated in Book III, 1: "there does be a power coming over me . . . from on high" (432.26). (Here Shaun seems to combine his priestly position with that of the Virgin, as he assumes a feminine stance with respect to that transcendence: "The Holy Ghost shall come upon thee, and the power of the Highest shall overshadow thee" [Luke 1:35].) But Shaun utters precise allusions to the New Testament Pentecost as well. To the "lawful" Father he adds the "consommation" of the Word (while repeating the priest's words: "those verbs he said to me. From above" [432.19]) and the "effusion" of the Holy Spirit. Shaun notes the date of Whitsuntide: "several sindays after whatsintime" (432.33). The double reference to sin indicates the parodic dimensions of Shaun himself, revealing his own concupiscence (gluttony, sadism, voyeurism, cupidity, etc.) in ecclesiastical remarks. Undone by his own desire, Shaun betrays the Catholic preoccupation with concupiscence.

Defeated by the Word, sin exceeds the limits of language: yet grace, the only possible Catholic absorption of sin, acts as *an excess of languages,* an entrance into their infinity, an effusion echoing that experienced by the Apostles: "Let us, the real Us, all ignite in our prepurgatory grade as aposcals" (446.36). Joyce celebrates Shaun's sacred and comic effusion in the exclamations of wind, *ruah,* glory, and voice: "Poof! There's puff for ye, egor, and planxty of it, all abound me breadth! Glor galore and glory be! . . . And the topnoted delivery you'd expected be me invoice!" (439.15). Shaun's "breadth," both breathing and eucharistic bread, situates Pentecost in the encounter of flesh not yet sublime and the poetic word of love. Shaun echoes the beginning of Hopkins's "Wreck of the Deutschland": "Thou mastering me / God! giver of breath and bread."[24]

Following Shaun's sermon of seduction, Joyce inscribes a Song of Songs in which Hce gives to Alp "shortcake nutrients for Paas and Pingster's pudding" (550.13),[25] or ingredients for the festival of Easter and Pentecost (in Flemish: *Paas* and *Pingster*). At this juncture, Joyce echoes the end of *Giacomo Joyce:* "Write it, damn you, write it! What else are you good for?"[26] Shaun condemns Shem and the seductions of his writing: "the wring wrong way to wright woman. Shuck her! Let him! What he's good for. . . . Could you wheedle a staveling encore out of your imitationer's jubalharp, hey, Mr Jingle-joys?" (466.15).[27] At the confluence of sexual *jouissance* and scriptural sublimation, Joyce signs his holy name of transmission, in the pentecostal figuration of Giacomo become Shem.

The expulsion of Judeo-Christian truth and of the passage toward Pentecost takes the form of Hce's sacrifice and Shem's persecution. In Book I, 4, "The Lion," the Four voyeurs argue about Hce and the two girls: "the great Howdoyoucallem, and his old nickname, Dirty Daddy Pantaloons . . . behind the war of the two roses" (94.34). The same question is asked once again: What happened at the beginning? The Four momentarily agree: "To give and to take! And to forego the pasht! And all will be forgotten!" (96.20). This attempt to establish total repression threatens the entire *Wake,* and particularly the Four. Here repression takes the form of a consummation of reconciliation, the decline of the Four. It annihilates passage: memory, ordained by God and destined to maintain the transmission of symbolic life saved from death, is undone.[28]

But Hce, like Shem, is the bearer of the symbolic passage toward Pentecost. Through the overturning of the failure associated with the Tower of Babel, language is resuscitated in its luminous infinity. Soon after the declaration of the Four, Hce's Pentecost takes place: "Mr Whitlock, gave him a piece of wood" (98.25). Someone asks: "What words of power were made fas between them, ekenames and auchnomes, *acnomina ecnumina?*" (98.26). In this sacred event (*fas:* divine law), the theophany of transmission gives rise to a gift or an exchange of nicknames (ekenames, auchnomes, *acnomina*). The offering of wood slips to *word,* via names of trees: "The war is in words and the wood is in the world. Maply me, willowy we, hickory he and yew yourselves" (98.34). Mr. Whitlock gave Hce the Irish alphabet, whose letters are the names of trees: he gave him *names.* Here Joyce parodies the Prologue to the Gospel of Saint John; the second sentence arranges the names of the Irish characters in a *conjugation of letters* according to the three persons. In Judaic mysticism, a name was posited at the origin of the Creation; the Creating Word is presented in the form of a name, even as "the juxtaposition of the Word and the Name."[29] The power of God is concentrated in His Name: with this Name, God created the world, according to the mystics.[30] The veritable mystical name of God would be not only the Tetragrammaton, but the sum of divine manifestations as well.[31] The Jezira, a neo-Pythagorean book of the Creation, states: "all that is created and speaking *comes from a name.* It is clear that this name from which everything derives is the name of God and not a group of consonants forming a name."[32] Joyce seals the Word to the Name YHWH by quoting the Genesis account of the Creation in proximity to the repetition of Genesis in Saint John's prologue. Hce-*Verbum* is also "I am," and the Spirit of Genesis 1:2 ("And the Spirit of God moved upon the face of the waters"): "he . . . was at his best . . . a rude breathing on the void of to be" (100.26).

The transmission of the Pentecost ("pinksir," "Whitweekend," "pentecostal jest") becomes even more explicit at the moment of Hce's "real murder": "On his pinksir's postern . . . at Whitweekend had been nailed an inkedup name and title, inscribed in the national cursives, accelerated, regressive, filiform, turreted and envenomoloped in piggotry" (99.27). This inscription, or "pentecostal jest," marks the entrance of Shem; he has apparently written a name and title in the form of letters—perhaps the Christly monograms of IHS or INRI. This beautiful Irish calligraphy written in all directions by the "fili" (son and Irish poet) reveals the transmission of the Pentecost through the text of *Finnegans Wake,* figuring and integrating the spectacular Irish illumination of the letter in the Book of Kells. This text illustrates the Joycean Pentecost: "Art is the gift of tongues." Joyce's illuminated letter is sought in the crossing ("Transocean") of the Red Sea or the journal *transition,* that published parts of the *Wake:* "Transocean ata-laclamoured him; The latter! The latter!" (100.1).

Hce's paschal death is announced in connection with the Pentecost in order to suggest that Joyce's languages are being crucified. His obituary is read: "after a lenty illness the roeverand Mr Easterling of pentecostitis, no followers by bequest" (130.8). His pentecostal death is prelude to the Resurrection in tongues, actualized in a thousand and one ways in the Joycean text—and particularly in Book IV. Especially concerning Hce and the Letter as symbolic document of sin and redemption, implicating all relations in the Joycean family: "Letter, carried of Shaun, son of Hek, written of Shem, brother of Shaun, uttered for Alp, mother of Shem, for Hek, father of Shaun" (420.16). The writing of the Letter is Shem's operation of the Resurrection in tongues. Shem functions in the *Wake* as the metaphorization of Joyce's relationship to his own textual act—*his written version of the gift of tongues.* Shem is the holy parody, reaching from Passover/Easter to the Pentecost: he is the "divine comic Denti Alligator" (440.6), according to the title given him. He is the Judaic Irish writer—in Hebrew: *name,* in Gaelic: *James:* Shem.

Shem's writing forms a Pentecost of language; Joyce transforms language into tongues of flame, delivered through fiction. In Book I, 7, the paschal aspect of Shem's writing is emphasized. As a sign of resurrection, Shem's Easter eggs, the spiritual nourishment taken in Thanksgiving and blessed on Easter Sunday, become the symbol of his writing: "chanting . . . his cantraps of fermented words . . . (his oewfs à la Madame Gabrielle de l'Eglise . . . his soufflosion of oogs . . . his Frideggs à la Tricareme" (184.23).[33] Shem's fermented words are evoked in terms of the Annunciation, Good Friday, and the effusion of the Holy Spirit at the Pentecost. This catalogue of scriptural cuisine follows a description of Shem's dwelling, covered with writing like the door posts and lintels of Exodus: "The warped flooring of the lair and soundconducting walls thereof, to say nothing of the uprights and imposts, were persianly literatured with burst loveletters, telltale stories, stickyback snaps, doubtful eggshells" (183.8). This writing traces the leap of the Exterminating Angel through the Word ("alphybettyformed verbage") and the Holy Spirit ("puffers" [183.13, .12]). This disguise of the persons of the Trinity raises the question of its status within monotheism and language: "imeffible tries at speech unasyllabled" (183.14). The triune God is approached through *Shem*, the holy name, "the magic word of messianic certainty."[34] This name, encoded by the Tetragrammaton as the one true name of God, plays a mystical role in Judaism. Gershom Sholem writes: "The name with which God designates Himself and with which he can be invoked removes itself from the acoustical sphere and becomes unpronounceable." This name "returns to the domain of the ineffable."[35] Beginning with the third century, the now unpronounceable Tetragrammaton is paradoxically called *Shem ha-meforash*, the simultaneously pronounced and hidden (*meforash*) name: the secret name.[36] The name of God is a condensation of holiness: as *Shem ha-meforash*, it vacillates between the virtual infinity of the ineffable, forbidden name and the creative infinity of the name as a signifying condensation, bursting forth in a Revelation, a Pentecost. It is said in the Hagaddah that the Torah was written with black fire on white fire:[37] prior to the tongues of fire, the Law of fire, an infinite nomination. The mystical Torah is written in the invisible forms of white light;[38] the infinite revelation to come is located in the divine fulguration through which writing itself approached the ineffable in the *invisibility of the Revelation*—forms, letters, names, significations.

Shem is named through this version of writing; he writes the infinity of the Name as the virtuality of the passage into languages, the fulguration of languages. This Pentecost is undergone by the drinker of "J. J. and S."; Shem covers his walls with souvenirs of the *passage* (the Crucifixion, the Mass, the Eucharist with its echoes of the Exodus): "lees of whine," "broken wafers" (183.32, .34). In the Eucharist, infinity (located in the ineffable name, according to the Kabbalists) is an invisible gift, metaphorized as the sacrament. Concerning the liturgical reference to daily bread, Augustine writes that one must "ask for the bread required by the body, the visible consecrated bread, and the invisible bread of the word of God."[39] This invisible mystery[40] of the eucharistic word must be examined through another of Shem's accessories: "Magnifying wineglasses" (183.21). The wineglass of the Magnificat alludes to the Annunciation; the grace of the Holy Spirit allows the Virgin to exalt the name of God: "And Mary said, My soul doth magnify the Lord" (Luke 1:46). Shem's glasses allude to the Pentecost as well, when the Apostles speak in tongues of "the wonderful works of God" (Acts 2:11); they are accused of being "full of new wine" (2;13). Shem's writing, the nomination in tongues that magnify God, operates via a reading of the invisible through the wineglass spectacles of the Magnificat—through the intoxication of the tongues of fire.

Elsewhere Joyce confirms the correspondence between eucharistic wine and the drunkenness of the Pentecost. At the end of the *Wake*, Alp alludes to Hce's mother: "losing her pentacosts after drinking their pledges" (624.34). This scandal founds the role of Shem in obscenity, intoxication, pentecostal contexts. Shem's "cantraps of fermented words," his naming in tongues and his magnification of God, stem from a reading of *invisibilia* through the magnifying drunkenness of the tongues of fire. The reading/writing of consecrated wine as the radiant body of Christ—of the gift of tongues rendered visible—is summed up by Saint Athanasius. Pentecost is "the new wine that is the Holy Spirit."[41] Joyce's Pentecost in Shem's scriptural passage toward art is the *eucharistic excess of languages*.[42] Shem in exile *sur place,* within himself ("self exiled in upon his ego" [184.6]) writes on his own body as *accident,* or species of the Eucharist: "the first till last alshemist wrote over . . . his own body . . . transaccidentated" (185.34). Shem's activity is "writing the mystery of himsel in furniture" (185.35). The "el" of himself is later heard as an Old Testament name of God: "God es el?" (246.6). The evocation of *mystery* locates Shem's writing within the dimensions of the Catholic *sacrament.* Saint Augustine conceives of the sacrament of the Eucharist as the result of "mystical prayer": the mystical quality of ritual utterance derives from the "transformations of matter" into body and blood of Christ. These changes occur only because discourse opens out toward what Aquinas will later call the "infinite agent"[43] of eucharistic conversion. Augustine emphasizes the Holy Ghost's invisible, *immutable* power as an extension of the *ineffable* Tetragrammaton. He writes: "When human hands have taken its visible appearance, the consecration which makes of this appearance such a great sacrament, comes only from the invisible action of the Spirit of God."[44] Joyce inscribes this mystery as "something supernoctural": "Panpan and vinvin are not alonety vanvan and pinpin" (598.17). Shem's "mystery of himsel in furniture" is the writing of this mystery in the furnishings of language, the "persianly literatured" interior of the exile. The languages named in affirmation counterpoint the holy passage through negativity ("seedy ejaculations," "fresh horrors from Hades") with an ecstatic gesture, recalling the Penelope of *Ulysses:* "ahs ohs ouis sis jos gias neys thaws sos, yeses and yeses and yeses" (183.23, .35, 184.1). As exiles we can receive only one gift: languages. The Tetragrammatic subject reveals itself as the mystery to be written, in the tongues appropriated as art: "his usylessly unreadable Blue Book of Eccles, *édition de ténèbres*" (179.26), darkness bringing forth light.

Shem rewrites the passage toward language of Exodus, named in Hebrew: *Shemot,* or Names. Joyce turns to mysticism in creating the Name as the center of language, the heart of sacred textuality. Nachmanides wrote that Torah "is not only made up of names of God but in reality forms as a whole the single sublime name of God."[45] According to Josef Gikatilla, Torah constitutes the explanation of the Tetragrammaton; the Torah is woven of the names of God.[46] He wrote: "The whole Torah is a fabric of appellatives, *kinnuyim*—the generic term for the epithets of God . . . and these epithets in turn are woven from the various names of God. But all these holy names are connected with the tetragrammaton YHWH and depend upon it. Thus the entire Torah is ultimately woven from the tetragrammaton."[47]

The Tetragrammaton is the visible and invisible signifying leitmotif—like the name of Joyce, opening a passage through all of *Finnegans Wake.* This mystical property could be attributed to a long series of names in the *Wake:* the invisible, ineffable proper name lends its subjective presence to multiple inscriptions. As a condensation of the subject's symbolic power (invisible, creative, scriptural: from Stern to Swift to Joyce himself, including the Tetragrammaton and the Trinity),[48] the permutations of the proper name in the *Wake* maintain the relationship between the subject's language and its infinite revelation—exceeding any particular close reading. Joyce un-

derwrites this realm of infinity in the *act of multiple naming.*
Art, the gift of tongues, is also, according to Shem, the gift of
names, "shemeries," fabricated by the "alshemist" (185.34,
187.35). He copies signatures; he *transnames:* "Transname me
loveliness, now and here me for all times!" (145.21). Making
his passage through names: "In the name of" (147.9). The
subject called name is anchored in language as the subject of
languages plural, of holy and bewildering symbolicity—out
of which comes the sacred and comic *Ulysses* and *Finnegans
Wake.* For Joyce, the name indicates the irreducible presence
of the subject capable of saying "I AM," with a tetragrammatic
gesture: this sets off the weaving of the Torah. The Pentecost
of *Finnegans Wake* delivers, in tongues, the Torah of the name
of Joyce. Shem's Letter is the figure of this text: gift, missive,
amorous excess, overflow of language singular into the plural
jouissance of the symbolic.

The subject of the Name is singularly sacred: he is voca-
tively present in the performative act of naming. But what
generates the divine and infinite quality of the Name? For
John Stuart Mill, names are "meaningless marks."[49] A. H.
Gardiner develops this hypothesis, insisting on the importance of the *referent* of the proper name and eliminating the
signified. The privileged signifier remains, and the identification that is its function: "A proper name is a word or group
of words which is recognized as having identification as its
specific purpose, and which achieves, or tends to achieve, that
purpose by means of its distinctive sound alone, without regard to any meaning possessed by that sound from the start
or acquired by it through association with the object or objects
thereby identified."[50] Whereas most words "directly convey
information," i.e., function as message, proper names refer
back to the *code,* or language as system, structure, virtuality.
Gardiner remarks: "Proper names merely provide the key to
information."[51] The name is the key, source, and guarantee
of language; Kabbalah posits the Holy Name as the origin of
language.[52] The proper name anchors the subject in linguistic virtuality with a signifier, a mark, a letter: the name takes
on the virtuality of language as an excess of symbolic meaning. Its signified is the singular being, incommunicable outside of the proper name. The Kabbalists say that the proper

name goes beyond meaning yet makes meaning possible.[53] Bereft of a specific significance, the proper name is comparable to the Holy Word of mystical revelation, to the holy letter of the signature of the finger of God or to the aleph—an infinite "I AM," echoed by Bloom on the beach in "Nausikaa."

At the Pentecost, the tongues of the Holy Spirit were rendered visible. For Joyce, Pentecost implies the visibility of the *name*. When Shaun condemns Shem's "root language," he evokes the hundred-lettered Holy Name, the Kabbalists' culmination of *Shem ha-meforash*.[54] Withdrawn from pronunciation, the name is infinitely serialized. The last name of a hundred letters rejoins the first name, the Tetragrammaton: "yav hace not one rpronouncable teerm . . . to signify majestate" (478.11). And Joyce's version: "Ullhodturdenweirmudgaardgringnirurdrmolnirfenrirlukkillokkibangimanddodrreringsurtkrinmgernrackinarockar! Thor's for yo!—The hundredlettered name again, last word of perfect language!" (424.20). The infinitized name, last "wholly words" of "Shemese" (424.33, 425.3), brings into relief the dissemination of the letter, dispersing its Mallarméan trace across the pages of *Finnegans Wake*. The "root language" suggests Hebrew, the language of revelation. In the passage toward Pentecost, Joyce sends his Name, his Letter, through the writing of a new tongue of Revelation. The roots hce and alp, the "trilitters," make of this Joycean enunciation a language of proper names, figured in illuminated monograms: art, the gift of tongues.

11

Punc
A Retrospective Arrangement

The progress of Joyce's working through language, his passage, leads him into the pentecostal multiplicity of tongues. The "progress" naming the last version of the book takes the direction of increasing complexity. Joyce's ever-widening scope leads him into the labyrinth of language—involution, meandering, a weave of knots. As art, this labyrinth constitutes the verbal version of Irish Catholic illumination: the interlace, or the labyrinth as infinitely beautiful. Our itinerary through the Joycean interlace—starting with *A Portrait of the Artist as a Young Man*—has in turn been widened and pluralized, through the innumerable ruptures and beginnings of *Ulysses,* through the saturation of the signifier and the engendering of paradoxical and limitless meaning in *Finnegans Wake.* The strange enterprise of reading Joyce itself takes on the turns and returns of invention. The attempt not to lose sight of the major configurations of the work (summarized, in this interpretation, as sacred and comic heterogeneity) leads to a labyrinth of readings of even the most minimal fragment of the Joycean enunciation. Through readings relayed by re-readings, weaving and unweaving, the text of exiles and passages in tongues demands to be heard *all or not at all:* impossibly, by an impassioned ear. For in this language, *sound* and *sense*—inseparable and yet perpetually at odds—are engaged in mortal combat.

For Joyce, the theological experience of Catholic perversion (in Lacanian colors: the turning toward the Father) is an experience of writing. Within it, the function of negativity falls into place; Joyce works through the underside of meaning, he exposes language as nocturnal. In *Ulysses,* the Passion of the Word is formulated as a comedy and as a theology. Tracing through this rendering of the Passion, Joyce articulates the limits of "common" language. His own language has become a gamut of styles, of singular subjectivities, that ceaselessly allow the passage of that which is usually left unsaid or considered unspeakable.

In *Ulysses,* the irony of the *Portrait* is turned into a vast production of comedy. Sexuality and the Passion are engaged or absorbed through humor, parody, and *Witz.* This process of Freudian "bewilderment and illumination," henceforth absorbed into Joycean style, is related to the symbolic enterprise of Joycean Catholicism—the Passion of the Word as an arrangement of theological and scriptural paternity. The voyage through love and sin gives rise to the question of theological infinity at the locus of the confrontation of Catholicism and negativity in *Ulysses:* Judaism.

The unspoken regions of Catholicism set off the creation of Bloom, that other exile. We have seen the symbolic constellation Joyce brings out of the dialogue between paternity and filiation: theological and sexual, the scriptural art of Catholicism puts the Word into musical form, into poetic language. Centering on the mystery of paternity, Stephen Dedalus formulates the Joycean aesthetic as a version of the Passion of Shakespeare.

The figure of Bloom, bearer of erotic wounds and Judaic paternity, brings the possibilities of Joycean sublimation into focus. On the one hand, there is Bloom's passion, his ear for music and poetic language; on the other, his biblical, prophetic, and Christlike speech. At their crossing: the *jouissance* of the letter, the true that has become the beautiful. Through Bloom, Joyce signs the accomplishment of the Scriptures. He does so through pluralized laughter—*Witz* and transcendent joy—in a symbolic transmission, or *transfiguration.* As demonstrated in "Cyclops" and "Circe," Joyce makes his writing shine with a biblical light. The reference to the Apocalypse indicates the ultimate destination of the Judeo-Christian trajectory: the infinite passage of the Trinity, rooted in the Joycean encounter between Christ and Shakespeare. Unraveling the doubled dimensions of light and darkness, a reading of theological discourse reveals its presence as the infinity of grace and marks Joyce's entry into the promised land of Judeo-Christianity. This entrance operates through the blackness of obscenity indicating the overflow or excess that must be talked or written out. The references to prophecy and to the Exodus are crucial. In *Ulysses,* Joyce initiates the Passover/Easter passage toward Resurrection that engages him until the end of *Finnegans Wake.*

Joyce figures the heterogeneity of his own Celtic-Catholic position in the encounter between Stephen and Bloom, i.e., the encounter of two languages, Gaelic and Hebrew. Out of this meeting, Joyce's English emerges in *Finnegans Wake* as a new tongue: as a language infinitely open to languages, to the gift of tongues. This opening is itself traced, metaphorized, in the Judeo-Catholic catechism uniting Bloom and Stephen. Joyce focuses here on the encounter between Hebrew and Irish sacred texts, specifically the Bible and the Book of Kells, that seems to catalyze the writing of Celtic-Catholic heterogeneity.

At the meeting point of the plurality of tongues, at the Celtic-Catholic crossroads of the sacred and comic text, Joyce lingers over the exchange of languages, the double gift of tongues. With Molly's monologue, he adds the figuration of the incarnation of the Word to this context: this leads to the Trinitarian enunciation, the instant of present speech, the letter of Blephen-Stoom. At this point, the disappearance of fictional characters becomes noticeable; Joyce will no longer need them to sustain his enunciation of the *contransmagnificand-jewbangtantiality.* In their place: the infinity of the proper name. Scriptural *jouissance,* discovered by Bloom-Joyce as the territory beyond the realism or *vraisemblable* of seduction. The end of *Ulysses* bears witness to the overturning of sin through grace—successful incest, taking place during the paschal night of the encounter with Nora, Martha, Marion . . . in Joyce's language. *Ulysses* indicates the trajectory leading from the first sin to sublime *jouissance:* June 16, 1904, opens its doors to *Finnegans Wake.*

The infinitized enunciation is theological and Freudian—transcendent and lapsed or dreamt. Its Celtic-Catholic, comic and sacred heterogeneity falls into place in the *Wake*. An analysis of the paschal constellation allows for a possible decoding of the Catholic access to symbolicity in *Finnegans Wake*. The Joycean text is deployed as a Judeo-Catholic *passage* in languages, in names, in voices—as a *paschal enunciation*. The itinerary of Passover/Easter filters the Joycean theology of writing.

In the *Wake*, liturgy becomes singularly Joycean, beginning with Good Friday. Through Hce's death, Joyce posits a structural arrangement of the sacred and the comic, focusing on sin and its engagement within the discourse of Catholicism. The Christly position—working through suffering and transgression, love and *jouissance*—engages Joyce in the writing of the Crucifixion. This scriptural initiation leads to the mysteries of Holy Saturday. Without the speaking voice of death heard during this night, there can be no resurrection. Obscene writing, the scripture of original sin, reveals the subject of the Joycean enunciation and the nocturnal position taken up by it in *Finnegans Wake*.

This nocturnal position springs forth in the paschal and Catholic cry of the *felix culpa*. The oxymoron of the holy night brings into relief the ambivalent position of Adam expelled from Milton's Paradise: Joyce returns to the drama of the first subject, his desire and his symbolic debt, in the *Wake*. A brief historical reading of the dogma of original sin facilitates the explication of the Catholic foundation for the Joycean *felix culpa*. At the heart of the enterprise of *Finnegans Wake*: the Catholic enunciation of culpability and grace has become the enunciation of the doubled *jouissance* of the Joycean subject—*felix culpa*. This cry of sublimation introduces the *Verbum* within the locus of the fault. In *Finnegans Wake* the (paschal) Letter of Shem acts as evidence that the sublimation has taken place, in multiple nomination, in the renewed and plural enunciation of *felix culpa*.

Joyce's paschal event is itself pluralized: Catholic, Exodic, Judaic. The sparing of the sacrifice at the moment of the first Passover marks the beginning of the itinerary leading to the Resurrection; since the creation of Bloom's Judaic paternity, the new scripture of the Joycean enunciation takes shape in the three-lettered Christly monograms—the last one being Hce. Having overturned the sacrifice, the people of the Name began to write their symbolic destiny; and in this writing, Joyce, the wandering Jew of Irish Catholicism, heard the Trinity. From Bloom to Hce, the sacred-comic father spurs the production or process of writing. Stephen's "apostolic succession" traces the Joycean relation to writing. Except for the laughter of obscenity and ecstasy.

It is the Father's *jouissance* that obsesses the Son in *Finnegans Wake*. Joyce writes out this *jouissance,* its knotted relation to grace and the Fall. For Joyce, in scriptural terms, this knot is first tied in the death of Father Flynn at the beginning of *Dubliners*—and his fallen, obscene, and Catholic laughter. The Mosaic path toward truth leads to Shem's writing—punctuated by proper names and signatures rendered as artistic monograms. Shem's Letter marks the resurgence of paternity: the conclusion of passage, the revelation of the *instant* founding paternal *jouissance* since the Fall. This is the symbolic *punctum* of the Resurrection, torn from the Jews by the Catholics eager to possess it as their own Passover, their own *jouissance.* Joyce the Irishman, both Jew and Catholic, here remarks the double *jouissance* of the symbolic, of paternity, constructed on the abyss. And he writes it as such: comic and sacred, fallen and transcendent, sacrificed and spared—slipping toward the writing, in the present, of the Name. Shem's Letter figures Joyce's writing as an illuminated page of revelation, a canticle of jubilation. The paschal enunciation, or the Resurrection. The Judeo-Christian subject becomes the subject of paternity, or Hce. *Naming* him as the present tense of Easter, Joyce signs the Resurrection in his own hand.

This paschal name is the Judaic symbolization of "to clear a passage." Following Saint Augustine, Joyce outlines the paschal experience as *transitus,* the heterogeneous working toward the Resurrection; Joycean writing adds to the Augustinian conception a passage toward the name, a revelation of the proper name. From *Work in Progress* to *Finnegans Wake,* the name of Joyce is in question, in waiting, as the scriptural and creative name. These variations on the name are received in the instant of their passage, in the consummation or transmission, as Joyce's paschal offering—the gift of tongues in his own language.

The end of the *Finnegans Wake* passage is the Pentecost, the moment of transmission. The divine light, the tongues of fire, indicate the mystical dimensions of speech. The transfigured presence of the *Verbum* and the *jouissance* of the Holy Spirit complete the Trinitarian arrangement of the Joycean gift of tongues. The *Wake* is Joyce's Torah, his fabric of proper names, the passage effected by Shem (*the name* who engenders names and scabrously signs them. Shem is the usurper, the obscene usurer of holy names) through the tenebrous language awaiting illumination, the nocturnal language. Through their mystery, the tongues of the Pentecost have been rendered *visible*. Beautiful signatures of the invisible: art. The writing of the Pentecost reproduces the illumination of the Celtic sacred manuscripts, and particularly the Book of Kells—the Irish Catholic version of the gift of tongues.

The invisibility of the Catholic text becomes visible: mysteriously signed as vision or revelation in Celtic illumination. Joyce appropriates the heterogeneity of the Book of Kells, the interlace style that infinitely translates the letter into color. This specifically Celtic stylization is emblematized by Joyce's relation to the *Tunc* page; its illumination is worked into the text of the *Wake,* where it is simultaneously absorbed and preserved in its singularity. The Joycean identification of the *Wake* with the Book of Kells manifests the focus of his poetic enterprise on the singularity of style itself, overflowing symbolic discourse. In the Book of Kells, Joyce singles out the *Tunc* page to encode the knot of passage. *Tunc* is the Celtic-Catholic letter of the Fall and its redemption, of sin and sublimation. Shem's letter (the entirety of *Finnegans Wake*) is sent infinitely far—"A way a lone a last a loved a long the"; it is engendered out of the interlace of names found in the Book of Kells. The illuminated letter is double: sexual and sublime.

In *Finnegans Wake,* the sacred and its lining of obscenity are infinitely written out, through an evocation of all possible forms of religious transcendence and scandalous desires (sins that must be rendered sublime). The Book of Kells figures this doubled dimension. Out of the heterogeneity formed by Judeo-Catholic scripture and Irish art springs an Irish comic tradition—i.e., an Irish tradition of *Catholic* comedy. In *Ulysses* and the *Wake,* Joyce's Celtic-Catholic position reveals the *beginning* (the primal scene, concupiscence, sin) as the eschatological entry into the world without end.

Sexual revelation and mystical sublimation maintain the sacred within the realm of comedy. Joyce's comedy takes the shape of paradox, like the oxymoron—that of the *felix culpa.* The sexual element implicates obscenity—concupiscent culpability—that *betrays* itself: the result is the laughter echoing the superego, expelling "sinse" as well as the guilty subject. The consequence: a death sentence, sacrifice, interdiction. These will later be undone, foiled by the *Witz;* at this moment, the subject takes possession of both the forbidden "sinse" and laughter—now freed of the superego. For the subject's greater *jouissance.* The laughter of the *Witz* gives evidence of a pleasure that was previously inaccessible. The saving or sparing of psychic energy now fills the space occupied by sacrifice (humor). The forbidden is still forbidden, but it is enjoyed. This paradoxical laughter of "bewilderment and illumination" slips toward the revelation of a *felix culpa* in the Joycean text. The No uttered by the superego gives way before a sublime Yes: the mystical *jouissance* of Dante's *Paradiso,* Bottom's vision in Shakespeare's *Midsummer Night's Dream.* This unspeakable infinite light of grace is figured as a Catholic Resurrection in *Finnegans Wake:* as a *divine comedy.* Bottom describes the "sweet comedy" he plays for the Duke as "very tragical mirth." The divine comedy of the *felix culpa* resembles it in Joyce's text as well as in that of Dante since it is the hell of desire and death that is "translated," like Bottom himself— *transsubstantiated.* This hell becomes a vision figured as song, "the concord of this discord." Out of tragedy: jubilation. Joyce's Celtic-Catholic heterogeneity is the fundamental discord of the *felix culpa,* or sacred comic art.

The moment of Celtic-Catholic origins becomes the climax of Joyce's sacred and comic art. According to Irish legend, the conversion of Ireland to Catholicism was the result of Saint Patrick's victory over the Druids. The Arch-Druid had forbidden Patrick to light the new fire of Holy Saturday, symbol of the Resurrection; but Patrick disobeyed the interdiction and sparked off the rejection of paganism. Joyce himself locates the acme of his art in the pagan-Catholic conflict opposing, at the end of *Finnegans Wake,* the philosopher Berkeley, in the guise of the Arch-Druid, to Saint Patrick. This opposition is played out in Berkeley's theory of colors. This text is also the ultimate trial of what is at stake in the writing of the *Wake.* Joyce commented: "Much more is intended in the colloquy between Berkeley the arch druid and his pidgin speech and Patrick the arch priest and his Nippon English. It is also the defense and indictment of the book itself, B's theory of colours and Patrick's practical solution of the problem."[1] Although Joyce never renders explicit what is implied by "Patrick's practical solution," Patrick seems to appropriate the colors of Berkeley's theory and render them performative: the colors are those illuminating the Book of Kells, encoded as "Tunc" (611.4). The final repetition of "Tunc" in the *Wake* occurs at the beginning of Berkeley's intervention. According to him, fallen man sees colors one by one while the druid sees them "in trues coloribus resplendent with sextuple gloria of light actually retained" (611.22). However, Berkeley's vision seems to be a seeing one by one, a spectrum composed exclusively of Irish greens. The color green evokes vegetation, nature, and paganism, ultimately a limited vision. But the resplendent prismatic colors of illuminated glory, the colors of the Book of Kells, will be revealed by Patrick. Moreover, at the moment of his intervention, *Tunc* will become an authentic signature, a monogram of the heterogeneity of Irish art: *"Punc."* (612.16). Out of this meeting, of this irreducible conflict, the Joycean Word is born.

Saint Patrick's practical solution is the vision of the resurrection of Hce now taking place: "Who his dickhuns now rearrexes from undernearth the memorialorum?" (610.3), "Hump cumps Ebblybally!" (612.15). Patrick invokes the illuminated Trinity. Balenoarch is *arcobaleno,* the rainbow of Father, Son, and Holy Ghost. It is with these illuminated names that *Finnegans Wake,* the Celtic interlace of Judeo-Catholic naming, reaches its culmination: "to Balenoarch (he kneeleths), to Great Balenoarch (he kneeleths down), to Greatest Great Balenoarch (he kneeleths down quitesomely), the sound sense sympol in a weedwayedwold of the firethere the sun in his halo cast. Onmen" (612.26). The Trinitarian name is the ultimate proper noun reuniting "sound" and "sense" in Joyce's symbolic art. Patrick's jubilation here recalls that which ends the *Divina Commedia,* the vision of celestial light: Dante's Father, Son, and Holy Ghost are named, in the Joycean text, as the fire, sun, and wheel of Dante's last lines in Paradise. They are named again, in the same passage, as "bygotter," "bogcotton," and "begad!" ending with the jubilatory exclamation point. Joyce's practical solution is the heterogeneous passage traced by his art: the call of the Holy Name, taken up by the colors of illumination, has become a signature without end.

Appendix
Notes
Bibliography
Index

The Tunc page of the book of Kells. Photo courtesy of The Rare Book Collection, Special Collections Division, The Milton S. Eisenhower Library, Johns Hopkins University.

Appendix

The Book of Kells
Irish Illumination and Joycean Writing

In order to be fully Irish, James Joyce went into exile. Any portrait of the artist begins with a gesture of negation, with the consummation of a rupture fraught with consequences. Joyce's passage, his exodus out of Ireland, enabled him paradoxically to know the Irish experience of the Dubliner in all its signifying dimensions. Joyce *created* Ireland out of nothing, in the *tohu* and *bohu* of exile. Out of nothing, *avec des riens:* thus Joyce described his writing of *Ulysses*. With nothing except a personal intensity, a rage capable of creating words and transfiguring tongues.

The specificity of Joyce's Catholicism functions through a series of reversals, torsions, and figurations of the Catholic position. In this sense, Joyce resembles the Irish saints who took the impossible path of exile all the way to eschatological truth. The love of wandering, *peregrinatio*, led them one by one to find their singular site of resurrection.[1] Joyce finds his site in Irish writing: a heterogeneous creation, both Catholic and Celtic. Outside the boundaries of the *lex romana*, Irish symbolism preserves its medieval character because of the juxtaposition of the sacred and the obscene.[2] The persistence of Irish paganism within the Catholic position produces Irish heterogeneity, or the sacred-comic doubling. Its model is the

Celtic illumination that anticipates the Joycean enterprise of making Catholicism into an art. Irish illumination is an important model for the new style, the "irish stew" of *Finnegans Wake*. Already in *Ulysses*, the Book of Kells is mentioned in the context of the infinitization and dissolution of fictional characters in Joycean discourse. In the *Wake*, the *Tunc* page of the Book of Kells (the illumination of Matthew 27:38) becomes an authentic signature, a monogram of the heterogeneity of Irish art. It signs the utterance of that other Irish exile, Saint Patrick: "*Punc*" (612.6.)

The Book of Kells, known as the Gospel of Saint Columba, is an Irish illuminated manuscript dating from the end of the eighth century or the beginning of the ninth. In 1914 Sir Edward Sullivan wrote a famous description of the manuscript, parodied by Joyce in the *Wake:* "Its weird & commanding beauty; its subdued & goldless colouring; the baffling intricacy of its fearless designs; the clean, unwavering sweep of rounded spiral; the creeping undulations of serpentine forms that writhe in artistic profusion through the mazes of its decorations; the strong & legible minuscule of its text; the quaintness of its striking portraiture; the unwearied reverence & patient labour that brought it into being; all of which combined go to make up the Book of Kells, have raised this ancient Irish volume to a position of abiding preeminence among the illuminated manuscripts of the world."[3] Sullivan here describes the spectacular Irish decoration of the Catholic text of the Gospels. The text becomes inseparable from its decoration; each sentence has its initial decorated with black lines or ornaments, accented with color or transformed into figures of people, animals, etc. Often, the letter is abandoned to interlace. The clear outline of its traced form gives way before a tress of ribbons, human figures, animal, plant, and geometric motifs. These motifs form a labyrinth of form and color. Their dazzling decoration sustains the text by bringing certain letters and words into symbolic or figurative relief with respect to the ensemble of a page or an evangelical text. The Book of Kells operates a double transmission of the written text and the text as painted figuration. This heterogeneity is displayed in the full-page illuminations. The intensity of the evangelical text is rendered through the isolation and high-

lighting of key phrases. These phrases are engaged by a decorative overabundance, by the *interlace* that brings out the
mysterious light of the words of the Gospel.

This interlace effect reveals the letter; it makes the letter
into a revelation. The mélange of ornaments, their sliding in
and out of each other, their clashes and conflicts—and the
juxtaposition of a multitude of *styles*—turn the traditional
repertoire of Celtic illumination into a wealth of forms that
animate the Catholic letter. Catholic writing becomes an extended figuration: dance, song, metaphor. This figuration is
infinitely evocative of the fantasies, dreams, and symbols of
the Celtic Other World, the legends that haunted the Irish
poets. Celtic illumination reveals the subjectivity specific to
the Gospel text while directing it toward its own ends—while
re-creating that text according to another subjectivity. The Book
of Kells recovers and re-creates the Gospel text in order to
take possession of it—in order to sign it forever with an Irish
signature, a beautiful and provocative arabesque. In order to
display it as a work of art.

Sullivan's edition of the Book of Kells accompanied Joyce
throughout his European exile. Aspiring to become "the poet
of his race," Joyce told Arthur Power: "You must write in your
own tradition. . . . You must write what is in your blood."[4] The
Book of Kells was the source of Irish art for Joyce; he advised
Power to use it as a *scriptural model.* As he began to compose
the *Wake,* Joyce marked the importance of the Book of Kells:
"It is the most purely Irish thing we have, and some of the
big initial letters which swing right across a page have the
essential quality of a chapter of Ulysses. Indeed, you can compare much of my work to the intricate illuminations."[5] The
letter is revealed through the interlace; illuminated, it becomes the signature of a singular vision. Joyce took as his model
the initials of the full-page decorations—the most spectacular
example of Celtic illuminated manuscript.

The heterogeneity of Celtic art is mirrored in the interlace
of names, the writing of *Finnegans Wake,* signed James Joyce.
This interlace is initialed in a series of portraits of the artist
(color and form) and signatures of the artist (letter and monogram): "thumb print, mademark or just a poor trait of the
artless" (114.32). "arabesque the page" (115.3), "So why, pray,

sign anything as long as every word, letter, penstroke, paperspace is a perfect signature of its own?" (115.6).

In Book I, 5, "The Hen," Joyce indicates a symbolic equivalence between Shem's letter (written for Alp, delivered by Shaun in order to save Hce) and the Book of Kells; Sullivan's commentary of the Book is turned into a parodic commentary of the Letter. Both the Letter and the Book of Kells dramatize Judeo-Catholic illumination and the culpability of original sin, the holy Resurrection and the Fall, sacred *jouissance* and Hce's comic downfall. These two texts are identified with the text of *Finnegans Wake,* Joyce's sacred-comic Letter, his interlace of "soundsense" (109.15, 121.15): the interlace of names is illuminated by the colors of the "rainbow girls," by voices, songs, metaphors, condensations cutting through the boundaries of languages.

Shem's letter as represented in Book I, 5, bears a particular resemblance to the *Tunc* page of the Book of Kells. It seems, then, that Joyce parodies Sullivan's interpretation and style not only as a description or discursive rendering of graphic art, but, ultimately, in order to appropriate the scripture and light glowing even now in the pages of the Book of Kells.

The full-page illumination called the *Tunc* page illustrates Matthew 27:38: *Tunc crucifixerant XPI cum eo duos latrones.* It is dominated by the initial T in the shape of a lion's body; its head devours a red snake. Another animal head (whose ribbon-shaped body intertwines with that of the devoured snake) becomes the ribbon framing the letters following the initial T. In the left margin, a second leonine head (barely distinct from the leonine body of the T) breathes fire. At the bottom of the page, the letters of the citation starting with the Christly monogram are arranged in a large initial X (described by commentators as a Saint Andrew's cross). The margins are decorated with ribbon motifs and primarily geometric interlace. They contain three groups of five spectators arranged in the form of a quincunx, probably intended to observe the Crucifixion.

In Book I, 5, Joyce rewrites the *Tunc* page through Shem's Letter and its commentary—the text of *Finnegans Wake.* The Letter is quoted: "with a beautiful present of wedding cakes for dear thankyou Chriesty and with grand funferall . . . with four crosskisses . . . tache of tch. The stain and that a teastain (. . . signing the page away)" (111.13). At the moment of Christ's funereal *jouissance,* he is thanked for his gift of beauty; halfway between tragedy and jubilation, an illumination of the Crucifixion takes shape. The four "crosskisses" echo the large X of the *Tunc* page. And the "teastain" or "tache of tch," rendered as the signature of the "masterbilker" or his portrait of the artist (114.32), engages the arabesque of the T, whose *presence* and *beauty* ("the beautiful presence of waiting kates" [116.21]) dominate the *Tunc* page.

The Letter is described in the following terms: "These ruled barriers along which the traced words, run, march, halt, walk, stumble . . . seem to have been drawn first of all in a pretty checker with lampblack and blackthorn. Such crossing is antechristian of course. . . . But by writing thithaways end to end and turning, turning and end to end hithaways writing and with lines of litters slittering up and louds of latters slettering down" (114.7, .16). This sounds like a description of the *Tunc* page. Most of its letters are framed by straight ribbons ("ruled barriers"); pre-Christian ("antechristian") motifs are used by the artist to illustrate the evangelical text; the major focus is on the large initial X ("crossing"). Letters ascend the X ("lines of litters slittering up") and descend it ("louds of latters slettering down") like the angels on the *ladder* dreamed by Jacob (the Latin translation of James). Letters follow the ribbons of the X in all directions—like Joyce's handwriting on the colored manuscripts of the *Wake.* The ascending and descending letters recall the origins of writing, noted at the beginning of the *Wake:* "A hatch, a celt, an earshare the pourquose of which was to cassay the earthcrust at all of hours, furrowards, bagawards, like yoxen at the turnpaht" (18.30). Boustrophedon writing figures the Celtic-Christian itinerary of Hce—fallen, resuscitated: "by writing thithaways end to end and turning, turning and end to end hithaways writing." Joyce's Celtic-Catholic passage is turned toward writing, from one end to the other. His conjugation of the letter (*litter, letter, latter*) leads him toward the prophetic signature, toward the monogram.

The turns of Joyce *polytropos* bring into relief the arabesque of Hce's monogram: "a round thousand whirligig glorioles, prefaced by (alas!) now illegible airy plumeflights, all tiberiously ambiembellishing the initials majuscule of Earwicker: the meant to be baffling chrismon trilithon sign ⊓ , finally called after some his hes hecitency Hec, which, moved contrawatchwise, represents his title in sign sigla" (119.14). The text parodies the beginning of Sullivan's introduction and, especially, his explication of the chrismon of the *Tunc* page: "The XPI, which seems to belong to the sentence, is, as pointed out by Sir John Gilbert, probably only the medieval note-mark composed of the monogram of 'Christi', which was arbitrarily used to call attention to remarkable passages. It was known as the Chrismon."[6] The Kells chrismon offers a "tiberiously ambiembellishing" version of the monogram; Shem the ambidextrous artist turns his Letter into a work of beauty. The Tiberian vocalization of the Hebrew Bible puts the Letter into Judaic enunciation.

As the chapter continues, Joyce's engagement of the *Tunc* page becomes more explicit. Through Hce and the "plumeflights" tracing the interlace of his title, name, sigla, illuminated monogram—his *chrismon*, or Christly monogram—Joyce re-creates the Celtic-Christian context of the Book of Kells in the illuminated letter, the infinite signature of the interlace that offers an image of the infinitely radiant and symbolic body of Christ (XPI). Hce's signature constitutes the splendor of the Word taken up by the interlace of names, Shem's Letter. Shem, the Joycean writer, is "cunctant that another would finish his sentence for him" (288.4); Shaun will tell him that he has read the message of his letter: "I've read your tunc's dimissage" (298.7).

A Sullivan-like voice evokes the art of the Book of Kells: "then . . . the cruciform postscript from which three basia or shorter and smaller *oscula* have been overcarefully scraped away, plainly inspiring the tenebrous *Tunc* page of the Book of Kells (and then it need not be lost sight of that there are exactly three squads of candidates for the crucian rose awaiting their turn in the marginal panels of Columkiller, chugged in their three ballotboxes, then set apart for such hanging committees, where two was enough for anyone, starting with old Matthew himself, as he with great distinction said then just as since then . . . when the third person is the person darkly spoken of, and then that last labiolingual *basium* might be read as a *suavium*" (122.20). Here Joyce specifically inscribes the *Tunc* page *through his own writing: Finnegans Wake*, or Shem's Letter. Colum Cille and Matthew are named via their Irish and Catholic text. The *Tunc* page is named—"then" (*tunc*) is repeated several times, rhythmically scanning the text with the hidden name of the "tenebrous *Tunc* page of the Book of Kells." The kiss ("basium," "suavium") of the Letter resembles the large initial X of the *Tunc* page, "the cruciform postscript."

Beginning with Tenebrae ("tenebrous," "darkly"), the three groups in the *Tunc* page margins are evoked in their context of the Crucifixion. Christ ("the third person," "the person darkly spoken of") sets off the lights and colors of illumination with his "beautiful presence." Through his Resurrection, and the jubilant *vision* it offers. Christ is identified as "the crucian rose," echoing the mystical rose of Dante's Trinitarian vision in the *Paradiso*. Joyce returns to the end of *Ulysses* and the Dantean rose he wove into the cascade of roses concluding "Penelope": "lastly when all is zed and done, the penelopean patience of its last paraphe, a colophon of no fewer than seven hundred and thirtytwo strokes tailed by a leaping lasso—" (123.4). The 732 pages of the first edition of *Ulysses*, its "last paraphe"—the "zed" ending its alphabet and its decorative, emblematic artistic signature, the "colophon": here is the end of the Letter. Or its beginning: the entry into the vision of the mystical rose, the entry into the Letter of *Finnegans Wake*, the new writing of *Tunc. Rosa mystica*, writes Joyce, since the letters to the Virgins (Nora, Martha . . .)—*Tunc* is also the feminine anagram. Through Catholic Latin and English slang, Joyce writes Molly's *jouissance* in a sacred and obscene text, signing his own signature in the writing of *Tunc*.

Tunc indicates the unnameable realm of the drives, in the entrails of the letter—close to the heart of *Finnegans Wake* and the possibilities of reading it. The letter is born of abjection and fright: indirectly it is spat out by the T of the lion's head and the devoured snake. The interlaced margins of the borders are also spat out by a lion (one of the evangelical symbols). This detritus of illumination figures the *ruah*, the creative breath: the light of the fire spat out in the beginning. The letter bears a masterly signature, X (and XPI as well). Ladder, cross, and monogram sign the darkness of divine murder, their tones of red and lavender, blue and green displaying the jubilation to come.

The driven aspect of the letter is translated into motifs, decorations, distortions. The paradox of Celtic-Catholic sublimation is this: in the Book of Kells, the more the letter operates as letter (signature, monogram, chrismon, the trace of the finger of the Spirit: *the invisible*), the more it operates as the contrary of the letter—illuminated decoration. This decoration is a mixture of representative forms and abstract tracing. The interlace summarizes the virtuosity of motifs, ribbons, colors, and geometrical forms.

Letter and non-letter: the Book of Kells reproduces, in reverse, the enigmatic itinerary of the alphabet and its writing from the hieroglyph (a thing-presentation) to the letter (a sound-presentation). In *Moses and Monotheism*,[7] Freud notes the potential role of the forbidden status of representation in the symbolic destiny of the Jews. A consideration of the development of the Hebraic alphabet starting from Egyptian hieroglyphics[8] reveals the gradual effacing of representative forms and the approach of an abstract architecture in the form of "ribbons," fragmented interlace, *letters* (of the Hebraic alphabet). This alphabet shifts the emphasis away from the form of a thing toward *the signature of a sound*. If less is seen, as compared to Egyptian hieroglyphics, it is because more can be heard: the sign of the voice, the encoded call of the voice. The focus of the writing system is no longer the recognition of a thing-presentation; the focus of the alphabet is the nonthing of language, of voice, serially monogrammatized in *the name of the letter*.

The animal on the *Tunc* page vomits the sacred letter of the desiring subject (figured in the gaze of the quincunx, the *coup de dés* burning the margins) aspiring toward God. The subject of the Book of Kells resembles Jonah in the belly of the whale: swallowed, spat out, cornered between fear and love of God. Jonah dives into the sea in order to flee his Yahweh, but he will be delivered, vomited by abjection itself, onto the beach whose border marks divine deliverance. Yahweh's commandment saves him. The Book of Kells (a swarm of bodies, tails, entrails) makes the sacred letter into a locus of multiple borderlines in which line and color bear witness to the oral, driven ferocity of the Celtic-Catholic subject. The fearful and fascinating decoration, grotesquely impassioned, overflows the confines of the letter. Each letter itself becomes a singular landscape of gestures, limbs, desires. As if to say that there can be no sacred sublimation without its discordant, abject, and serpentine double—inseparable from sin and the Fall. The Catholic who operates Judeo-Christian transcendence cannot help but see these pagan images of sin as comical. Turning to a scheme that has become classic, the prophet or victorious Son makes the fallen Father Adam into a comical and ridiculous character . . . the cuckold of Paradise and of the Redemption.[9]

In the eyes of the letter, the drives are comical: but their presence, intruding into the sacred, threatens and overflows the limits that constitute the letter. Translated into Irish art, paganism turns the sacred, theological letter of Scripture into *a vision, a sublimation, an illumination of the invisible. Tunc* is the Celtic-Catholic letter of fall and redemption, of sin and sublimation. The Letter of Shem that is all of *Finnegans Wake* is engendered as an interlace of names, mediated by the Book of Kells. Judeo-Catholic writing and Irish art found the heterogeneity of the Book of Kells, giving rise to an Irish comic tradition—i.e., an Irish *Catholic* comic tradition. Joyce's Celtic-Catholic position reveals, in *Ulysses* and *Finnegans Wake*, the beginning as the eschatological entry into the world without end.

Notes

PREFACE

1 Richard Ellmann, *James Joyce* (New York: Oxford University Press, 1959), p. 345.

2 Stanislaus Joyce, *My Brother's Keeper* (London: Faber and Faber, 1958), pp. 27, 29.

3 Ellmann, *Joyce*, p. 30.

4 Stanislaus Joyce, *Recollections of James Joyce* (New York: James Joyce Society, 1950), p. 7.

5 Ellmann, *Joyce*, p. 133.

6 Ibid., p. 134.

7 During Holy Week, Joyce seemed to suspend his dramatic exile from the Church with an equally dramatic return: "You had better not look for Joyce during the week before Easter, because he is not available to anyone. On the morning of Palm Sunday, then during the four days that follow Wednesday of Holy Week, and especially during all the hours of those great symbolic rituals at the early morning service, Joyce is at church . . . following the liturgy attentively in his book of the Holy Week Services, and often joining in the singing of the choir" (Alessandro Francini Bruni, "Joyce Stripped Naked in the Piazza," in *Portraits of the Artist in Exile*, ed. Willard Potts [Seattle: University of Washington Press, 1979], pp. 35, 37).

8 Mary Colum and Padraic Colum, *Our Friend James Joyce* (Garden City, N.Y.: Doubleday, 1958), pp. 205, 207.

9 Ellmann, *Joyce*, p. 27.

10 Frank Budgen, "Further Recollections," in *James Joyce and the Making of 'Ulysses' and Other Writings* (London: Oxford University Press, 1972), p. 352.

11 Ibid., p. 186.

12 Ellmann, *Joyce*, p. 372; Louis Gillet, *Stèle pour James Joyce* (Marseille: Sagittaire, 1946), p. 144; Joyce, *My Brother's Keeper*, p. 173.

13 Budgen, *James Joyce*, p. 191. Budgen later writes: "Joyce's attitude toward the Christian religion was twofold. When he remembered his own youthful conflict with it in its Irish-Roman form he could be bitterly hostile, but in general, viewing it as a whole as an objective reality and as epitomized human experience and from a position well out of reach of any church's authority and sanctions it was for him a rich mine of material for the construction of his own myth. Then he was a collector displaying all a collector's ardour" (ibid., p. 352).

14 Joyce, *My Brother's Keeper*, p. 140.

15 Ellmann, *Joyce*, p. 406.

16 Colum and Colum, *Our Friend James Joyce*, p. 183.

17 Jacques Mercanton, *Les Heures de James Joyce* (Lausanne: L'Age d'Homme, 1967), p. 32.

READING JOYCE

1 Stanislaus Joyce wrote that Joyce "is trying to commit the sin against the Holy Ghost for the purpose of getting outside the utmost rim of Catholicism" (*The Complete Dublin Diary of Stanislaus Joyce* [Ithaca: Cornell University Press, 1962], p. 55, n. 5).

2 Because of the richness and complexity of the *Wake*, textual quotation, paraphrasing, and explication are inevitably fragmentary. This fragmentation is perhaps compensated by the reading of heterogeneity in the text of the *Wake*, indicative of the plurality essential to its structural and signifying dimensions. Wherever possible, the explication attempts to illustrate both the argument and the interpretation of the text in question, without legislating the possible resonances of the latter.

3 Julia Kristeva, *Polylogue* (Paris: Seuil, 1977), p. 122. The multiplicity of the theme seems accentuated when its content represents *états-limites* that can be related to the Joycean experience of Catholicism.

4 James Joyce, *Dubliners* (Great Britain: Jonathan Cape, Ltd., 1967). Joyce wrote *Dubliners* between 1904 and 1907. According to Theodore Spencer's "Introduction to the First Edition," Joyce wrote *Stephen Hero* between 1904 and 1906; between 1907 and 1914 he rewrote it as *A Portrait of the Artist as a Young Man*. Between 1914 and 1921 he wrote *Ulysses*.

5 James Joyce, *Stephen Hero* (Great Britain: Jonathan Cape, Ltd., 1944). James Joyce, *A Portrait of the Artist as a Young Man* (New York: Viking Press, 1964). Subsequent page references to these works will appear in parentheses in the text.

6 "He [Joyce] once said to me, 'A voice is like a woman—you respond or you do not; its appeal is direct'" (Colum and Colum, *Our Friend James Joyce,* p. 185).

7 Letter of October 29, 1934, in James Joyce, *Letters of James Joyce,* ed. Richard Ellmann (New York: Viking Press, 1966), vol. 3.

8 In her Introduction to Saint Augustine, *Sermons pour la Pâque* (Paris: Cerf, 1966), p. 15, Suzanne Poque writes: "Pâque est le sacrement du passage. Le mot lui-même l'indique: *Pascha* en hébreu signifie *transitus.*"

9 [Saint] Thomas d'Aquin, *Somme théologique: La Trinité,* trans. Hyacinthe Dondaine, O.P. (Paris: Cerf, 1943), q. 27, sol. 3.

10 Saint Augustine interprets the *"jouissance"* of the Holy Spirit according to Saint Hilary as "the ineffable enflaming of the Father and the Image" (*De Trinitate* [Paris: Desclée de Brouwer, 1955], L. VI; C. X, 11).

11 Letter of August 21, 1912, in Joyce, *Letters of James Joyce,* vol. 2. Joyce alludes to the Angelus, quoted in the text.

AND THE LIGHT SHINETH IN DARKNESS

1 Regarding the Catholic position implicit in Joycean writing, see *Tel Quel,* 83 (1980), and Jacques Aubert, "Sur James Joyce," *Ornicar? Analytica, Mélanges,* 4 (n.d.): 10.

2 James Joyce, *Ulysses* (New York: Random House, 1960), p. 47. Page references to this edition will appear in parentheses in the text. Except where indicated, biblical quotations are taken from *The Holy Bible: Authorized (King James) Version* (New York: New York Bible Society, n.d.); quotations in French are from *La Bible de Jérusalem* (Paris: Cerf, 1978), and quotations in Latin are from the *Biblia Vulgata* (Madrid: Biblioteca des Autores Cristianos, Edica, 1977).

3 Italian quotations of the *Divina Commedia* are taken from Dante, *Le Opere di Dante Alighieri,* ed. Giorgio Petrocchi (Milan: Arnold Mondadori, 1966–1967). English quotations are taken from Dante, *The Divine Comedy,* trans. Charles Singleton (Princeton: Princeton University Press, 1970). As regards Daedalus and Icarus, see David Hayman, "Forms of Folly in Joyce: A Study of Clowning in Ulysses," *ELH,* 34 (June 1967): 261. According to the *Oxford English Dictionary* (OED), s.v. "lapwing," the lapwing is "a wellknown bird of the plover family. . . . Allusions are frequent . . . to the notion that the newly hatched lapwing runs about with its head in the shell." The OED quotes John Gower (*Confessio Amantis,* II: 329): "A lappewinke has lost his feith And is the brid falsest of alle."

4 Since the demoniacal is rooted in the subject as speaking subject, it is situated *within* Catholicism. Hereditary *punishments* (Gen. 3)

resulting from Adam's Fall do not constitute the inherited *fault:* the doctrine of original sin is given by Paul in Romans 5. Christianity makes sin an integral part of being, whereas Judaism, at least before the prophets, attempts to maintain a separation between sin and being (see Julia Kristeva, *Pourvoirs de l'horreur* [Paris: Seuil, 1980], pp. 125–142; and Jean-Louis Houdebine and Philippe Sollers, "La Trinité de Joyce," *Tel Quel,* 83 (1980): 51, 55, 79). In "A 17th Century Demonological Neurosis," Freud writes: "The evil demon of the Middle Ages—was, according to Christian mythology, himself a fallen angel and of a godlike nature. It does not need much analytic perspicacity to guess that God and the Devil were originally identical—were a single figure which was later split into two figures with opposite attributes. In the earliest ages of religion God himself still possessed all the terrifying features which were afterwards combined to form a counterpart of him" (*The Standard Edition of the Complete Psychological Works of Sigmund Freud,* ed. James Strachey [London: Hogarth Press, and the Institute of Psychoanalysis, 1953–74], 19:86). This edition will be henceforth designated as *SE.*

5 John Milton, *Paradise Lost,* I, 125, in *The Complete Poetry* (Garden City, N. Y.: Anchor Books, Doubleday, 1971).

6 In his "Remarks on Oedipus," Hölderlin evokes the *"transport, which, in the measuring of syllables, is named caesura,* pure speech" (*Oeuvres* [Paris: Gallimard, 1967], pp. 951–958). The "uprooting" of tragedy, "the drama, like that of a trial for heresy," creates a confrontation between God and man; this face-to-face pulls knowledge out of the Augustinian enigma. We are establishing a link between the *jouissance* of tragic sublimation and that of the Christian revelation; the narratives of Apocalypse designate their crossing.

7 Compare the mortal cut of the sword in the final catastrophe of *Hamlet* and the "twoedged sword" coming from Christ's mouth (Apoc. 1:16). The latter is a metaphor for the word: "He fears the lancet of my art as I fear that of his. The cold steelpen" (*U* 7).

8 *U* 428. "Sinned against the light and even now that day is at hand when he shall come to judge the world by fire." Cf. pp. 434, 583, 598.

9 Relations of fraternal enemies play an increasingly important role in Joyce's trilogy. Regarding Byrne ("Cranly"), Joyce wrote to Nora on August 29, 1904: "When I was younger I had a friend to whom I gave myself freely—in a way more than I give to you and in a way less. He was Irish, that is to say, he was false to me" (Joyce, *Letters,* vol. 2).

10 According to Freud, the family romance helps to free the child from parental authority but exalts the parents as well by recapitulating the over-valuation of the parents during the child's first years. Family romance is often motivated by an unavowable incestuous desire (*SE* 9:235–241). At the time of Stephen's "descent" into sin, he sees himself as irremediably distanced from his family. He evokes "the restless shame and rancour that divided him from mother and brother and sister. He felt that he was hardly of the one blood with them but stood to them rather in the mystical kinship of fosterage" (Joyce, *Portrait*, p. 90).

11 Ulick O'Connor notes that Gogarty (Mulligan's model) "had never acquired the penitential habit as Joyce had, when the hellfire sermons of the Jesuits terrified him with visions of damnation." He quotes a letter Gogarty wrote to C. Bell in January 1905: "I cannot but think that religious people who live in ostrich holes and let their reason atrophy have disobeyed the very injunction they fancy they are following—they have not taken up their cross" ("Joyce and Gogarty," in John Ryan, ed., *A Bash in the Tunnel: James Joyce by the Irish* [London: Clifton Books, 1970], p. 98).

12 According to René Girard, the sacred plays a fundamental role in hominization—it is the source of culture (*Anthropologie fondamentale*, livre 1 in *Des Choses cachées depuis la fondation du monde* [Paris: Grasset, 1978]). The separation between man and nature is reinforced in Judeo-Christianity by the definitive rejection of cyclical time (see Jean Guitton, *Le Temps et l'éternité chez Plotin et Saint Augustin* [Paris: Vrin, 1971], pp. 403–404.)

13 In his seminar on "Le Sinthome," Lacan writes: "Les pulsions, c'est l'écho dans le corps du fait qu'il y a un dire" (*Ornicar? Analytica, Mélanges*, 6 [n.d.]:8.). He defines psychoanalysis as a "court-circuit passant par le sens, le sens comme tel que j'ai défini tout à l'heure de la copulation du langage, puisque c'est de ça que je supporte l'inconscient, avec notre propre corps" (ibid., 9 [n.d.]:34). On the subject of the knot, he says: "C'est une façon d'articuler que cette sexualité humaine est perverse, si nous suivons bien ce que dit Freud" (ibid., 11[n.d.]:8).

14 The anti-Semitic Mulligan delights in having seen Bloom admire the statue of Venus; he accuses Bloom of being homosexual (cf. regarding the distance from femininity, Mulligan's remarks on masturbation and homosexuality in "Scylla and Charybdis.")

15 "L'érotisation de l'abjection, et peut-être toute abjection pour autant qu'elle est déjà érotisée, est une tentative d'arrêter l'hémorragie: un seuil devant la mort, un arrêt ou un palier?" (Kristeva, *Pouvoirs de l'horreur*, p. 67.). In *My Brother's Keeper*, Stanislaus Joyce notes the nickname given Joyce by Gogarty: "the virginal kipran-

ger," the virginal explorer of whorehouses. According to Stanislaus Joyce, this erotic bias comes directly from Catholicism (p. 160).

16 In this passage and elsewhere, our reading of Joycean abjection owes a great deal to Kristeva's *Pouvoirs de l'horreur*. In regard to the prayer, "Liliata rutilantium" (*U* 10, 23, 190, 580, 704), Aubert notes the perversity of the confessor and Joyce's doubled position: "Mais tout se passe comme si Joyce jouait les deux jeux à la fois, s'efforçait d'occuper *en même temps*, pour sa plus grande jouissance, *deux* positions par rapport au symbolique, l'une faisant vrai, l'autre faux trou. . . . Joyce choisit de confesser avec *et* contre le confesseur pervers, de jouer à la fois le jeu de la casuistique, du cas comme récupérable, et de ce qui tombe à côté du tout. C'est-à-dire le jeu de l'hérésie" ("Sur James Joyce," p. 10).

17 The mourning for the mother and the fantasized mourning for the young Jewish woman (desired by Giacomo Joyce) come together in the desire attributed to God. All love for women is incestuous, all objects are substitutes for the mother, the original object. (See Freud, *Totem and Taboo*, I, "The Horror of Incest" [*SE* 13]; *Three Essays on the Theory of Sexuality*, III, 5, "The Finding of an Object" [*SE* 7]; "On the Universal Tendency to Debasement in the Sphere of Love" [*SE* 11], pp. 180, 183, 189. See also Jacques Lacan, *Séminaire XI* [Paris: Seuil, 1973], p. 173.)

18 "Mais Freud nous révèle . . . que la Loi est au service du désir qu'elle institue par l'interdiction de l'inceste. Car l'inconscient montre que le désir est accroché à l'interdit, que la crise de l'Oedipe est déterminante pour la maturation sexuelle elle-même" (Jacques Lacan, *Ecrits* [Paris: Seuil, 1966], p. 852). On the subject of the "terme autrifié de la pulsion orale," Lacan says: "Puisque nous nous référons au nourrisson et au sein, et que le nourrissage, c'est la succion, disons que la pulsion orale, c'est le *se faire sucer*, c'est le vampire" (*Séminaire XI*, p. 178).

19 "The way in which dreams treat the category of contraries and contradictions is highly remarkable. It is simply disregarded. 'No' seems not to exist so far as dreams are concerned. They show a particular preference for combining contraries into a unity or for representing them as one and the same thing" (Sigmund Freud, *The Interpretation of Dreams*, VI.C, [*SE* 4], p. 318).

20 Irish parody seems particularly apt to sustain ambivalence (of sense and the non-sense that attacks it), thanks to the primordial role of the signifier in the Irish comic tradition. The verbal magic of the Druids is at the source of the wordplay, puns, assonances, and alliterations so important in Irish comedy from the ninth century to the present. (See Vivian Mercier, *The Irish Comic Tra-*

dition [New York: Oxford University Press, 1969], pp. 3, 6, 9, 10.) Regarding the opposition between serious discourse and parody, see Houdebine and Sollers, "La Trinité de Joyce," pp. 41–42; and David Hayman, *Ulysses: The Mechanics of Meaning* (Englewood Cliffs, N.J.: Prentice-Hall, 1970), pp. 17, 37–42, 55–61. See also Hayman's "Forms of Folly in Joyce," pp. 260–283.

21 Georges Bataille, *Le Coupable,* in *Oeuvres complètes* (Paris: Gallimard, 1973), vol. 5, p. 251.

22 "The Renaissance, to be concise, has put the journalist in the monk's chair. . . . We might say indeed that modern man has an epidermis rather than a soul" (James Joyce, "The Universal Literary Influence of the Renaissance," in Louis Berrone, *James Joyce in Padua* [New York: Random House, 1977], p. 90. Berrone notes: "Joyce wished to retain the medieval ability to depict the various planes of the human soul in art and architecture, but as a modern writer he realized that he must also base his work to a large extent on realism" (ibid., p. 47). See also Arthur Power, *Conversations with James Joyce* (New York: Barnes and Noble, 1974).

23 The major Trinitarian heresies: the modalism of Sabellius underlines the unity of divine substance at the expense of the three Persons (third century); subordinationism maintains the three Persons but denies their equality, culminating in the heresy of Arius, who devalues the Word in order to preserve the privileged position of the Father (fourth century). (Arianism persisted in the Christological conflicts in the East during the fifth and sixth centuries.) The word *filioque,* added to the Nicene Creed in order to specify the procession of the Holy Spirit from the Son as well as from the Father, is denounced by Photius (ninth century). The *filioque* controversy, central in the ninth century, contributed to the break in 1054 between the Roman Church and the Byzantine Church, and still separates the Orthodox Church and the Roman Catholic Church. See [Saint] Thomas d'Aquin, *Somme théologique: La Trinité.* See in addition *Des Origines à Grégoire le Grand* and *Le Moyen Age,* vols. 1 and 2 of *Nouvelle Histoire de l'Eglise* (Paris: Seuil, 1963 and 1968).

24 Saint Augustine, *De Trinitate,* I. II, 4; XV. VIII, 14; V. IX, 10; XV. XXVIII, 43.

25 Lacan, *Ecrits,* p. 272. See for "la symbolisation dans l'être," p. 275.

26 Julia Kristeva, "La Musique parlée ou remarques sur la subjectivité dans la fiction à propos du "Neveu de Rameau," in Michèle Duchet and Michèle Jalley, *Langue et langages de Leibniz à l'Encyclopédie* (Paris:10/18, 1977). "Moment décisif et lourd de conséquence: le sujet trouvant son identité dans le symbolique, se *sé-*

pare de son implication dans la mère, *localise* sa jouissance comme génitale, et transfère la motilité sémiotique dans l'ordre symbolique." "Il faut que la castration ait été un problème, un trauma, un drame, pour qu'à travers la position symbolique qu'elle cause, le sémiotique puisse faire retour" (Julia Kristeva, *La Révolution du langage poétique* [Paris: Seuil, 1974], pp. 45, 49).

27 See Sigmund Freud, *Civilization and Its Discontents*, chaps. 2 and 3 [*SE* 21].

28 John Lyons writes that proper names "are *particular* (or 'singular') terms, denoting some definite, *individual* substance" (*Introduction to Theoretical Linguistics* [Cambridge: Cambridge University Press, 1968], 8.1.3). The proper name is the signifier representing the singular subject; it occupies a privileged "sacred" space, and can only be defined, according to Jakobson, as a reference to the code of language itself ("Les embrayeurs, les catégories verbales et le verbe russe," in Roman Jakobson, *Essais de linguistique générale* vol. 1. [Paris: Ed. de Minuit, 1963]). Set apart from communication, the enunciation of the proper name creates an event, either by its vocative function or by its performative capacity to name, so crucial in religious discourse (rites of passage, taboos, etc.). (See John Lyons, *Eléments de sémantique* [Paris: Larousse, 1978], 7.5.) The proper name is thus part of being itself.

29 The father of his grandfather evokes Dante's "vergine madre, figlia di tuo figlio," which will be discussed in "*Modus Peregrinus: The Trinity.*"

1 Joycean criticism has catalogued the multiple circumstances of this resemblance. See Richard Ellmann, *Ulysses on the Liffey* (New York: Oxford University Press, 1972), and *The Consciousness of Joyce* (London: Faber and Faber, Ltd., 1977); Marilyn French, *The Book as World* (Cambridge, Mass.: Harvard University Press, 1976), esp. pp. 88–89, 191–195; Clive Hart and David Hayman, *James Joyce's "Ulysses": Critical Essays* (Berkeley: University of California Press, 1974); Jean Kimball, "The Hypostasis in 'Ulysses,'" *James Joyce Quarterly*, 10, (1972–1973):422–438. The coming together of Bloom and Stephen takes effect beginning with their shared *lack,* extended through various details of their daily lives: their wounds, exiles, mourning, and expulsions are linked by a signifying pathway or chain in the letter itself. Hayman notes the predominance of these "signifying clusters" (*Ulysses,* p. 18). (See, in addition, the articles of Leo Knuth: "The Ring and the Cross in

Joyce's Ulysses," in Louis Bonnerot, Jacques Aubert, and Claude Jaquet, *Ulysses cinquante ans après* (Paris: Marcel Didier, 1974), pp. 181–188; "A Bathymetric Reading of Joyce's *Ulysses,* 'ch. X,' *James Joyce Quarterly,* 9 [1971–1972]; "Joyce's Verbal Acupuncture," *James Joyce Quarterly,* 10 [1972–1973].) These "symbolic clusters" seem to function along the lines of Mallarméan "suggestion," allowing the writer to retreat into the "disparition élocutoire du poète, qui cède l'initiative aux mots, par le heurt de leur inégalité mobilisés" (see Stéphane Mallarmé, *Crise de vers* in *Oeuvres complètes* [Paris: Gallimard, 1945], p. 366.). Jacques Aubert writes: "C'est que le langage dans *Ulysses,* perversement fidèle à sa nature secrète, est trompeur, est là pour faire glisser, sans heurt, sans transgression douloureuse, le lecteur de l'autre côté de sa transparence" ("Remarques sur quelques études critiques," in *Ulysses cinquante ans après,* p. 295).

2 All day long Bloom thinks about the erotic wound caused by Milly's absence and sexual maturity (see pp. 285, 542, 692–695). Molly too thinks about her daughter's eroticism (see pp. 766–768). Cf. the incestuous relations between HCE and Isabel in *Finnegans Wake*.

3 On the subject of the role of the mother in the Gospels, Julia Kristeva remarks that the filial relationship eludes the corporeal, matrilinear element and invests itself exclusively in the proper name ("Héréthique de l'amour," *Tel Quel,* 74 [1977]:32–33).

4 Cf. *U* 609, 652–654, 695. Concerning the spiritual union of two men through the body of a woman (including, perhaps, the resonance of the unity of Father and Son when the latter is engendered in the body of the Virgin), Joyce writes: "Bertha wishes for the spiritual union of Richard and Robert and *believes* (?) that union will be effected only through her body, and perpetuated thereby" ("Notes by the Author," in *Exiles* [New York: The Viking Press, 1951], p. 123).

5 See Ellmann, *Ulysses on the Liffey,* p. 35.

6 The question of paternity is also present in this narrative; God commands the transmission of Aaron's vestments to his son Eleazar (Num. 20:26–29).

7 "La Loi morale n'est rien d'autre que cette refente du sujet qui s'opère de toute intervention du signifiant: nommément du sujet de l'énonciation au sujet de l'énoncé." "Le drame du sujet dans le verbe, c'est qu'il y fait l'épreuve de son manque à être" (Lacan, *Ecrits,* pp. 770, 655. See also pp. 840–844, and "La Signification du phallus," pp. 685–695).

8 Sigmund Freud, Draft 67-1-1895, quoted by Kristeva, *Pouvoirs de l'horreur,* p. 67.

9 James Joyce, *Giacomo Joyce* (New York: The Viking Press, 1968), p. 16.

10 Kristeva, "La Musique parlée," pp. 184–203.

11 Regarding the reconciliation between Joyce and his father in 1909, Louis Gillet notes that John Joyce played an aria on the piano and asked his son: "Tu as reconnu l'air que je jouais tantôt?—Oui, c'est celui du père d'Armand dans la pièce de Verdi." Gillet adds: "Il n'en fut pas dit davantage," "Un air de piano tenait lieu d'un discours" (*Stèle pour James Joyce*, pp. 130–131, 148). "Notons dans *Ulysse* le rapport très mystérieux que constate Bloom entre la voix de Simon Dedalus et celle de Stephen, rapport qui s'effectue au-delà et à l'encontre de tout ce qui peut séparer la personne factuelle du géniteur et celle de 'l'engendré'; et de fait, il ne s'agit nullement d'un banal et phénoménal rapport de ressemblance de l'une à l'autre, puisque la performance vocale de Stephen est à elle seule parfaitement originale, et que de toute façon, c'est avec Bloom, et non avec Simon Dedalus, que le 'colloque' s'établit. Il semble bien à cet égard que le vecteur principal de cet 'état mystique' qu'est la paternité pour Joyce soit précisément la voix: celle qui s'exprime dans le chant" (Houdebine and Sollers, "La Trinité de Joyce," p. 60, n. 26).

12 For the names of Mary and Martha, see *U* 79. Bloom comes very close to a fantasy of Christ's preaching as a *relationship* with women, thus bringing into proximity Christ/Bloom and Mary, Martha (Luke 10:38; John 11—12)/Molly, Martha Clifford/the two prostitutes.

13 Cf. the liturgical "*consummatus est*," in *Stephen Hero*, p. 110. (In Luke 13:32, "et tertia die consummor," the Resurrection is evoked.)

14 Girard, *Des Choses*, p. 275. "Jésus est le dernier et le plus grand des prophètes, celui qui les résume et les transcende tous. . . . Avec lui un déplacement à la fois minuscule et gigantesque se produit qui se situe dans le prolongement direct de l'Ancien Testament mais qui constitue aussi une rupture formidable" (ibid., p. 223).

15 See Roderick Davis, "The Fourfold Moses in Ulysses," *James Joyce Quarterly*, 7 (1970): 120–131.

16 On the subject of Mosaic exile, Stephen makes the explicit parallel between Jew and Irishman. Davis writes: "Joyce was captivated by this analogy of Israel and Ireland, Egyptian rule and English, Moses and Parnell" (ibid., p. 123).

17 Cf. for this passage *U* 122. The pertinent biblical passages are the following: Exod. 12; Matt. 26:2; Mark 14:1; Luke 22:1; John 13:1.

18 Cf. the exile of Stephen upon his return to Ireland. The writer

is an exile, whether at home or far away: those pertinent to *Ulysses* are Dante, Shakespeare, Ibsen, and Joyce himself.

19 See Jacques Lacan, *Séminaire XX* (Paris, Seuil, 1975), pp. 26–27, 41, 45, 48, 57, 65–70, 81, 85, 89, 103.

20 "Les figures ne seraient rien d'autre que *le langage perçu en tant que tel;* autrement dit, un emploi du langage dans lequel celui-ci cesse plus ou moins de remplir sa fonction de signification (c'est-à-dire de renvoyer à quelque chose d'absent) pour acquérir une existence opaque" (Oswald Ducrot and Tzvetan Todorov, *Dictionnaire encyclopédique des sciences du langage* [Paris: Seuil, 1972], pp. 351–352).

21 *La Bible de Jérusalem* (Paris: Cerf., 1978), p. 122, n. f. See as well Matt. 17:2 and 28:3.

22 Girard interprets this passage according to his non-sacrificial reading of Christianity (*Des Choses,* pp. 449–450). He situates the origin of this non-sacrificial analysis in "une tendance indubitable chez les écrivains bibliques à se situer moralement du côté des victimes, à prendre le parti et la défense des victimes" (ibid., p. 171).

23 See Philip Herring, *Joyce's "Ulysses" Notesheets in the British Museum* (Charlottesville: University of Virginia Press, 1972), p. 17; and Ellmann, *Joyce,* p. 477. On Judaism, anti-Semitism, and virility, see David Hayman, "Cyclops," in Hart and Hayman, *James Joyce's "Ulysses,"* pp. 243–275; and French, *Book as World,* pp. 138–156.

24 *U* 345. Cf. Hayman, "Cyclops," pp. 272–273. Hayman notes the ambiance of Irish pantomime in this scene as well as in "Circe."

25 Joyce described "Oxen of the Sun" to Budgen in a letter written on March 20, 1920: "Bloom is the spermatozoon, the hospital the womb, the nurse the ovum, Stephen the embryo" (Joyce, *Letters,* vol. 1). Budgen himself remarked on the particularly "symbolical" aspect of the chapter (*James Joyce* p. 221).

26 Herring, *Joyce's "Ulysses" Notesheets,* includes the following note for "Oxen": "SD I am the eternal son" (6:44). Cf. the three notes on the Eucharist (3:7, 5:6, 5:7). Cf. also *U* 393, where Stephen utters his own version of the Reproaches of Holy Friday.

27 According to Ellmann's schema, in "Circe," the soul and the body coincide in a symbolic act of love that leads to unity of being; such are the circumstances of the Eucharist (*Ulysses on the Liffey,* pp. 182–185).

28 "They sinned against the light, Mr Deasy said gravely. And you can see the darkness in their eyes. And that is why they are wanderers on the earth to this day" (*U* 34). Stephen sees this "sin" as universal; when he replies: "Who has not?" the perversion inherent in Deasy's anti-Semitism is revealed. Deasy continues: "A

woman brought sin into the world." His attempt to elude femininity, sin, the blackness of flesh, motivates his quasi-sacrificial expulsion of Judaism: Deasy's fetishistic anti-Semitism protects him against the menace of castration, displacing the horror inspired by femininity to the "race of sinners." (Cf. Sigmund Freud, "Fetishism," in *SE* 21, pp. 147–157.) In the Bible, the wandering of the Jews receives particular emphasis as concerns the prophets, including Christ. According to the *Bible de Jérusalem* (p. 398, n. c), Elijah is subject to sudden disappearances: he is *transported by the Spirit.*

29 The correspondence between Moses-Bloom and Judaic sin evokes the mysterious sin of Moses, forbidden entry into the Promised Land, as well as the sin of Adam overturned by Christ; cf. J. C. Doyle (Jesus Christ the Anointed) and "Love's Old Sweet Song" (*U* 63).

30 Cf. Mal. 3:24; Matt. 17:10; Luke 1:17. The return of Elijah is an important element of Judaic eschatology.

31 Cf. the analysis of Hugh Kenner, in Hart and Hayman, *James Joyce's "Ulysses,"* p. 356.

32 Kristeva, *Pouvoirs de l'horreur,* pp. 9–10, 23.

33 "ZOE: Are you looking for someone? He's inside with his friend. . . . You're not his father, are you?" (*U* 475). In his desire, Bloom imagines that Zoe (life, the incarnation of sin) is Jewish.

34 Cf. Joyce, *Giacomo Joyce,* p. 10.

"MODUS PEREGRINUS": THE TRINITY

1 For the Judaic and Kabbalistic element of *Ulysses,* see "*Ulysses:* Joyce's Kabbalah" in Jackson Cope, *Joyce's Cities* (Baltimore: Johns Hopkins University Press, 1981). Cope's work is particularly illuminating as regards the historical ambiance of the late nineteenth century; he describes the resurgence of "mysticism," the new attention given to the Zohar, the importance of forgeries, the mysticism of Yeats, and the use of myth by D'Annunzio—all extremely important for an assessment of Joyce's symbolic context, both in *Ulysses* and *Finnegans Wake.* Cope's reading of the Kabbalistic revival on the part of Mathers and Waite, and its influence on Yeats, is also of interest as regards Joyce. The emphasis, however, on the importance of their work is problematic in that it denies Joyce's specificity in the domain of Judeo-Catholic symbolic discourse, and in its tendency to equate the Kabbalah with Dublin hermeticism.

2 Of substance suppressed as substance (marking the entry into aesthetic religion), G. W. F. Hegel writes: "This form is the night

in which substance was betrayed and made itself into Subject": it is thus that "Spirit brings itself forth as object." This "negative activity" evolves in the sense of symbolic negativity: confronting the present and absent Other, the subject finds itself absorbed, fascinated by the alternation of mimetic violence and its sacrificial dénouement in an enigmatic vacuum. Hegel writes: "The animal sacrificed is the *symbol* of a god" (*Phenomenology of Spirit*, trans. A. V. Miller with Analysis and Foreword by J. N. Findlay [New York: Oxford University Press, 1977], pp. 426, 434). Sacrifice as a connection between heterogeneous terms ("the link between the objective and the subjective, between bread and individuals") is evoked in *L'Esprit du christianisme et son destin* (Paris: Vrin, 1971), p. 72, concerning the Last Supper. Hegel writes that it is a "mystical act," elusive for those who have not understood Christ's utterances: "Just as when separating friends keep fragments of a ring they have broken into pieces, the observer sees only the breakage of a usable ring into unusable pieces which are without value; he does not grasp the mystical quality of the fragments" (ibid., p. 71; author's translation). The mystical act is *symbolic:* the Hegelian ring resembles the Greek (and, later, Christian) *symbolum*. In his analysis of the "mystical act," Hegel seems to enter an area of thought far from the sacrificial realm (according to the opposition between paganism and the Judeo-Christianity of Girard); the gift Christ makes of himself in the Last Supper (the Eucharist, or the Christly Passover) recalls the Judaic Passover. God orders the Israelites to immolate the paschal lamb; because of the marks of its blood on the doorposts, the Angel of Death spares them. Thus begins the slippage from the sacrifice/expulsion of Passover toward the non-sacrificial symbolic joy of the resurrected Christ.

3 "Pater innotescit quidem paternitate et communi spiratione, per respectum ad personas ab eo procedentes: inquantum autem est principium non de principio, innotescit per hoc, quod non est ab alio: quod pertinet ad proprietaten innascibilitatis, quam significat hoc nomen 'ingenitus'" ([Saint] Thomas d'Aquin, *Summa Theologica*, t. 2, q. 33, art. 4, conclusion); author's translation.

4 In early December 1918, Joyce wrote to Martha Fleischmann: "Puis, en vous regardant, j'ai observé la mollesse des traits réguliers et la douceur des yeux. Et j'ai pensé: une juive. Si je me suis trompé il ne faut pas vous offenser. Jésus Christ a pris son corps humain: dans le ventre d'une femme juive" (*Letters*, vol. 2).

5 In popular culture, he who "has horns" is cuckold. The stag is one of Joyce's preferred images; he applies it to himself in "The Holy Office" ("I flash my antlers in the air") and to Stephen in

"A Portrait of the Artist" (see Robert Scholes and Richard M. Kain, *The Workshop of Dedalus* [Evanston: Northwestern University Press, 1965], p. 61) and in *Stephen Hero* (p. 36). For "The Holy Office," see James Joyce, *Critical Writings* (New York: The Viking Press, 1964), p. 152. This transformation scene seems to echo the fourth act of *A Midsummer Night's Dream*. Bottom, a highly polysemic character, has a Pauline vision following Puck's transformation of his head into that of an ass (see Robert Boyle, S. J., *James Joyce's Pauline Vision* [Carbondale: Southern Illinois University Press, 1978], pp. vii–xiii, 1–12).

6 Sigmund Freud, *SE* 14:249.

7 Cf. the theophanies in which the shadow of God plays an important role (Exod. 33:22; Matt. 17:5; Mark 9:7; Luke 9:34; Acts 1:9), including the Annunciation (Luke 1:35): "And the angel answered and said unto her, The Holy Ghost shall come upon thee, and the power of the Highest shall overshadow thee: therefore also that holy thing which shall be born of thee shall be called the Son of God."

8 "Clouding over. No black clouds anywhere, are there?" (*U* 50).

9 See M. Littmann and C. Schweighauser, "Astronomical Allusions, Their Meaning and Purpose, in *Ulysses*," *James Joyce Quarterly,* 2 (1964–1965):238–246. Bloom's paternity is invested in the letter and in languages: he desires a son as reader of the holy text (cf. *U* 609, the vision of Rudy) and he is interested in Stephen partly as writer, and as speaker of Italian. In regretting the death of his son, he thinks that he could have taught him German (*U* 89); he inherited from his father "an ancient haggadah book" (*U* 723), the liturgical text of Passover.

10 See *La Bible de Jérusalem,* p. 1107, n. g, and Isaiah 14:12. Concerning the morning star as emblem of the Virgin, see *A Portrait of the Artist as a Young Man,* p. 127.

11 See Weldon Thornton, *Allusions in "Ullyses"* (Chapel Hill: University of North Carolina Press, 1968), pp. 66–67.

12 What is this *jouissance* if not the miracle through which the subject's love endures in writing, eluding the wear and passage of time? "Shall Time's best jewel from Time's chest lie hid?
>   Or what strong hand can hold his swift foot back?
>   Or who his spoil of beauty can forbid?
>   O! None, unless this miracle have might,
>   That in black ink my love may still shine bright" (Shakespeare, *Sonnet LXV*).

13 See on Joyce's writing Jacques Aubert, *Introduction à l'esthétique de Joyce* (Paris: Didier, 1973), pp. 171, 176–80. For Joyce, the only possible redemptor is a singular one, and the position of redemp-

tion is taken up with respect to the letter. This singularity which saves (itself) is the counterpart of the equally singular experience of the *Fall* (named according to its Judeo-Christian conception) which, in various real and symbolic forms, impressed Joyce all his life. Regarding Joyce the potential redemptor, see the remarks of Aubert and Lacan, "Le Sinthome," *Ornicar?*, 8 (1976):7–9. It is in this irreducible experience of the Fall that the unspeakable quality of death slips into multiple symbolizations surrounding the listener; his ear, first refined in the intensely Catholic (Verbal) ambiance of the Jesuits, leads him into the night that takes the shape of a labyrinth: "Darkness is in our souls." This labyrinth is subjectivity itself, agitated by eroticism and its Falls and by the light of the Resurrection, threading their way through poetic language.

14 It is possible that Stephen does not intend to share his mother with *dio boia*, the libidinous God more Roman than Catholic (*U* 213), to whom she has sacrificed herself: "With me all or not at all," he cries at the moment of his refusal (*U* 582).

15 Genesis 2:17. Original sin: the exile from paradise lost, the entrance into the human structure of desire and death. The sexual knowledge acquired in the Garden of Eden at the moment of turning away from the Law (the eyes of Adam and Eve *are opened*: seduction, orality, perversion) institutes exile and repression: the first cut, negation, is the result of this *scene* that, at least with respect to the permanent scandal it sets off *après-coup* in Judeo-Christianity, is *primal*.

16 Stephen's failed flight bears witness to his ties to the mother: "*Amor matris*, subjective and objective genitive, may be the only true thing in life" (*U* 207, cf. *U* 28). The desire maintaining Stephen in mourning, under the shadow of the dead mother, hinders (until June 16, 1904) his access to women. *Amor matris* as incestuous fixation is summed up by the term *lapwing*, according to an exchange in *Hamlet*, V, ii: "Horatio: This lapwing runs away with the shell on his head. Hamlet: He did comply with his dug before he sucked it."

17 Joyce's enthusiasm for Yeats—and his reservations regarding Yeats's engagement in the Irish Renaissance—are well known. Ellmann writes that Joyce "conceded to a friend that Yeats was a greater writer than he, a tribute he paid to no other contemporary. It was Yeats's imagination which always dazzled him: 'No surrealist poet can equal it,' he said. One day he was reading *Wuthering Heights* when Eugene Jolas came in, and Joyce said to him, 'This woman had pure imagination; Kipling had it too, and certainly Yeats.' . . . Joyce often recited Yeats's poems from mem-

ory, and seemed to wonder if his own work was imaginative enough" (*Joyce*, p. 673). Cf. Mercanton, *Les Heures*, p. 68, and Budgen, *James Joyce*, p. 182 and concerning the meeting of Joyce and Yeats as it is presented in *FW* 348. "Who Goes with Fergus?" can be found in William Butler Yeats, *The Collected Poems* (New York: Macmillan, 1946), p. 49.

18 *U* 432, and Scholes and Kain, *Workshop*, pp. 70, 86, 97: "Art has the gift of tongues." Cf. the analysis of the Paris and Pola notebooks in Aubert, *Introduction*, pp. 142–171.

19 See Boyle, *Joyce's Pauline Vision*, pp. 13–30. "La mort du Christ est l'intuition même de cet amour absolu non pour autre chose, non à cause d'autre chose, mais c'est la divinité en cette identité universelle avec l'altérité, la mort." "Une conversion se produit; Dieu se conserve dans ce processus lequel n'est que la mort de la mort" (G. W. F. Hegel, *La religion absolue*, III, 1 in *Leçons sur la philosophie de la religion* [Paris: Vrin, 1959], pp. 152, 159–160.)

20 See Herring, *"Ulysses" Notesheets*, p. 82; Cyclops 1:54, 1:55: "The cuckoo's a fine bird He sings as he flies." Cf. *U* 212, 335, 382.

21 See "Ireland, Island of Saints and Sages" (1907), in Joyce, *Critical Writings*, pp. 153–174. Joyce remarks that the Irish reputation for holiness was applied to the Ireland of the Druids (who were ultimately Egyptian, according to him) as well as to the Ireland of the Catholic Church (ibid., p. 156). As regards the heterogeneity of religion in Ireland, see Liam de Paor and Mary de Paor, *Early Christian Ireland* (London: Thames and Hudson, 1958) and Françoise Henry, *L'Art irlandais*, vols. 1 and 2 (Zodiaque, la nuit des temps 18 & 19, 1963, 1964: Les Cahiers de l'atelier du coeur-meurtry).

22 "Après le VIIIe siècle de notre ère, lorsque le Cantique fut utilisé dans la liturgie pascale, il devint l'un des cinq 'megillot,' ou rouleaux, qu'on lisait aux grandes fêtes" ("Introduction," Cantique des Cantiques, *La Bible de Jérusalem*, p. 945).

23 Except fiction: after all, it is not clear that Joyce considers what he writes as being fictitious, given the material that sustains it. Joyce told Arthur Power that the task of the writer was to seek out what truth remained in life (Power, *Conversations*, p. 36) and that the writer's work should be solidly sustained by facts (ibid., p. 95). Joyce often invokes subjective truth and the truth of daily life which must be written. In his oeuvre, the narrative as such slips progressively toward nominations, toward the paradigmatic, metaphoric, and Freudian dimensions of language. Thus, in *Finnegans Wake*, all that remains of narrative is in the form of fragments, sustained by the plurality of tongues and by the im-

mense work of condensation. ("Ainsi la soumission rigoureuse aux phénomènes du langage doit lui garantir la vérité, de sa connaissance et de sa représentation des événements.—-La seule différence, déclare-t-il, c'est que, à l'imitation du rêve, j'opère en quelques minutes ce qu'il a fallu parfois des siècles pour produire" (Mercanton, *Les Heures,* p. 36).

24 See the writings of Françoise Henry.

25 Thus Bloom's potential careers: priest, lawyer (giver of the Law), actor, and their respective connotations of the Trinity, rhetoric FROM THE FATHERS, the art of Shakespeare.

26 See Boyle, *Joyce's Pauline Vision,* pp. 21–30.

27 James Joyce, *Finnegans Wake* (New York: The Viking Press, 1974), p. 184, line 26 (184.26). This edition will henceforth be indicated as *FW*.

28 Bloom-Moses is also Bloom-Shakespeare: cf. *U* 152, 235, 280; cf. Bloom the poet, *U* 678.

29 See Julia Kristeva, "Le Vréel," in *Folle vérité: Ouvrage collectif* (Paris: Seuil, 1979). For Bloom, Christly heterogeneity is seen in its negative aspect: he is *neither* masculine self *nor* feminine other, *neither* meat *nor* milk (according to the rules of *kashruth,* cf. *U* 724). The Citizen attacks Bloom: "Half and half I mean, says the citizen. A fellow that's neither fish nor flesh" (*U* 321). Joyce's strand resembles the desert of the prophets—a site of uprooting, a "lieu sans lieu" (Maurice Blanchot, *Le Livre à venir* [Paris: Gallimard, 1959], p. 119).

30 Letter to Budgen, end of February 1921, in Joyce *Letters,* vol. 1.

31 See Joyce, *Giacomo Joyce*.

32 "Cette béance inscrite au statut même de la jouissance en tant que dit-mension du corps, chez l'être parlant, voilà ce qui rejaillit avec Freud par ce test—je ne dis rien de plus—qu'est l'existence de la parole. Là où ça parle, ça jouit" (Jacques Lacan, *Séminaire XX* [Paris: Seuil, 1975], p. 104). Concerning Joyce and the letter, see Jean-Louis Houdebine, "James Joyce: Obscénité et Théologie," *Tel Quel,* 83 (1980).

33 See Jean Starobinski, *Les Mots sous les mots* (Paris: Gallimard, 1971); and Julia Kristeva, *Recherches pour une sémanalyse* (Paris: Seuil, 1969), pp. 174–207, 255.

34 See Fritz Senn, "Nausikaa," in Hart and Hayman, *Joyce's Ulysses,* pp. 277–311. In early December 1918, Joyce wrote to Martha Fleischmann: "J'ai 35 ans. C'est l'âge que Shakespeare a eu quand il a conçu sa douleureuse passion pour la 'dame noire.' C'est l'âge que le Dante a eu quand il est entré dans la nuit de son être" (*Letters,* vol. 2.). H. Straumann writes, concerning this letter: "Ac-

cording to Martha's statement, she tore off the lower right-hand edge of the second sheet of Letter 1 because it contained what she considered an indelicate expression" (ibid., 2:430).

35 Letter to H. S. Weaver, August 6, 1919, in ibid., vol. 1.

36 See Lacan, *Ecrits,* pp. 506–509. Correspondence can be seen as the letter that answers itself—thus Swedenborg's theory, taken up by Baudelaire: "Nous arrivons à cette vérité que tout est hiéroglypique et nous savons que les symboles ne sont obscurs que d'une manière relative" (Charles Baudelaire, "Réflexions sur quelques-uns de mes contemporains," 1, "Victor Hugo," in *Oeuvres complètes* [Paris: Gallimard, 1961], p. 705).

37 See Joyce, *Letters,* 2: *Selected Letters.*

38 See ibid., 2:428.

39 In the letters to Nora, Joyce represents himself either as her son or as her father: Nora is a pure maid or a sinful mother. Joyce is interested in the incestuous possibilities between mother and son but also in those between father and daughter: cf. in the *Wake,* the love between a fatherly man and a very young woman (Yeats, Swift, etc.).

40 See Fritz Senn, ed., *New Light on Joyce from the Dublin Symposium* (Bloomington: Indiana University Press, 1972), p. 289.

41 Bloom the writer resembles Shem; cf. *FW* 181.

42 The writing of God on the tablets of stone marks the fundamental context of Judeo-Christian writing: the relationship between God and his people is crystallized in the text of the Law given to Moses (*U* 143).

43 "Letter? No. Can't read. . . . Page of an old copybook" (*U* 381). The unreadable page reappears as the fragmentary and mysterious letter of *Finnegans Wake.*

44 On the image and narcissism in the borderline case, see D. W. Winnicott, "Le Rôle de miroir de la mère et de la famille dans le développement de l'enfant," *Nouvelle Revue de psychanalyse,* 10 (1974): 79–86, and Kristeva, *Pouvoirs de l'horreur,* pp. 74–79.

45 "Le 'je' ne dénomme donc aucune entité lexicale. . . . *Je* se réfère à l'acte de discours individuel où il est prononcé, et il en désigne le locuteur. . . . C'est dans l'instance de discours où *je* désigne le locuteur que celui-ci s'énonce comme 'sujet'" (Emile Benveniste, *Problèmes de linguistique générale* [Paris: Gallimard, 1966], 1: 261–262).

46 Letter written November 8, 1926, to H. S. Weaver, in Joyce, *Letters,* vol. 1.

47 Gillet, *Stèle pour James Joyce,* p. 151.

48 According to the Haggadah, or Passover ritual, it is necessary to pour a cup of wine for Elijah and to open the door for him while

saying: "May the Spirit of Elijah, who enters our home at this hour, enter the hearts of all men." Rabbi S. Ganzfried writes: "It is customary to fill one extra cup of wine, and it is called 'The Cup of Elijah.'" "After Grace, the cup is filled for the fourth time. The door is opened according to custom, to signify that this is a night of vigil, and nothing is to be feared. Because of this belief, our righteous Messiah will come." (*Code of Jewish Law* [*Kitzur Schulchan aruch*], trans. H. E. Goldin [New York: Hebrew Publishing Co., 1961], 3: 48, 51).

49 Lacan, *Ecrits,* pp. 44–61.

50 "Nous voilà ainsi devant un chiasme: l'accès à la réalité est dans le registre du vraisemblable; l'accès à la vérité est du seul signifiant mais au prix d'une éclipse de la réalité" (Kristeva, "Le Vréel," p. 21). The fictional paternity of Bloom with relation to Stephen is perhaps in between the two terms of the chiasma: in the narrative, it is true but not real. Once filtered by the narrative marking the gap of the *symbolum,* its symbolicity is challenged by the *vraisemblable* (or realistic appearance) guaranteeing reality: it is thus that the encounter between Bloom and Stephen changes *everything* or *nothing* in the reality (or *vraisemblance*) sometimes attributed to the fictional characters. (In *Finnegans Wake,* Joyce seems to modify the problem of the *vraisemblable:* he enters into the domain of the dream.)

51 "The moment of the divinity could only be an instant . . . just the amount of time during which the imagination can fulfill the heavy task of retaining love in the object" (Hegel, *L'Esprit du christianisme et son destin,* p. 74), author's translation). Cf. Guitton, *Le Temps,* pp. 234–235.

52 Stephen says: "Paternity may be a legal fiction" (*U* 207). According to the legal formula quoted by Freud: "*Pater semper incertus est*" ("Family Romances," *SE* IX).

53 "Where there is neither Greek nor Jew . . . but Christ *is* all, and in all" (Col. 3:11). Cf. Jean Kimball, "The Hypostasis in 'Ulysses,'" *James Joyce Quarterly,* 10 (1972–1973): 436.

54 The name is a-temporal, according to Aristotle (*Poetics* XX).

55 See Harold Bayley, *The Lost Language of Symbolism* (London: E. Benn, Ltd., 1968), p. 72.

56 "Le trauma, en tant qu'il a une action refoulante, intervient *après-coup, nachträglich.* A ce moment-là, quelque chose se détache du sujet dans le monde symbolique, même qu'il est en train d'intégrer." "Entre la frappe et le refoulement symbolique, il n'y a aucune différence essentielle" (Jacques Lacan, *Séminaire I* [Paris: Seuil, 1975], p. 215).

57 Cf. Stephen's meditation: "Hold to the now, the here, through

which all future plunges to the past" (*U* 186). French sees in this passage a citation from Augustine (*The Book as World*, p. 282). The experience of the present tense evokes Georges Bataille's theory of the instant: "L'extase elle-même est proche de nous: qu'on imagine l'enchantement provocant de la poésie, l'intensité d'un fou rire, un vertigineux sentiment d'*absence*, mais ces éléments simplifiés, réduits au point géometrique, dans l'indistinction" (*Oeuvres complètes*, 5:228).

58 December 24, 1909, Joyce wrote to Nora: "My little mother, take me into the dark sanctuary of your womb" (*Letters*, vol. 2). "Theyre all mad to get in there where they came out of" (*U* 760).

59 In Joyce's first letter to M. Fleischmann, he wrote: "Je m'en irai, un jour, n'ayant rien compris, dans l'obscurité qui nous a enfantés tous" (*Letters*, vol. 2). (Cf. Job 1:21: "Nu, je suis sorti du sein maternel, nu, j'y retournerai.")

60 Cf. *U* 91, 241, 277, 413, 444.

61 The "message" of Shakespearean tragedy is that one cannot cheat or trick the Other. The murder of the king by his brother is an act of mimetic violence, hiding an incestuous desire: it is impossible to enjoy the brother's happiness without ousting him from his position.

62 Joyce, *Giacomo Joyce*, p. 16.

63 Cf. Girard, *Des Choses*, pp. 204–205.

64 [Saint] Thomas d'Aquin, *Summa Theologica*, Q. 39, art. 2.

65 [Saint] Thomas d'Aquin, *Summa Theologica*, 2: 339–340, n. 72. Concerning Arius, see *Des Origines à Grégoire le Grand*, pp. 290–294.

66 Saint Augustine *De Trinitate*, L. III, c. IV, 10.

67 "L'Eucharistie est un *sacramentum:* il faudrait traduire 'mystère' autant que 'sacrement' au sens formel du terme" (ibid., t. 1, p. 581, n. 26).

68 See *Le Moyen Age*, pp. 289–291.

69 Saint Augustine, *De Trinitate*, L. III, c. IV, 10.

70 The Holy Spirit comes upon all who are *carnally* concerned with the coming of Christ: Mary, Elizabeth, Zachariah, John the Baptist (Luke 1).

71 Language in exile is comparable to poetic language, simultaneously inside and outside the Law, i.e., legal and outlaw.

72 Saint Augustine addresses God: "You ceaselessly hit the weakness of my vision with the violence of your rays on me, and I trembled with love and horror" (*Les Confessions* t. 13 and 14 [Paris: Desclée de Brouwer, 1962], L. VII. c. X, 16; author's translation). Augustine sees himself listening to the divine response, which seems to focus on the Eucharist: "And you will not alter me in-

side you, like the aliment of your flesh, but it is you who will be altered in me." Kristeva describes confession as "la transgression la plus subtile de la loi qu'est l'énonciation du péché face à l'Un" (*Pouvoirs de l'horreur*, p. 153). Regarding the complicity between the law and the outlaw, see Georges Bataille, *L'Erotisme* (Paris: 10/18, 1957), especially the remarks on interdiction and transgression. René Girard seems to draw his inspiration from Bataille's hypothesis when he writes: "Dans tous les phénomènes du religieux primitif . . . on retrouve cette dualité étrange du comportement sacrificiel; le rite se présente toujours sous la forme d'un meurtre . . . d'une transgression d'autant plus désirable en fin de compte qu'elle est plus sacrilège" (*La Violence et le sacré* [Paris: Grasset, 1972], pp. 269–270).

73 Jacques Turmel, *Histoire des dogmes* (Paris: Rieder, 1936), 6:20, 60, 88–89.

74 First homily on Psalm 37:1, quoted by Turmel in ibid., p. 89.

75 Saint Augustine, *Les Confessions*, L. VII, c. XII, 18.

76 Turmel, *Histoire*, p. 66. Origen, in the eleventh homily on Leviticus 11:2, writes: "Currently, the body is no longer punished, and sin is no longer erased by corporeal torture, but by means of penitence" (quoted in ibid., pp. 91–92).

77 See Lacan, *Séminaire XX*, esp. pp. 61–82.

78 S. Poque, "Le Sacrement de Pâques," in Saint Augustine, *Sermons* p. 21 (author's translation).

79 There is abundant evidence of Joyce's interest in Dante. Joyce discusses him in "The Universal Literary Influence of the Renaissance" (see Berrone, *Joyce in Padua*, p. 22, and Berrone's analysis, pp. 45–53) and in the *Critical Writings* (see especially "William Blake" [1912], pp. 214–222). "Italian literature begins with Dante and finishes with Dante. . . . I love Dante almost as much as the Bible. He is my spiritual food the rest is ballast" (Ellmann, *Joyce*, p. 226; cf. pp. 193, 369–371). Cf. Stanislaus Joyce, *Recollections of James Joyce by His Brother* (New York: James Joyce Society, 1950), p. 7; Joyce, *My Brother's Keeper*, p. 53; Constantine Curran, *James Joyce Remembered* (New York: Oxford University Press, 1968), p. 9. Regarding *Ulysses*, see Father Boyle, *Joyce's Pauline Vision*, p. 53.

The most complete treatment to date of Joyce's reading of Dante is Mary T. Reynolds' *Joyce and Dante: The Shaping Imagination* (Princeton: Princeton University Press, 1981). This work reveals the extent of Joyce's preoccupation with Dante and demonstrates the breadth of allusions to the *Divina Commedia* (cf. the Appendix), particularly as concerns *Ulysses*. Reynolds remarks on Joyce's Dantean context and his doubling of the Vergil-Dante relationship. But as regards this relationship, the questions raised by Joyce's reading/writing seem highly complex. Dante's autobiographical figure of the poet and of the relationship between Vergil and the poet is fictionalized as being completely *outside* fiction, whereas Joyce employs the opposite strategy by inscribing the relationship between the paternal and filial figures *within* fiction and, in most of *Ulysses,* in the terms of fiction—however autobiographical. Joyce's conversion of identity involves taking on Judaic paternity, or a fantasy of it, which is not eliminated in the way that Dante must eliminate Vergil's pagan identity as Latin poet. The germ of that Judaic paternity as Joyce conceives it, through Molly's monologue, moves toward creation through a new enunciation, a vision of language leading to the *Wake.* For Joyce's Judeo-Catholic stance, see my "L'Ecriture joycienne: juive ou catholique?" *L'Herne* (forthcoming).

80 Dante, *Tutte le opere di Dante: Edizione del Centenario,* ed. Fredi Chiappelli (Milano, U. Mursia, 1965). Regarding Dante's use of Psalm 113, see Dante, *Divine Comedy,* vol. 2, pt. 2, p. 31.

81 At least since the Vulgate, sexual relations are biblically described as "knowledge," as in Genesis 4:1: "And Adam knew Eve his wife." This idiom can perhaps be interpreted according to Genesis 3:7; their error first strikes Adam and Eve through vision, when they *know* their nudity.

82 "The sensual current that has remained active seeks only objects which do not recall the incestuous figures forbidden to it. . . . The whole sphere of love in such people remains divided in the two directions personified in art as sacred and profane (or animal) love. Where they love they do not desire and where they desire they cannot love" (Sigmund Freud, "On the Universal Tendency to Debasement in the Sphere of Love," *SE* 11: 182–183).

83 Ibid., p. 180.

84 "This very relation of the sharpest contrast between 'mother' and 'prostitute' will however encourage us to enquire into the history of the development of these two complexes and the unconscious relation between them, since we long ago discovered that what, in the conscious, is found split into a pair of opposites often occurs in the unconscious as a unity. . . . Brutal pieces of information . . . now acquaint him with the secret of sexual life. . . . The aspect of these disclosures which affects the newly initiated child most strongly is the way in which they apply to his own parents. This application is often flatly rejected by him . . . : 'Your parents and other people may do something like that with one another, but *my* parents can't possibly do it'" (Sigmund Freud, "A Special Type of Choice of Object Made by Men," in ibid., p. 170).

85 Cf. Freud's remark: "The ascetic current in Christianity created psychical values for love which pagan antiquity was never able to confer on it. This current assumed its greatest importance with the ascetic monks, whose lives were almost entirely occupied with the struggle against libidinal temptation" (ibid., p. 188).

86 *U* 663. Joyce, *Giacomo Joyce,* p. 16: Cf. Ellmann's Introduction, p. xviii.

87 "O rosa mistica, ora pro me!" (letter of February 2, 1919, in Joyce, *Letters,* vol. 2).

88 In his analysis of *FW* 502, Boyle discusses the representation of the Virgin through images of roses and other flowers in certain Christmas hymns (*Joyce's Pauline Vision,* p. 5).

89 Cf. the perverse desire of Gerty, in love with Father Conroy. It is to him that she confesses her femininity, and for him that she desires to become a nun: "And if ever she became a Dominican nun in their white habit perhaps he might come to the convent for the novena of Saint Dominic. He told her that time when she told him about that in confession . . . that that was no sin because that came from the nature of woman instituted by God, he said, and that Our Blessed Lady herself said to the archangel Gabriel be it done unto me according to Thy Word" (*U* 358).

90 My thanks to Gregory Lucente for pointing out this parallel.

91 Joyce wrote to Nora on August 7, 1909: "O Nora! Nora! Nora! I am speaking now to the girl I loved, who had red-brown hair and sauntered over to me and took me so easily into her arms and made me a man." And on September 5, 1909: "*Everything that is noble and exalted and deep and true and moving in what I write comes, I believe, from you. O take me into your soul of souls and then I will become indeed the poet of my race*" (Joyce, *Letters,* vol. 2).

92 *Ulysses* takes place June 16, 1904; *Finnegans Wake* takes place Easter weekend, 1904.

93 The formulation of Joycean fiction might be located in the Augustinian clash of the backward glance and the anticipation of the future. Their meeting point is the instant of the present. (Cf. the clash of the enunciated declaration and the enunciation at the point of the future perfect in Lacan, *Ecrits,* p. 808.)

TOWARD "WORK IN PROGRESS"

1 See Kristeva, "La Productivité dite texte," in *Recherches,* pp. 208–245.

2 See Joyce, *Letters,* 1:126; and Budgen, *James Joyce,* p. 107. Joyce told Budgen: "I have just got a letter asking me why I don't give Bloom a rest. The writer of it wants more Stephen. But Stephen

no longer interests me to the same extent. He has a shape that can't be changed."

3 For a very different reading of Joycean language, see Margot Norris, *The Decentered Universe of "Finnegans Wake"* (Baltimore: Johns Hopkins University Press, 1978).

4 Saint Augustine, *De Trinitate*, L. VI, C. X, 11. Thomas Aquinas comments on this passage in *Somme théologique*, Q. 39, art. 8.

5 Cf. "Ireland, Island of Saints and Sages," in Joyce, *Critical Writings*, p. 156.

6 Power, *Conversations*, p. 127.

7 See Lacan, "Le Sinthome," in *Ornicar?*, 11 (n.d.):9.

8 Ellmann, *Joyce*, p. 597.

9 *SE* 14: 214.

10 Potts, ed., *Portraits of the Artist in Exile*, p. 64; and Budgen, *James Joyce*, p. 347.

11 "Pas seulement des êtres vivants. Ma paternité s'étend aux végétaux, aux minéraux, même aux signes d'algèbre" (Mercanton, *Les Heures*, p. 60).

12 "Exposé dogmatique: Pâques," in Dom Gaspar Lefèbvre and the Benedictines of the Abbaye de Saint André, *Missel quotidien et vespéral* (Bruges: Apostolat Liturgique, 1942), p. 1107.

EASTER: THE CRUCIFIXION

1 Several critics have found allusions to Catholic liturgy in the *Wake*. See James S. Atherton, *The Books at the "Wake,"* expanded and corrected edition (Mamaroneck, N.Y.: Appel, 1979), chap. 10; Boyle, *Joyce's Pauline Vision;* Edward A. Kopper, Jr., "Some Additional Christian Allusions in the *Wake*," *The Analyst*, no. 24 (1965):5–22; Roland Bates, "The Feast Is a Flyday," *James Joyce Quarterly*, 2 (1964–1965). See as well Michael H. Begnal and Fritz Senn, *A Conceptual Guide to "Finnegans Wake"* (University Park: Pennsylvania State University Press, 1974); Clive Hart, *Structure and Motif in "Finnegans Wake"* (Evanston: Northwestern University Press, 1962); William T. Noon, *Joyce and Aquinas* (New Haven: Yale University Press, 1957); Hugh Kenner, *Dublin's Joyce* (Bloomington: Indiana University Press, 1956); Roland McHugh, *Annotations to "Finnegans Wake"* (Baltimore: Johns Hopkins University Press, 1980); Clive Hart and Fritz Senn, *A "Wake" Newslitter* (Essex: University of Essex, 1962–1980). According to Bates ("The Feast") the "plot" of the *Wake* unfolds during the Easter holiday in 1904. The author's conclusion regarding the date of 1904 is the result of a comparison of Dublin newspapers with certain passages of the *Wake*.

2 This infinity cannot be confused with a collectivity; it may perhaps be conceived as a condensation of singularities.

3 Cf. Shaun's sermon: "Words taken . . . from the sufferant pen of our jocosus inkerman militant of the reed behind the ear" (*FW* 433.7). Shaun *delivers* Shem's signature.

4 Cf. Hce's "christlikeness" (*FW* 33.29).

5 "There extand by now one thousand and one stories, all told, of the same" (*FW* 5.28).

6 Luke 23:34. Luke's Passion is part of the liturgy for Wednesday of Holy Week.

7 Cf. "wet good Friday" (*FW* 399.22); cf. "(*doerehmoose genuane!*) (*letate!*)" (*FW* 53.18), where McHugh notes a reference to the Mass of the Presanctified (*Annotations,* p. 53).

8 Cf. Joyce, *Portrait,* p. 97.

9 Joyce explains this passage to Miss Weaver in a letter of August 8, 1928 (Joyce, *Letters,* vol. 1).

10 See David Hayman, *A First Draft Version of "Finnegans Wake,"* (Austin: University of Texas Press, 1963), p. 165.

11 Cf. "me ah err eye ear marie" (*FW* 300.12).

12 Cf. the section of "Love's bitter mystery: *Blumenlied*" entitled "Elijah is coming": the whirlwind of the prophetic word.

13 St. Gregory applies these pentecostal images to Mary Magdalene: "Voyez avec quelle force l'amour divin s'était allumé dans l'âme de Marie-Madeleine, qui ne quittait point le sépulcre du Seigneur alors que les disciples s'étaient retirés. . . . Elle pleurait en le cherchant, et toute embrasée du feu de son amour, elle brûlait du désir de retrouver celui qu'elle croyait enlevé" (quoted by Lefèbvre, *Missel quotidien,* p. 1135). Where love encounters the Word, the key signifier of the proper name emerges. According to John 20:15, 16, Mary Magdalene only recognizes Christ when he calls her by name: "She, supposing him to be the gardener, saith unto him, Sir, if thou have borne him hence, tell me where thou hast laid him, and I will take him away. Jesus saith unto her, Mary. She turned herself, [variant: she recognized him] and saith unto him, Rabboni; which is to say, Master."

14 Cf. my remarks on the subject of biography, and the first chapter of the *Portrait.*

15 Ellmann, *Joyce,* p. 25.

16 According to Joyce, J. J. and S. is the dirtiest (the most beautiful?) of Irish whiskies (*James Joyce,* p. 604).

17 Hayman, *First Draft,* p. 120.

18 Cf. *U* 47: "Morose delectation Aquinas tunbelly calls this, *frate porcospino.* Unfallen Adam rode and not rutted."

19 Definitions of these four terms are from the *Oxford English Dictionary.*

20 Emile Benveniste, *Pouvoir, droit, religion,* vol. 2 in *Le Vocabulaire des institutions indo-européennes,* (Paris: Minuit, 1969), p. 165.

21 Ibid., p. 172. This analysis is in chap. 8, on "Le Serment en Grèce," of which the author writes: "C'est un rite qui garantit et sacralise une affirmation" (p. 164). Cf. chap. 3, "*ius* et le serment à Rome," where Benveniste explains the meaning of *ius iurandum* as "formule à formuler" (p. 111).

22 Joyce, *Stephen Hero,* p. 106.

23 Cf. 3a Q. 15, art. 4; suppl., Q. 82. Cf. 3a Q. 16, art. 4 as well.

24 "Etre passible, c'est être corruptible: 'Toute passion qui s'accentue tend à détruire la nature.' Or S. Paul dit du corps des élus: 'Semé dans la corruption, il ressuscitera incorruptible,' donc impassible" ([Saint] Thomas d'Aquin, *Somme théologique: La Résurrection,* trans. J. D. Folghera, O.P. [Paris: Cerf, 1938], Q. 82, art. 1).

25 [Saint] Thomas d'Aquin, *Somme théologique: Le Verbe incarné,* trans. Ch. V. Heris, O.P. (Paris: Cerf, 1927), 3a Q. 15, art. 4 (author's translation).

26 Ibid., 3a Q. 15, art. 10 (author's translation).

27 Caxton, *Vitas Patrum,* V, XI, quoted in the *Oxford English Dictionary.*

HOLY SATURDAY

1 Mercanton, *Les Heures,* pp. 25–26.

2 Ibid., p. 27.

3 Saint Augustine, *Sermons,* p. 75 (author's translation).

4 Christine Mohrmann, "Pascha, Passio, Transitus," in *Etudes sur le latin des chrétiens,* (Rome: Editore di storia e letteratura, 1958), p. 205.

5 Saint Augustine, *Sermons,* pp. 213, 215.

6 Henri de Lubac, *Meditations sur l'Eglise* (Paris: Aubier-Montaigne, 1968), p. 112–113.

7 See Mercanton, *Les Heures,* p. 24.

8 Lacan, *Séminaire XI.*

9 Bloom fills several roles with respect to death—he is father, son, and perhaps spouse as well.

10 Cf. Kristeva, *Pouvoirs de l'horreur,* pp. 153–54.

11 Emile Benveniste, "La blasphémie et l'euphémie," in *Problèmes,* 2: 254–257.

12 Girard, *Les Choses.*

13 "Après la bénédiction du feu nouveau, un acolyte apporte le cierge pascal au milieu, devant le célébrant. Celui-ci, avec un poinçon, trace une croix entre les ouvertures extrêmes destinées à recevoir les grains d'encens. Au-dessus de cette croix, il trace ensuite la

lettre grecque *Alpha,* au-dessous la lettre *Omega,* et entre les bras de la croix, quatre chiffres, ceux du millésime pour l'année courante" (*La Semaine Sainte: Édition française avec chant grégorien par les Bénédictins de Solesmes* [Paris: Desclée et Cie, 1962], p. 166).

14 See the remarks of Brendan O'Hehir on the linguistic phenomenon marking the separation of the Celtic languages from the Indo-European languages ("P/K split," in *A Gaelic Lexicon for "Finnegans Wake"* [Berkeley: University of California Press, 1967], pp. 403–405).

15 See Charles Mauron, *Psychocritique du genre comique* (Paris: J. Corti, 1964).

16 According to Sollers, theology "a pour fonction de dire la vérité sur la *culpa,* et de montrer la seule façon qu'elle devienne *felix*" ("La Trinité de Joyce II," *Tel Quel,* 83 [1980]: 72).

17 This explains the expulsion of Shem, "expulled for looking at churches from behind" (*FW* 488.22).

18 Walter William Skeat, *A Concise Etymological Dictionary of the English Language* (Oxford: Oxford Univ. Press, 1911), p. 598.

19 "Joyce le symptôme," in *Joyce et Paris,* Actes du cinquième symposium international James Joyce, Paris, 16–20 juin, 1975, ed. Jacques Aubert and Maria Jolas (Lille: Publications de l'Université de Lille III/CNRS, 1979), pp. 13–17.

20 Letter of March 7, 1924, in Joyce, *Letters,* 1: 213.

21 See Adaline Glasheen, *Third Census of "Finnegans Wake"* (Berkeley: University of California Press, 1977), pp. 214–215; and Hayman, *First Draft,* p. 59.

22 Letter of May 13, 1927, in James Joyce, *Selected Letters* (New York: The Viking Press, 1975). Joyce's commentary marks the distance separating him from the first cries of *Non serviam.* In fact, Lucifer is only marginally evoked in the Exultet, as "that star which knows no setting" ("lucifer qui nescit occasum"). It would seem that his role in Joyce's explanation owes much to Milton; for although the Exultet eliminates Lucifer as a dramatic character, his presence is central in *Paradise Lost.* Regarding difficulties of interpretation raised by the importance of Lucifer in the poem, see W. H. Marshall, "*Paradise Lost: Felix Culpa* and the Problem of Structure," *MLN,* 76 (1961): 15–20.

23 Arthur O. Lovejoy, "Milton and the Paradox of the Fortunate Fall," *ELH,* 4 (1937): 172.

24 See the letter of May 13, 1927. According to Lovejoy, this expression can be traced back to Gregory the Great (ibid., p. 173).

25 For Miltonian influences in other passages of *Finnegans Wake,* see Atherton, *The Books at the Wake,* p. 272.

26 Milton, *Paradise Lost,* Book XII, in *Complete Poetry,* pp. 469–476.

27 Sören Kierkegaard, *Le Concept de l'angoisse* (Paris: Gallimard, 1935), pp. 36, 51, 69.
28 See Turmel, *Histoire*, 1: 5, 6; and Kristeva, *Pouvoirs de l'horreur*.
29 Lovejoy, "Milton," p. 171.
30 Kierkegaard, *Le Concept de l'angoisse*.
31 Lovejoy, "Milton," p. 163.
32 Joyce was aware of Milton's Dantean position as well as of the specifically Catholic dimension lacking in Milton. Joyce made the following remark at a lecture he gave in Trieste in 1912: "Il [sic] *Paradiso Perduto* di Milton è une trascrizione puritanica delle *Divina Commedia*" (Joseph Prescott, "*Daniel Defoe* by James Joyce," *Buffalo Studies*, 1 [1964]: 7).
33 "BLOOM: (*In a seamless garment marked I.H.S. stands upright amid phoenix flames*)" (*U* 498). See the description of the phoenix in Pierre de Beauvais's *Bestiaire*, in the *Bestiaire divin* by Guillaume le Clerc de Normandie, and in the *Livre du Trésor* by Brunetto Latini. All of these texts are in Giorgio Bianciotto, *Bestiaires du Moyen Age* (Paris: Stock, 1980), pp. 30–31, 79–80, 204–205. See also Glasheen, *Third Census*, p. 233.
34 According to Kierkegaard, culpability "belongs to the individual" (*Le Concept*, p. 66).
35 "C'est donc que la rédemption, liée au péché, n'avait pas avec le péché originel comme tel le lien que souligneront plus tard saint Augustin ou saint Anselme" (Henri Rondet, S. J., *Le Péché originel dans la tradition patristique et théologique* [Paris: Fayard, 1967], p. 35).
36 Turmel, "Le Péché originel," in *Histoire*, 1: 38–41.
37 Quinti Septimi Florentis Tertulliani, *De Anima*, ed. Jan Hedrik Waszink, (Amsterdam: J. M. Meulenhoff, 1947), 16.2.
38 *In. ps. 136, 5*, quoted by Turmel, *Histoire*, 1: 55.
39 Sigmund Freud, "La Dénégation," trans. Bernard This and Bernard Thèves, *Le Coq-Héron*, 52 (1975): 7–15.
40 A. Gaudel, "Péché originel," in *Dictionnaire de Théologie Catholique* (Paris: Letouzey et Ané, 1933), 12, 1: 362.
41 Ibid., p. 371.
42 See Turmel, *Histoire*, 1: 79.
43 Gaudel, "Péché originel," p. 378.
44 *Ad Simplicianum*, I, II, 20, quoted by Gaudel in ibid., p. 378 (author's translation).
45 *Ad Simplicianum*, I, I, 9, quoted by Gaudel in ibid., p. 379 (author's translation).
46 *De Nupt.*, I, XXV, 28, quoted by Gaudel in ibid., p. 397 (author's translation).
47 *De Peccatorum meritis*, quoted by Turmel in *Histoire*, 1: 138 (author's translation).

48 Gaudel, "Péché originel," p. 435.

49 Rondet, *Le Péché originel*, p. 177.

50 Duns Scotus, *Op. Ox.*, II, dist. 32 n. 7, quoted by Gaudel in "Péché originel," p. 504.

51 "Thanks, beloved, to Adam . . . for his beautiful crossmess parzel" (*FW* 619.3).

52 See Glasheen, *Third Census*, p. 101.

53 David Hayman, *Joyce et Mallarmé* (Paris: Lettres Modernes, 1956), 2: 161.

54 The daughter will "rekindle the flame on Felix Day" (*FW* 27.13).

55 Edward A. Kopper, Jr., "Earwicker's Tavern Feast," in Begnal and Senn, *Conceptual Guide*, pp. 116–138.

56 See the narrative of Adam's sin ending with: "Oh Findlay's coldpalled!" (*FW* 506.9). It includes the declaration of Hce-Finn's death, the result of original sin.

57 Turmel, *Histoire*, 1: 96–104.

58 "A Portrait of the Artist," in Scholes and Kain, *Workshop*, p. 60. Cf. L. F. Céline's remark: "Au commencement était l'émotion."

59 This list is the parodic repetition of that in the *Divine Names* of Pseudo-Denys. See Maurice de Gandillac, ed., *Oeuvres complètes de Pseudo-Denys l'Aréopagite* (Paris: Aubier, 1943), pp. 74–75.

60 See Hayman, *First Draft*, p. 94, and the letter of March 24, 1924, to H. S. Weaver (Joyce, *Letters*, vol. 1).

61 See the letter of July 10, 1927, to H. S. Weaver (Joyce, *Letters*, vol. 3); Ellmann, *Joyce*, p. 721; Eugene Jolas, "My Friend James Joyce," in Sean Givens, *James Joyce: Two Decades of Criticism* (New York: Vanguard Press, 1948), pp. 16–17.

62 Cf. Stephen's meditation on precious stones as he stands before the window of the lapidary: "Born all in the dark wormy earth . . . evil lights shining in the darkness. Where fallen archangels flung the stars of their brows" (*U* 241).

63 See Freud's remarks on the primal scene in *From the History of an Infantile Neurosis* [*SE* 17].

64 See Hayman, *First Draft*, p. 179.

65 Ibid., p. 194.

66 Saint Cyprian discusses the penitence of the "fallen" (*lapsi*) (Turmel, *Histoire*, 6: 107).

67 "For as in Adam all die, even so in Christ shall all be made alive" (1 Cor. 15:22).

68 Saint Augustine, *City of God*, ed. David Knowles (Harmondsworth: Pelican Books, 1972), XIV, 16.

69 "Leading him the life of the damned. Wear the heart out of a stone, that" (*U* 96).

70 Augustine writes: "Sin is father to death." "What is there in pro-

fusion? Birth and death" (*Sermons,* pp. 247, 17). Sin, birth, and death provide the novelistic frame of *Ulysses* with a Catholic version of the Real.

71 "I uses goggles reading. Sand in the Red Sea done that" (*U* 659). Cf. *U* 51, 77.

72 John Joyce's friend Matthew Kane is (since the story "Grace") Joyce's model for Cunningham; he drowned in 1904, the year of *Ulysses* (Ellmann, *Joyce,* p. 138, and Glasheen, *Third Census,* p. 152).

73 Ellmann, *Joyce,* p. 411.

74 Gershom C. Scholem, "Le Nom de Dieu," *Diogène,* 79 (1972): 70.

75 Nelson's statue in Dublin (cf. *Ulysses;* "The Parable of the Plums" in "Aeolus" commemorates the victory at Trafalgar).

76 According to Jean-Louis Houdebine, in Joycean paternity the proper name should not be interpreted as a signifier: the name is "habité par une voix, qui opère en lui la signature par laquelle l'infinité du langage s'actualise" (seminar of March 19, 1981). The *call* emanating from the beyond of infinity is destined to give to the subject the singular voice of his Name: since the *Portrait,* this biblical path works its way through the Joycean signature of the letter.

77 H. Haag, "Pâques," in *Supplément au Dictionnaire de la Bible* (Paris: Letouzey et Ané, 1966), 6: 1120–1121.

78 Sigmund Freud, *Moses and Monothesism* [*SE* 23].

79 Cf. Girard, *Les Choses,* pp. 176–177.

80 Freud, *Moses and Monotheism.*

81 On the cad as James Joyce, see Ellmann, *Joyce,* p. 196; and Joyce, *Letters,* 2: 424–425.

82 Cf. *FW* 63.29: "a'top o'it."

83 "The engine of the laws declosed unto Murray" (*FW* 63.26).

84 See "Ivy Day in the Committee Room," in Joyce, *Dubliners.*

85 The section of the Mishna called Pesahim, quoted by Haag, in "Pâques," p. 1140.

86 Cf. in this passage, "the free, the froh, the frothy freshener, puss, puss, pussyfoot" (*FW* 553.27) and "and she lalaughed in her diddydid, domino" (*FW* 554.7).

87 See Alp's remark to Hce: "Amid the soleness. Tilltop, Bigmaster!" (*FW* 624.11).

88 Cf. possible allusions to the Flood and the building of the Tower of Babel (Gen. 8:13 and 11:3): "floodmud, now all loosebrick and stonefest" (*FW* 552.4).

89 Benveniste, *Le Vocabulaire,* 2: 14.

90 Ibid.

91 Brendan O'Hehir and John Dillon, *A Classical Lexicon for Finnegans Wake* (Berkeley: University of California Press, 1977), p. 465.

92 Quoted by Odo Casel, *La Fête de Pâques dans l'Eglise des Pères* (Paris: Cerf, 1963), p. 87.

PASCHAL TIME: THE CALENDAR

1 Cf. Arnold van Gennep, *Cérémonies périodiques, cycliques, 1, Carnaval-Carême-Pâques*, vol. 1, III in *Manuel de folklore français contemporain*, (Paris: Picard, 1947), pp. 866, 1321–1322, 1335, 1339. In some places, Easter eggs are blessed on the Sunday of the Resurrection.

2 See *The Scarlet Letter* by Nathaniel Hawthorne: the "A" of adultery, worn by Hester Prynne (as evidence of *passion*, according to Hawthorne himself) is invested with a *jouissance* that is simultaneously sinful and penitential: "On the breast of her gown, in fine red cloth, surrounded with an elaborate embroidery and fantastic flourishes of gold-thread, appeared the letter A. It was so artistically done, and with so much fertility and gorgeous luxuriance of fancy" (*The Scarlet Letter* [New York: Holt, Rinehart, and Winston, 1961], p. 49). This double *jouissance* of the *passion* is elaborated like a work of *artistic* imagination and beauty: Hester's art is the metaphor of Hawthorne's art. And Joyce, the "carpetweaver," who considered his work to be a fabric or tapestry (see the letter to H. S. Weaver of November 9, 1927, in *Letters*, vol. 1) was certainly sensitive to the image of the scarlet letter, evoked several times in the *Wake* (see Atherton, *The Books at the Wake*, p. 255).

3 See Eric Partridge, *The Penguin Dictionary of Historical Slang* (Harmondsworth: Penguin Books, 1972).

4 Cf. Henry Campbell Robinson, "Hardest Crux Ever," in Marvin Magalaner, ed., *James Joyce Miscellany*, 2d ser. (Carbondale: Southern Illinois University Press, 1959), p. 206.

5 Nora K. Chadwick, *The Celts* (Harmondsworth: Penguin Books, 1970), pp. 204–206.

6 According to de Paor and de Paor, *Early Christian Ireland*, p. 69. According to Henry, *L'Art irlandais*, 1:38, the discovery was made by Saint Columba himself. Cf. Chadwick, *The Celts*, pp. 207–211. Regarding the unique character of the Celtic Church, see *Nouvelle Histoire de l'Eglise*, 1: 507.

7 At Iona, the Roman form of calculation did not come into use until 718. It is to this ardently Celtic monastery that we owe the Book of Kells.

8 Cf. Bates, "The Feast Is a Flyday," p. 176.

9 Dom Louis Gougaud, *Les Chrétientés celtiques* (Paris: J. Gabalda, 1911), pp. 197–198.

10 McHugh, *Annotations*, p. 43.

11 Gougaud, *Les Chrétientés*, p. 176.

12 Ibid.

13 Henry notes that Saint Columba is "accused, completely gratuitously, of participating in the heresy of the quarto-decimans" (*L'Art irlandais*, 1:38).

14 Ireneus is quoted by Jean Daniélou in *Nouvelle Histoire de l'Eglise*, 1: 136.

15 Cf. *FW* 254.8: "eye . . . eye, aye."

16 Turmel, *Histoire*, 3: 17–18.

17 See *La Psychanalyse est-elle une histoire juive?* (Paris: Seuil, 1981).

18 Sigmund Freud, *Jokes and Their Relation to the Unconscious* [*SE* 8].

19 Heterogeneity catalyzes writing. At the moment of the paschal controversy, the Irish (who until then content themselves with an exclusively oral tradition) suddenly began to produce a vast sacred literature in order to define their position (Chadwick, *The Celts*, p. 210). Chadwick observes that these writings were of a *personal* character: "These writings consisted chiefly of martyrologies, rules and penitentials and saints' *Lives*." "The most widespread literary development of the period however is the *vita*, the narrative form of a saint's Life. . . . The *Vitae* were indeed the greatest literary development of the Celtic Church from the seventh century onwards" (ibid., pp. 210–211). The Irish continued the tradition begun by Athanasius in the *Life of Saint Anthony*, a work of crucial literary importance. The doubled position of Irish heterogeneity leads from the paschal controversy to Christian fiction and, perhaps, from there to the great Irish literature of the modern period.

THE RESURRECTION

1 Joyce, *Letters*, 2: 432.

2 Ellmann, *Joyce*, p. 350.

3 Cf. the passage preceding that of the dance of the paschal sun: "But are you solarly salemly sure . . .—Siriusly and selenely sure" (*FW* 512.35–513.1).

4 See Haag, "Pâques."

5 On the subject of "root language," Shaun scorns his brother: "I have the outmost contempt for. . . .—But for what, . . . Shaun of grace? . . .—For his root language, if you ask me whys, Shaun replied" (*FW* 424.8, .14, .23). See also "aprioric roots for aposteriorious tongues" (*FW* 83.11).

6 See Ivan Fonagy, "Les Bases pulsionnelles de la phonation," *Re-*

vue française de psychanalyse, nos. 34 and 35 (January 1970 and July 1971).

7 Cf. Mark L. Troy, *Mummeries of Ressurection: The Cycle of Osiris in "Finnegans Wake"* (Uppsala: University of Uppsala Press, 1976), p. 80.

8 Joyce, *Portrait,* p. 200. Jolas tells the following anecdote: "Once he celebrated on the same day, his fiftieth birthday and the tenth anniversary of the publication of *Ulysses.* . . . The birthday cake was decorated with an ingenious candy replica of a copy of *Ulysses,* in its blue jacket. Called on to cut the cake, Joyce looked at it a moment and said: '*Accipite et manducate ex hoc omnes: Hoc est enim corpus meum*'" (Jolas, "My Friend James Joyce," in Givens, *James Joyce,* p. 8).

9 Cf. the sermon on the "Four Last Things" in Joyce, *Portrait.*

10 Jolas, "My Friend James Joyce," p. 9.

11 Letter of July 22, 1932, in Joyce, *Letters,* vol. 3.

12 McHugh, *Annotations,* p. 193.

13 Cf. the repeated "because" of Molly and Gerty in "Penelope" and "Nausikaa."

14 Cf. van Gennep, *Manuel de folklore,* p. 1374.

15 Ellmann, *Joyce,* p. 520.

16 Cf. Hayman, *First Draft,* p. 285.

17 Cf. *FW* 583.10.

NAME, MEANING, AND TIME: THE PASCHAL ENUNCIATION

1 Cf. Joyce's remark to Jolas: "'Really, it is not I who am writing this crazy book,' he said in his whimsical way one evening. 'It is you, and you, and you, and that man over there, and that girl at the next table'" (Jolas, "My Friend James Joyce," p. 13).

2 The expression is from Hughes de St. Victor, quoted by Turmel in *Histoire,* 5: 505.

3 Haag, "Pâques," p. 1121.

4 Cf. Saint Patrick *Confession, La Lettre à Coroticus* (Paris: Cerf, 1978).

5 See, in *Dubliners,* the declined and terrifying fathers of "A Little Cloud" and "Counterparts."

6 Cf. Haag, "Pâques," pp. 1120–1122, and the notes in the *Bible de Jérusalem,* pp. 95–96. See also 1 Kings 18:21, 26.

7 Haag, "Pâques," p. 1140.

8 The treatise of Pesahim, quoted by Haag in ibid., p. 1140.

9 Mohrmann, *"Pascha, Passio, Transitus,"* in *Etudes,* pp. 205–222.

10 Ibid., pp. 211–214.

11 Ibid., p. 211.

12 *EP,* 55, 1, 2, quoted by Mohrmann in ibid., p. 218.

13 See Mauron's treatment of the father in comic theater in *Psycho-critique*.

14 "(*Stephen . . . chants with joy the introit for paschal time. . . . Vidi aquam egredientem de templo a latere dextro. Alleluia*" (*U* 431). On the next page, Stephen speaks of "the gift of tongues."

15 See the following works concerning Saint Patrick: Oliver St. John Gogarty, *I Follow Saint Patrick* (London: Rich and Cowan, 1938); Whitley Stokes, *The Tripartite Life of Patrick* (London: 1887); John B. Bury, *The Life of Saint Patrick* (London: Macmillan, 1905); and Dom Gougaud, *Les Chrétientés,* pp. 45–54. The italicized definitions of pass and passage are taken from the *Oxford English Dictionary*.

16 See Hart, *Structure and Motif*.

17 Cf. the allusion to Dante's paschal enunciation: "ghimbelling on guelflinks" (*FW* 567.36).

18 See Louis Réau, *Iconographie de l'art chrétien* (Paris: PUF, 1959), 3: 1031–1033.

19 See Hayman, *First Draft*, p. 278.

20 James Joyce, *Pomes Penyeach* (London: The Bodley Head, Ltd., 1960), p. 13. Cf. Ellmann, *Joyce*, p. 142.

21 Boyle, *Joyce's Pauline Vision*, pp. 84–85.

22 Gerard Manley Hopkins, *The Complete Poems*, ed. W. H. Gardner and N. H. Mackenzie, 4th ed. (London: Oxford University Press, 1967), pp. 105–106.

23 McHugh, *Annotations*, p. 563.

24 "La Lutte avec l'Ange: Analyse textuelle de Genèse 32.23–33," in *Analyse structurale et exégèse biblique* (Neuchâtel: Delachaux et Niestlé, 1971), p. 35.

THE PASSAGE TOWARD PENTECOST

1 "Pentecost," in *The Jewish Encyclopedia* (New York: Funk and Wagnalls, 1905), 9: 592.

2 M. Delcor, "Pentecôte," in *Supplément au Dictionnaire de la Bible* (Paris: Letouzey et Ané, 1966), 7: 865–867.

3 Ibid., p. 875.

4 *De Decalogo*, pp. 46–47, quoted by Delcor in ibid., p. 875.

5 See Gershom C. Scholem, *On the Kabbalah and Its Symbolism* (New York: Schocken Books, 1965), p. 62.

6 Delcor, "Pentecôte," pp. 875–876.

7 *De Baptismo*, 19, quoted by Odo Casel, *La Fête de Pâques*, pp. 41–43.

8 *Sur Elcana et Anne,* quoted by Casel in ibid., p. 50.

9 Letter to the bishop of Tarragon, quoted by Delcor in "Pentecôte," p. 879.

10 *De Baptismo,* quoted by Casel in *La Fête de Pâques,* p. 44.

11 See "Exposé liturgique: Pentecôte," in Lefèbvre, *Missel quotidien,* pp. 1200–1201.

12 Cf. David Hayman, "Nodality and the Infra-structure of *Finnegans Wake," James Joyce Quarterly,* 16 (1979). (This article was first published in *Poétique,* 26 [1976]).

13 See the discussion of holidays in Irwin Epstein, *Le Judaïsme* (Paris: Payot, 1959), pp. 150–168.

14 Ibid., p. 154.

15 Scholem, *The Kabbalah,* p. 62.

16 Ibid., p. 30.

17 Ibid.

18 Cf. *FW* 415.29, when the Ondt excludes the Gracehoper with a cry of "Nixnixundnix": "He is not on our social list."

19 Epstein, *Le Judaïsme,* p. 185.

20 "I called you naughty boy because I do not like that other world. Please tell me what is the real meaning of that word" (*U* 77).

21 See Kristeva, *La Révolution,* esp. A.I and B.I.

22 See Mohrmann, *Etudes,* on the language of Saint Bernard v. II).

23 Joyce compared his method of composition (revisions, insertions of fragments, meticulous work on what Hayman (*Ulysses*) calls the "micro-structure," interlineated notes in color) to the creation of a mosaic. The comparison was taken up, perhaps on cue, by Valéry Larbaud and Frank Budgen (*James Joyce,* p. 178). Cf. the remarks of A. Walton Litz, *The Art of James Joyce* (London: Oxford University Press, 1964), pp. 11–12.

24 See the beginning of "The Wreck of the Deutschland": "Thou mastering me / God! giver of breath and bread" (Hopkins, *Complete Poems,* p. 51).

25 Cf. McHugh, *Annotations,* p. 550.

26 Joyce, *Giacomo Joyce,* p. 16.

27 The harp of David is alluded to here. See Edmund L. Epstein, *The Ordeal of Stephen Dedalus* (Carbondale: Southern Illinois University Press, 1971), pp. 104–169.

28 "Memory is a function of the mind which Joyce equated with imagination" (Frank Budgen, "Resurrection," in James Dalton and Clive Hart, *Twelve and a Tilly* [London: Faber and Faber, 1966], p. 14). The function of memory is at the heart of creative symbolic power.

29 Scholem, "Le Nom de Dieu," *Diogène,* 79 (1972): 70.

30 Scholem, *The Kabbalah,* p. 38.

31 Ibid., p. 36.

Notes to Pages 165–179

32 Chap. II, quoted by Scholem in *The Kabbalah*, pp. 167–168.

33 Cf. for this passage, Hayman, *First Draft*, pp. 117–118.

34 Henri Cohen, quoted by Scholem in "Le Nom de Dieu," p. 67.

35 Scholem, *The Kabbalah*, p. 35, and "Le Nom de Dieu," p. 66.

36 Ibid., p. 68. Scholem remarks: "This sort of mystical names existed in the strictly rabbinical tradition."

37 Ibid., pp. 77–78 and Scholem, *The Kabbalah*, p. 38.

38 Ibid., pp. 48–50.

39 *De sermone Domini in monte*, 2, 26, quoted by Turmel in *Histoire*, 5: 355–356.

40 In *De Mysteriis*, 52, Saint Ambrose writes: "This sacrament that you receive is effected by the word of Christ" (Turmel, ibid., p. 306).

41 Athanasius, First Paschal Letter, quoted by Casel in *La Fête*, p. 84.

42 Shem slides toward Joyce when the latter names him "Tumult, son of Thunder" (*FW* 184.6)—or *James*, nicknamed "Boanerges, which is, The sons of thunder" by Christ (Mark 3:17). The nomination of the Apostles by the Word prefigured the descent of the Holy Spirit at the Pentecost.

43 [Saint] Thomas d'Aquin, *Somme théologique*, 3, 75, 4, ad. 3, quoted by Turmel in *Histoire*, 5: 471.

44 *De Trinitate*, L. III, C. IV, 10.

45 Scholem, *The Kabbalah*, p. 39.

46 Ibid., p. 42.

47 *Sha'are Ora* 2b, quoted by Scholem in *The Kabbalah*, p. 42.

48 The Judaic and Catholic presence of the Tetragrammatic and Trinitarian Name can be found throughout the *Wake*. In this passage, the trajectory moves from Hebrew to Latin, and then to English: "*Petries and violet ice* (*I am yam*, as Me and Tam Tower, used to jagger pemmer it, over at the house of *Eddy's Christy*, meaning *Dodgfather, Dodgson and Coo*) and *spiriduous sanction!*" (*FW* 481.35; author's italics).

49 *System of Logic*, quoted by Sir A. H. Gardiner in *The Theory of Proper Names*, 2d ed. (London: Oxford University Press, 1954), p. 1.

50 "Retrospect," 1953, in ibid., p. 73.

51 Ibid., p. 75.

52 Scholem, "Le Nom de Dieu," p. 195.

53 Ibid., and *The Kabbalah*, p. 31.

54 Scholem, "Le Nom de Dieu," p. 69.

"PUNC": A RETROSPECTIVE ARRANGEMENT

1 Letter to Frank Budgen, August 20, 1939, in Joyce, *Letters*, vol. 1.

THE BOOK OF KELLS: IRISH ILLUMINATION
AND JOYCEAN WRITING

1 Chadwick, *The Celts,* p. 206.

2 Power, *Conversations,* p. 127.

3 Sir Edward Sullivan, ed., "Introduction," *The Book of Kells* (London: The Studio Ltd., 1933), p. 1. Joyce owned a copy of Sullivan's edition of the Book of Kells. In the *Wake,* he often parodies Sullivan's Introduction; see Joseph Campbell and Henry Morton Robinson, *A Skeleton Key to "Finnegans Wake"* (New York: Harcourt, Brace and Co., 1944), pp. 103–104; and Atherton, *The Books at the Wake,* pp. 62–65.

4 Ellmann, *Joyce,* p. 520.

5 Ibid., pp. 558–559.

6 Sullivan, *Book of Kells,* p. 119.

7 Freud, *SE* 23: 43.

8 See James Février, *Histoire de l'écriture* (Paris: Payot, 1948); and David Diringer, *The Alphabet* (London: Hutchinson's Scientific and Technical Publications, n.d.). The permanent collection of the British Museum, Room 56, "Ancient Writing," contains documents comparing hieroglyphic, proto-Sinaitic, Arabic (Southern Semitic), Phoenician and Aramaic, Hebraic, and Greek forms.

9 Mauron, *Psychocritique.*

Bibliography

JAMES JOYCE: WORKS AND MANUSCRIPTS

Berrone, Louis. *James Joyce in Padua*. New York: Random House, 1977.

Connolly, Thomas E. *James Joyce's Scribbledehobble*. Evanston: Northwestern University Press, 1961.

Hayman, David. *A First Draft Version of "Finnegans Wake."* Austin: University of Texas Press, 1963.

Herring, Philip. *Joyce's "Ulysses" Notesheets in the British Museum*. Charlottesville: University of Virginia Press, 1972.

Joyce, James. *Chamber Music*. London: Jonathan Cape, 1971.

Joyce, James. *Critical Writings*. New York: Viking Press, 1964.

Joyce, James. *Dubliners*. London: Jonathan Cape, 1967.

Joyce, James. *Exiles*. New York: Viking Press, 1951.

Joyce, James. *Finnegans Wake*. New York: Viking Press, 1974.

Joyce, James. *Giacomo Joyce*. New York: Viking Press, 1968.

Joyce, James. *Letters of James Joyce*. Edited by Richard Ellmann. 3 vols. New York: Viking Press, 1959–1966.

Joyce, James. *Pomes Penyeach*. London: Bodley head, 1960.

Joyce, James. *A Portrait of the Artist as a Young Man*. New York: Viking Press, 1964.

Joyce, James. *Selected Letters*. New York: Viking Press, 1975.

Joyce, James. *Stephen Hero*. London: Jonathan Cape, 1944.

Joyce, James. *Ulysses*. New York: Random House, 1961.

Prescott, Joseph. *"Daniel Defoe* by James Joyce." Buffalo Studies, 1 (1964).

Rose, Danis. *James Joyce's The Index Manuscript, "Finnegans Wake" Holograph Workbook VI.B.46*. Colchester: A Wake Newslitter Press, 1978.

Scholes, Robert, and Richard M Kain. *The Workshop of Dedalus*. Evanston: Northwestern University Press, 1965.

SECONDARY WORKS

Adams, Robert M. *Surface and Symbol.* New York: Oxford University Press, 1962.

Analyse structurale et exégèse biblique. Neuchâtel: Delachaux et Niestlé, 1971.

Aristotle. *Poetics.* New York: Hill and Wang, 1961.

Atherton, James S. *The Books at the Wake.* Expanded and corrected ed. Mamaroneck, N.Y.: Appel, 1979.

Atti del Third International James Joyce Symposium. 14–18 giugno 1971. Trieste: Università degli Studi, 1974.

Aubert, Jacques. *Introduction à l'esthétique de Joyce.* Paris: Marcel Didier, 1973.

Aubert, Jacques, and Maria Jolas. *Joyce et Paris.* Actes du cinquième symposium international James Joyce, Paris, 16–20 juin 1975. Paris: Publications de l'Université de Lille III/CNRS, 1979.

Augustine, Saint. *City of God.* Edited by David Knowles. Harmondsworth: Pelican Books, 1972.

Augustine, Saint. *Les Confessions.* Paris: Desclée de Brouwer, 1962.

Augustine, Saint. *De Magistro.* Paris: Desclée de Brouwer, 1941.

Augustine, Saint. *Sermons pour la Pâque.* Edited by Suzanne Poque. Paris: Cerf, 1966.

Augustine, Saint. *De Trinitate.* Paris: Desclée de Brouwer, 1955.

Austin, J. L. *How to Do Things with Words.* Cambridge, Mass.: Harvard University Press, 1975.

Barthes, Roland. *Le Degré zéro de l'écriture.* Paris: Seuil, 1953, 1972.

Barthes, Roland. *Eléments de sémiologie. Communications 4.* Paris: Seuil, 1964.

Barthes, Roland. *L'Empire des signes.* Geneva: Skira, 1970.

Barthes, Roland. *Fragments d'un discours amoureux.* Paris: Seuil, 1977.

Barthes, Roland. *Mythologies.* Paris: Seuil, 1970.

Barthes, Roland. *Sade, Fourier, Loyola.* Paris: Seuil, 1971.

Barthes, Roland. *S/Z.* Paris: Seuil, 1970.

Bataille, Georges. *L'Erotisme.* Paris: 10/18, 1957.

Bataille, Georges. *Oeuvres complètes.* Vols. 4–6. Paris: Gallimard, 1971–1976.

Bayley, Harold. *The Lost Language of Symbolism.* London: E. Benn, 1968.

Begnal, Michael H., and Fritz Senn. *A Conceptual Guide to "Finnegans Wake."* University Park: Pennsylvania State University Press, 1974.

Benstock, Bernard. *James Joyce: The Undiscover'd Country.* Dublin: Gill and Macmillan, 1968.

Benstock, Bernard. *Joyce-again's Wake.* Seattle: University of Washington Press, 1965.

Benveniste, Emile. *Problèmes de linguistique générale.* 2 vols. Paris: Gallimard, 1974.

Benveniste, Emile. *Le Vocabulaire des institutions indo-européennes.* Paris: Minuit, 1969.

Bianciotto, Giorgio. *Bestiaires du Moyen Age.* Paris: Stock, 1980.

Bieler, L. *The Life and Legend of Saint Patrick.* Dublin: Clonmore and Reynolds, 1949.

Blanchot, Maurice. *Le Livre à venir.* Paris: Gallimard, 1959.

Bonheim, Helmut. *Joyce's Benefictions.* Berkeley: University of California Press, 1964.

Bonheim, Helmut. *A Lexicon of the German in "Finnegans Wake."* Berkeley: University of California Press, 1967.

Bonnerot, Louis, Jacques Aubert, and Claude Jacquet. *"Ulysses" cinquante ans après.* Paris: Marcel Didier, 1974.

The Book of Common Prayer. New York: The Church Pension Fund, 1945.

Boyle, Robert, S. J. *James Joyce's Pauline Vision.* Carbondale: Southern Illinois University Press, 1978.

Budgen, Frank. *James Joyce and the Making of "Ulysses" and Other Writings.* London: Oxford University Press, 1972.

Bury, John B. *The Life of Saint Patrick.* London: Macmillan, 1905.

Byrne, J. F. *Silent Years.* New York: Farrar, Strauss and Co., 1953.

Campbell, Joseph, and Henry Morton Robinson. *A Skeleton Key to "Finnegans Wake."* New York: Harcourt, Brace and Co., 1944.

Casel, Odo. *La Fête de Pâques dans l'Eglise des Pères.* Paris: Cerf, 1963.

Chace, W. M., ed. *Joyce: A Collection of Critical Essays.* Englewood Cliffs, N.J.: Prentice-Hall, 1974.

Chadwick, Nora K., *The Celts.* Harmondsworth: Penguin Books, 1970.

Christiani, Dounia B. *Scandinvian Elements of Finnegans Wake.* Evanston: Northwestern University Press, 1965.

Code of Jewish Law [*Kitzur Shulchan aruch*]. Translated by H. E. Goldin. New York: Hebrew Publishing Co., 1961.

Colum, Mary, and Padraic Colum. *Our Friend James Joyce.* Garden City, N.Y.: Doubleday and Co., 1958.

Cope, Jackson. *Joyce's Cities.* Baltimore: Johns Hopkins University Press, 1981.

Curran, Constantine. *James Joyce Remembered.* New York: Oxford University Press, 1968.

Dalton, James, and Clive Hart. *Twelve and a Tilly.* London: Faber and Faber, 1966.

Derrida, Jacques. *La Dissémination.* Paris: Seuil, 1972.

Diringer, David. *The Alphabet.* London: Hutchinson's Scientific and Technical Publications, n.d.

Ducrot, Oswald, and Tzvetan Todorov. *Dictionnaire encyclopédique des sciences du langage.* Paris: Seuil, 1972.

Eco, Umberto. *L'Oeuvre ouverte.* Paris: Seuil, 1965.

Ellmann, Richard. *The Consciousness of Joyce.* London: Faber and Faber, Ltd., 1977.

Ellmann, Richard. *James Joyce.* New York: Oxford University Press, 1959.

Ellmann, Richard. *Ulysses on the Liffey.* New York: Oxford University Press, 1972.

Epstein, Edmund L. *The Ordeal of Stephen Dedalus.* Carbondale: Southern Illinois University Press, 1971.

Epstein, Irwin. *Le Judaïsme.* Paris: Payot, 1959.

Février, James. *Histoire de l'écriture.* Paris: Payot, 1948.

La Folie. Actes du colloque de Milan, 1976. Edited by Armando Verdiglione. Paris: 10/18, 1977.

Foucault, Michel. *Les Mots et les choses.* Paris: Gallimard, 1966.

French, Marilyn. *The Book as World.* Cambridge, Mass.: Harvard University Press, 1976.

Freud, Sigmund. *On Aphasia.* New York: International University Presses, 1953.

Freud, Sigmund. *The Standard Edition of the Complete Psychological Works of Sigmund Freud.* 24 vols. Edited by James Strachey. London: Hogarth Press and the Institute of Psychoanalysis, 1953–1974.

Gandillac, Maurice de, ed. *Oeuvres complètes de Pseudo-Denys l'Areopagite.* Paris: Aubier, 1943.

Gardiner, Sir A. H. *The Theory of Proper Names.* 2d. ed. London: Oxford University Press, 1954.

Garvin, John. *James Joyce's Disunited Kingdom and the Irish Dimension.* Dublin: Gill and Macmillan, 1976.

Genette, Gérard. *Figures I.* Paris: Seuil, 1966.

Gennep, Arnold van. *Cérémonies périodiques, cycliques, 1, Carnaval-Carême-Pâques.* I, III, *Manuel de folklore français contemporain.* Paris: Picard, 1947.

Gilbert, Stuart. *James Joyce's "Ulysses."* New York: Random House, 1952.

Gillet, Louis. *Stèle pour James Joyce.* Marseille: Sagittaire, 1946.

Gilson, Etienne. *Philosophie et incarnation selon Saint Augustin.* Montréal: Université de Montréal, 1947.

Girard, René. *Des Choses cachées depuis la fondation du monde.* Paris: Grasset, 1978.

Girard, René. *La Violence et le sacré.* Paris: Grasset, 1972.

Givens, Sean. *James Joyce: Two Decades of Criticism.* New York: Vanguard Press, 1948.

Glasheen, Adaline. *Third Census of "Finnegans Wake."* Berkeley: University of California Press, 1977.

235
Bibliography

Gogarty, Oliver St. John. *I Follow Saint Patrick*. London: Rich and Cowan, 1938.

Gogarty, Oliver St. John. *It Isn't This Time of Year at All!* London: MacGibbon & Kee, 1954.

Goldberg, L. S. *The Classical Temper*. London: Routledge and Kegan Paul, 1966.

Gougaud, Dom Louis. *Les Chrétientés celtiques*. Paris: J. Gabalda, 1911.

Gross, John. *Joyce*. Great Britain: Fontana/Collins, 1971.

Guitton, Jean. *Le Temps et l'éternité chez Plotin et Saint Augustin*. Paris: Vrin, 1971.

Hart, Clive. *Structure and Motif in "Finnegans Wake."* Evanston: Northwestern University Press, 1962.

Hart, Clive and David Hayman. *James Joyce's "Ulysses": Critical Essays*. Berkeley: University of California Press, 1974.

Hayman, David. *Joyce et Mallarmé*. Paris: Lettres Modernes, 1956.

Hayman, David. *"Ulysses": The Mechanics of Meaning*. Englewood Cliffs, N.J.: Prentice-Hall, 1970.

Hegel, G. W. F. *The Christian Religion*. George Lasson, ed. Peter C. Hodgson, trans. Chico: Scholars Press, 1979.

Hegel, G. W. F. *Lectures on the Philosophy of Religion*. 3 vols. E. B. Speirs and J. B. Sanderson, trans. Atalantic Highlands: Humanities, 1968.

Hegel, G. W. F. *Phenomenology of Spirit*. A. V. Miller, trans., with analysis and foreward by J. N. Findlay. New York: Oxford University Press, 1977.

Henry, Françoise. *L'Art irlandais*. Vols. 1 and 2. Zodiaque, la Nuit des temps 18 & 19, 1963, 1964; Les cahiers de l'atelier du coeurmeurtry.

Hodgart, Matthew. *James Joyce: A Student's Guide*. London: Routledge and Kegan Paul, 1978.

Hutchins, Patricia. *James Joyce's Dublin*. London: Grey Walls Press, 1950.

Jacquet, Claude. *Joyce et Rabelais*. Paris: Didier, 1972.

Jakobson, Roman. *Essais de linguistique generale*. Paris: Minuit, 1963.

Jacobson, Roman. *Questions de poétique*. Paris: Seuil, 1973.

Jolas, Maria. *A James Joyce Yearbook*. Paris: Transition Press, 1949.

Joyaux, Julia. *Le Langage, cet inconnu*. Paris: Denoël, 1969.

Joyce, Stanislaus. *The Complete Dublin Diary of Stanislaus Joyce*. Ithaca: Cornell University Press, 1962.

Joyce, Stanislaus. *My Brother's Keeper*. London: Faber and Faber, 1958.

Joyce, Stanislaus. *Recollections of James Joyce by His Brother*. New York: James Joyce Society, 1950.

Kain, Richard M. *Fabulous Voyager*. Chicago: University of Chicago Press, 1947.

Kenner, Hugh. *Dublin's Joyce*. Bloomington: Indiana University Press, 1956.

Khatibi, Abdelkabir. *La Blessure du nom propre*. Paris: Denoël, 1974.

Kierkegaard, Sören. *Le Concept de l'angoisse*. Paris: Gallimard, 1935.

Kierkegaard, Sören. *La Répétition*. Vol. 5, *Oeuvres complètes*. Paris: Edition de l'Orante, 1972.

Klein, Melanie. *Essais de psychanalyse*. Paris: Payot, 1978.

Kristeva, Julia. *Folle vérité. Ouvrage collectif*. Paris: Seuil, 1979.

Kristeva, Julia. *Polylogue*. Paris: Seuil, 1977.

Kristeva, Julia. *Pouvoirs de l'horreur*. Paris: Seuil, 1980.

Kristeva, Julia. *Recherches pour une sémanalyse*. Paris: Seuil, 1969.

Kristeva, Julia. *La Révolution du langage poétique*. Paris: Seuil, 1974.

Kronegger, Maria E. *James Joyce and Associated Image Makers*. New Haven: College and University Press, 1968.

Lacan, Jacques. *Ecrits*. Paris: Seuil, 1966.

Lacan, Jacques. *Séminaire I*. Paris: Seuil, 1975.

Lacan, Jacques. *Séminaire II*. Paris: Seuil, 1978.

Lacan, Jacques. *Séminaire XI*. Paris: Seuil, 1978.

Lacan, Jacques. *Séminaire XX*. Paris: Seuil, 1975.

Laplanche, Jean, and J. B. Laplanche. *Vocabulaire de la psychanalyse*. Paris: PUF, 1967.

Lefèbvre, Dom Gaspar, and the Benedictines of the Abbaye de Saint André. *Missel quotidien et vespéral*. Bruges: Apostolat Liturgique, 1942.

Litz, A. Walton. *The Art of James Joyce*. London: Oxford University Press, 1964.

Lubac, Henri de. *Méditations sur l'Eglise*. Paris: Aubier-Montaigne, 1968.

Lyons, John. *Eléments de sémantique*. Paris: Larousse, 1978.

Lyons, John. *Introduction to Theoretical Linguistics*. Cambridge: Cambridge University Press, 1968.

MacCabe, Colin. *James Joyce and the Revolution of the Word*. New York: Harper and Row, 1957.

McHugh, Roland. *The Sigla of "Finnegans Wake."* London: Edward Arnold, 1976.

McHugh, Roland. *Annotations to "Finnegans Wake."* Baltimore: Johns Hopkins University Press, 1980.

Magalaner, Marvin, ed. *James Joyce Miscellany: First Series*. Carbondale: Southern Illinois University Press, 1957.

Magalaner, Marvin. *James Joyce Miscellany: Second Series*. Carbondale: Southern Illinois University Press, 1959.

Magalaner, Marvin. *James Joyce Miscellany: Third Series*. Carbondale: Southern Illinois University Press, 1965.

Magalaner, Marvin, and Richard M. Kain. *Joyce the Man, the Work, the Reputation.* New York: New York University Press, 1956.

Marin, Louis. *Sémiotique de la Passion.* Paris: Bibliothèque des Sciences Religieuses, 1971.

Mauron, Charles. *Psychocritique du genre comique.* Paris: J. Corti, 1964.

Mayoux, Jean-Jacques. *Joyce.* Paris: Gallimard, 1965.

Mercanton, Jacques. *Les Heures de James Joyce.* Lausanne: L'Age d'Homme, 1967.

Mercier, Vivian. *The Irish Comic Tradition.* New York: Oxford University Press, 1969.

Mink, Louis O. *A "Finnegans Wake" Gazeteer.* Bloomington: Indiana University Press, 1978.

Mohrmann, Christine. *Etudes sur le latin des chrétiens.* Rome: Editore di storia e letteratura, 1958.

Morse, J. Mitchell. *The Sympathetic Alien.* New York: New York University Press, 1959.

Noon, William T. *Joyce and Aquinas.* New Haven: Yale University Press, 1957.

Norris, Margot. *The Decentered Universe of "Finnegans Wake."* Baltimore: Johns Hopkins University Press, 1978.

Nouvelle Histoire de l'Eglise. Vol. 1: *Des Origines à Grégoire le Grand.* Paris: Seuil, 1963.

Nouvelle Histoire de l'Eglise. Vol. 2: *Le Moyen Age.* Paris: Seuil, 1968.

O'Brien, Darcy. *The Conscience of James Joyce.* Princeton: Princeton University Press, 1968.

O'Hehir, Brendan. *A Gaelic Lexicon for "Finnegans Wake."* Berkeley: University of California Press, 1967.

O'Hehir, Brendan, and John Dillon. *A Classical Lexicon for "Finnegans Wake."* Berkeley: University of California Press, 1977.

O'Suilleabhain, Sean. *Irish Wake Amusements.* Dublin: The Mercier Press, 1967.

Our Exagmination Round His Factification for Incamination of Work in Progress. New York: New Directions, 1939.

Paor, Liam de, and Mary de Paor. *Early Christian Ireland.* London: Thames and Hudson, 1958.

Paris, Jean. *James Joyce par lui-même.* Paris: seuil, 1957.

Partridge, Eric. *The Penguin Dictionary of Historical Slang.* Harmondsworth: Penguin Books, 1972.

Potts, Willard, ed. *Portraits of the Artist in Exile.* Seattle: University of Washington Press, 1979.

Power, Arthur. *Conversations with James Joyce.* New York: Barnes and Noble, 1974.

La Psychanalyse est-elle une histoire juive? Paris: Seuil, 1981.

Récits du temps de Pâques. Paris: Seuil, 1967.

Reynolds, Mary T. *Joyce and Dante: The Shaping Imagination.* Princeton: Princeton University Press, 1981.

Rondet, Henri, S. J. *Le Péché originel dans la tradition patristique et théologique.* Paris: Fayard, 1967.

Ryan, John, ed. *A Bash in the Tunnel: James Joyce by the Irish.* London: Clifton Books, 1970.

Scholem, Gershom C. *On the Kabbalah and Its Symbolism.* New York: Schocken Books, 1965.

Schutte, William M. *Joyce and Shakespeare.* New Haven: Yale University Press, 1957.

La Semaine Sainte: Edition française avec chant grégorien par les Bénédictins de Solesmes. Paris: Desclée et Cie, 1962.

Senn, Fritz, ed. *New Light on Joyce from the Dublin Symposium.* Bloomington: Indiana University Press, 1972.

Sharkey, J. *Celtic Mysteries: The Ancient Religion.* London: Thames and Hudson, 1975.

Shechner, Mark. *Joyce in Nighttown.* Berkeley: University of California Press, 1974.

Sibony, Daniel. *L'Autre incastrable.* Paris: Seuil, 1978.

Skeat, William Walter. *A Concise Etymological Dictionary of the English Language.* Oxford: Oxford University Press, 1911.

Smidt, Kristian. *James Joyce and the Cultic Use of Fiction.* Oxford: Blackwell, 1955.

Sollers, Philippe. *Logiques.* Paris: Seuil, 1968.

Solomon, Margaret C. *Eternal Geomater.* Carbondale: Southern Illinois University Press, 1969.

Soupault, Philippe. *Souvenirs de James Joyce.* Alger: E. Charlot, 1957.

Starobinski, Jean. *Les Mots sous les mots.* Paris: Gallimard, 1971.

Stokes, Whitley. *The Tripartite Life of Patrick.* London: 1887.

Strong, L. A. G. *The Sacred River.* New York: Pellegrini & Cudahy, 1951.

Sullivan, Sir Edward. *The Book of Kells.* London: The Studio Ltd, 1933.

Thomas d'Aquin [Saint]. *Somme théologique: La Résurrection.* Translated by J. D. Folghera. O.P. Paris: Cerf, 1938.

Thomas d'Aquin. *Somme théologique: La Trinité.* Translated by Hyacinthe Dondaine, O.P. Paris: Cerf, 1946.

Thomas d'Aquin. *Somme théologique: Le Verbe incarné.* Translated by C. V. Heris, O.P. Paris: Cerf, 1927.

Thornton, Weldon. *Allusions in "Ulysses."* Chapel Hill: University of North Carolina Press, 1968.

Tindall, William York. *James Joyce: His Way of Interpreting the Modern World.* New York: Charles Scribner's Sons, 1950.

Tindall, William York. *A Reader's Guide to "Finnegans Wake."* London: Thames and Hudson, 1969.

Tindall, William York. *A Reader's Guide to James Joyce.* New York: Farrar, Strauss & Giroux, 1959.

Troy, Mark L. *Mummeries of Ressurection: The Cycle of Osiris in "Finnegans Wake."* Uppsala: University of Uppsala Press, 1976.

Turmel, Jacques. *Histoire des dogmes.* 6 vols. Paris: Rieder, 1931–1936.

Tysdahl, Bjorn. *Joyce and Ibsen.* Oslo: Norwegian University Press, 1968.

Ussher, Arlen. *Three Great Irishmen: Shaw, Yeats and Joyce.* London: Gollancz, 1952.

Vico, Giambattista. *The New Science.* Revised and abridged ed. Ithaca: Cornell University Press, 1970.

Wilson, Edmund. *Axel's Castle.* New York: Charles Scribner's Sons, 1931.

Zohar: Basic Readings from the Kabbalah. New York: Schocken, 1949.

JOURNALS AND ARTICLES

Hart, Clive and Fritz Senn. *A "Wake" Newslitter.* Essex: University of Essex, 1962–1980.

Change, 11 (1972).

James Joyce Quarterly. 1964–1981.

Nouvelle Revue de Psychanalyse. 1974–1975.

Poétique, 26 (1976).

Tel Quel, 83 (1980).

Aubert, Jacques. "Sur James Joyce." *Ornicar? Analytica, Mélanges,* 4 (n.d.): 7–15.

Coleman, Elliot. "Heliotropical Noughttime." *Texas Quarterly,* 1961: 162–176.

Copper, Edward A., Jr. "Some Additional Christian Allusions in the Wake." *The Analyst,* 24 (1965): 5–22.

Delcor, M. "Pentecôte." In *Supplément au Dictionnaire de la Bible,* 7:858–879. Paris: Letouzey et Ané, 1966.

Fonagy, Ivan. "Les Bases pulsionnels de la phonation." *Revue française de psychanalyse,* 34 (1970): 101–136; and 35 (1971): 543–591.

Freud, Sigmund. "La Dénégation." Translated by Bernard This and Bernard Thèves. *Le Coq-Héron,* 52 (1975): 7–15.

Gaudel, A. "Péché originel." In *Dictionnaire de théologie catholique,* 12:275–606. Paris: Letouzey et Ané, 1933.

Haag, H. "Pâques." In *Supplément au Dictionnaire de la Bible,* 6:1120–1149. Paris: Letouzey et Ané, 1966.

Hayman, David. "Forms of Folly in Joyce: A Study of Clowning in *Ulysses. ELH,* 34 (1967): 260–283.

Hayman, David. "From *Finnegans Wake:* A Sentence in Progress." *PMLA* 74 (1958): 136–154.

Heath, Stephen. "Ambiviolences." *Tel Quel,* 50 (1972): 22–43.

Hodgart, M. J. C. "Shakespeare and *Finnegans Wake.*" *Cambridge Journal,* 6 (1953): 735–752.

Houdebine, Jean-Louis. "L'avoir-été de Hölderlin." *Documents Sur,* 2/3 (1978): 19–28.

Houdebine, Jean-Louis. "Joyce l'examen." *Documents Sur,* 4/5 (1979): 18–43.

Houdebine, Jean-Louis. "Joyce et Jung." *Tel Quel,* 80 (1979): 63–65.

Houdebine, Jean-Louis. "La signature de Joyce." *Tel Quel,* 80 (1979): 52–62.

Kristeva, Julia. "Héréthique de l'amour." *Tel Quel,* 74 (1977): 30–49.

Kristeva, Julia. "La Musique parlée ou remarques sur la subjectivité dans la fiction à propos de 'Neveu de Rameau.'" In Michèle Duchet and Michèle Jalley. *Langues et langage de Leibniz à l'Enclyclopédie,* pp. 153–202. Paris: 10/18, 1977.

Lacan, Jacques. "Séminaire." *Ornicar?,* 2 (n.d.): 87–105; 3 (n.d.): 95–110; 5 (n.d.): 3–66.

Lacan, Jacques. "Le Sinthome." *Ornicar?* 6 (n.d.): 3–20; 7 (n.d.): 3–18; 8 (1976): 5–20; 9 (n.d.): 32–40; 10 (n.d.): 5–12; 11 (n.d.): 2–9.

Lacan, Jacques. "Lituraterre." Littérature, 3 (1971): 3–10.

Lesêtre, H. "Pentecôte." In *Dictionnaire de la Bible,* pp. 119–123. Paris: Letouzey et Ané, 14. 1922.

Lovejoy, Arthur O. "Milton and the Paradox of the Fortunate Fall." *ELH,* 4 (1937): 161–179.

Marshall, W. H. "*Paradise Lost: Felix Culpa* and the Problem of Structure." *MLN,* 76 (1961): 15–20.

"Pentecost." In *The Jewish Encyclopedia,* 9:592. New York: Funk and Wagnalls Co., 1905.

Réau, Louis. "Saint Patrick." In *Iconographie de l'art chrétien,* 3:1031–1033. Paris: PUF, 1959.

Richard, M. "La Question pascale au second siècle." *L'Orient syrien,* 6 (1961): 179–213.

Scholem, Gershom C. "Le Nom de Dieu." *Diogène,* 79 and 80 (1972): 60–80.

Simone, Raphaele. "Sémiologie augustinienne." *Semiotika,* 7 (1972): 1–31.

Sollers, Philippe, and Stephen Heath. "Joyce in Progress." *Tel Quel,* 54 (1973): 4–24; and 64 (1975): 15–24.

Worthington, Margaret P. "Nursery Rhymes in *Finnegans Wake.*" *Journal of American Folklore* (1957): 37–48.

Index

DESIGNED BY BILL BOEHM
COMPOSED BY GRAPHIC COMPOSITION, INC.,
ATHENS, GEORGIA
MANUFACTURED BY INTER-COLLEGIATE PRESS, INC.
SHAWNEE MISSION, KANSAS
TEXT IS SET IN BASKERVILLE, DISPLAY LINES IN
BOOKMAN LIGHT

Library of Congress Cataloging in Publication Data
Schlossman, Beryl, 1955–
Joyce's Catholic comedy of language.
Bibliography: pp. 231–240.
Includes index.
1. Joyce, James, 1882–1941—Religion and ethics.
2. Joyce, James, 1882–1941—Humor, satire, etc.
3. Holy, The, in literature. 4. Catholic Church in literature.
5. Christianity in literature. I. Title.
PR6019.09Z7943   1985   823'.912   84-40503
ISBN 0-299-10160-6